Parapsychology and Psychology

Parapsychology and Psychology

Matches and Mismatches

GERTRUDE R. SCHMEIDLER

McFarland & Company, Inc., Publishers
Jefferson, North Carolina, and London

Library of Congress Cataloguing-in-Publication Data

Schmeidler, Gertrude Raffel.
Parapsychology and psychology.

Includes references.
Includes index.
1. Psychical research. I. Title.
BF1031.S36 1988 133.8 88-42505

ISBN 0-89950-350-0 (lib. bdg.; 50# acid-free natural paper) ∞

Manufactured in the United States of America.

McFarland & Company, Inc., Publishers
Box 611, Jefferson, North Carolina 28640

Acknowledgments

Many have helped me directly or indirectly in preparing this book. My thanks go to them all: to the subjects who cheerfully and even eagerly cooperated in experiments, to the students and other associates whose ideas were often so keen and stimulating, and especially to the parapsychologists whose research and theorizing are the base for my own. The References omit many of their important writings which have helped to shape my thinking.

Here is a short list of those whose help was most direct. It begins with Gardner Murphy, that wisest and kindest of men. His seminar roused my interest in parapsychology; he helped finance and guide my research; and he then in a variety of ways encouraged it and my other professional activities. For the setting that made my first studies possible, I must thank G.W. Allport, E.G. Boring, and H.A. Murray, who provided facilities for work on a topic in which their own interest was only mild. For similar help in later years I thank two groups at the City University of New York: the Department of Psychology at the City College and the Social-Personality faculty at the Graduate Center, who tolerated my unconventional interests in the best tradition of academic freedom.

Both help and stimulation came from a succession of graduate students whose lively ideas and active cooperation made work with them a pleasure. Outstanding, in the last decade, were the members of our informal parapsychology seminar. This was a shifting group, with several who joined us for a short time, and a core (in alphabetical order, so as not to be invidious) of Steven Berman, Michaeleen Maher, Janet Mitchell, Ruth Reinsel, Carolyn Snyder, Nancy Sondow, Miriam Wollman.

Parts of the work that follows have benefitted from critical comments by Michaeleen Maher, Ruth Reinsel, Katherine Schmeidler Sapiro, James Schmeidler, Nancy Sondow. Three others had the fortitude to read through the whole text and I owe a special thanks to them: to Joan Healy for her patience with a book that was not the one she wanted written, to Richard L. Schmeidler for his incisive criticisms that showed how much of the manuscript needed rewriting, and to Robert Schmeidler for his help whenever I asked for it and for his unfailing encouragement.

Table of Contents

I. Introduction: A Theory

1. A Personal Introduction

This is a book about parapsychology, or in other words, about the scientific study of ESP*, PK*, and possible kindred processes. It states a theory about ESP and PK, then reviews the relevant research to see if the results support the theory. (Some do, some don't.) But you will find that it never seriously considers the basic question of whether ESP and PK deserve a theory, of whether they actually occur.

Some of you may think this is like my trying to build the second story of a house without putting in the floor below it. The rest of my introduction first explains and then tries to justify the omission.

The explanation demands some personal history. In 1942, seven years after my doctorate, I went back to Harvard for war work and out of idle curiosity also audited Gardner Murphy's seminar on parapsychology. I found myself with two quick, knee-jerk reactions to ESP and the other material Murphy presented. One was: "This is absurd. It can't happen in the world as I know it." The other, equally automatic, was the result of my training as an experimental psychologist. It was: "Here are data that look good. Good data should be accepted."

It was uncomfortable to be swinging between two judgments that couldn't be reconciled. A chance to discard one or the other came when Murphy offered me money from Harvard's Hodgson Fund to do an experiment on ESP. Doing the experiment could let me see for myself whether or not evidence for ESP showed up in carefully controlled research, and I accepted.

With half of the Harvard Department of Psychology looking over my shoulder and making excellent suggestions, I ran an experiment which we all agreed was properly tight. My subjects, as was customary in psychology

**A glossary at the back of the book gives the meanings of technical terms and also of some everyday words that are used technically, like "blind" and "call" and "run." Read it if you need it, but with the caution that Samuel Johnson suggested when he said, "Dictionaries are like watches; the worst is better than none, and the best cannot be expected to go quite true."*

then, were any and all who volunteered their time. The results showed significant evidence for ESP. My feelings were a mix of excitement and disbelief, and I ran the experiment again. Again it came up with significant results. A third run gave the same outcome. By then the data had bullied me into recognizing that, like it or not, I must accept ESP and consequently must accept the disquieting idea that the world I lived in was not the world I had thought it was.

Since those far off days, my students and I have done dozens of psi experiments. (Psi is a collective term for ESP and PK.) I knew the research conditions intimately and think that most of the projects were well controlled although a few had loopholes. A large number of the well controlled ones, far more than would be expected by chance, had significant findings.

Meanwhile others were doing psi research, some with beautifully controlled conditions. Many of the well controlled experiments gave highly significant affirmative results. Further, the cumulative result of all research that uses a particular method is often impressive (see, e.g., the meta-analysis by Radin, May, & Thomson, 1986, summarized in Chapter 17). It seems to me that even if all the work of my students and myself were ignored, or all the work from any other single laboratory or single investigator, the evidence for psi from the remaining work would still be compellingly strong.

All this adds up to my personal reason for not discussing the question of whether psi occurs. The question no longer interests me. In my judgment, the evidence for psi has become so strong that evaluating it would not be a challenge.

But there is an impersonal reason too, and it alone (I think) justifies omitting the topic. This reason is integrally tied to problems of the scientific method, and a few general comments about empirical or scientific methods will have to come in here before we reach the reason itself.

Scientific tests of a hypothesis typically begin by stating what the hypothesis predicts. They then check out whether or not, under well controlled conditions, those predicted outcomes are found. If the predictions are not verified, all is clear. The hypothesis has been disconfirmed or disproved.

But what if the predictions are verified? Is the hypothesis proved? No. Logicians tell us that calling this a proof would be a fallacy: the fallacy of affirming the consequent. Their argument puts scientific method into the form of: if A is true, then B is true—or, specifically: If the hypothesis is true, then the prediction about the outcome will be true. Scientific tests examine B. If B is false, A was false. But if B is true, A may still be false. (If tomtoms beat and the sun then emerges from eclipse, this does not prove that the beating of tomtoms caused the emergence.) Logicians tell us that verifying a prediction is never proof of a hypothesis.

Where does this leave the scientific method? It can disprove a hypothesis, but can never prove one. If tests of the hypothesis show that its predictions panned out, the most we have a right to say is that tests did not disconfirm it. The statement is almost (but not quite) a double negative. The way it is usually stated affirmatively is to say: The hypothesis was supported.

This sounds like a weak affirmation, and to some people it seems inadequate when there are very many, very strong supportive findings. What the most daring sometimes do then is to step beyond what is logically correct by making a personal value judgment. They assert that the hypothesis is so strongly supported that any reasonable person will (tentatively) accept it.

You can see how all this applies to my reviewing the evidence for psi. No matter how much evidence strongly supports the psi hypothesis, that evidence has not proved that psi occurs. An attempt to marshal scientific data for proof is a lost cause.

But the scientific method is a strong one; it can guide reasonable persons into deciding what should be tentatively accepted. This book therefore depends on conventional scientific methods to see how well its theory's predictions stand up to testing. The theory is about the way psi functions. It predicts that ESP and PK scores will change when there is a change in certain other conditions.

The theory, obviously, takes it for granted that psi can occur. The technical way of putting this is to say that the theory takes the occurrence of psi as one of its working hypotheses. (A couple of other working hypotheses will be added near the end of Chapter 4.)

Now suppose that examination of the theory finds support for it or for a substantial part of it. Although this does not prove correctness, it surely implies that whatever parts of the theory are supported should be tentatively accepted; they look as if they are moving in the right direction. And simultaneously, those supportive findings also imply support for the working hypotheses on which the theory is based, so that the working hypotheses should be tentatively accepted too. Thus, to wrap up the argument, a careful check on a theory about how psi functions will have a byproduct: It will provide a check on the occurrence of psi. The topic of whether psi occurs does not need a separate examination.

2. A Theory of Parapsychology

Two major deficiencies in parapsychology have long been stated both by its adherents and its critics, and still are widely accepted as true. Taken together, they seem so devastating that we can wonder why parapsychology has any adherents at all. They are:

> Parapsychology does not have a theory.
> Parapsychology does not have a repeatable experiment.

It is time to deny the first and to question the second.

Slowly, over the years, it began to dawn on me that the first statement was not true even in 1942, when Gardner Murphy introduced me to the field. Ever since the 1880s parapsychology (or psychical research, its earlier name) had had "a" theory, although it did not have the ultimate, grand unified theory. We in parapsychology, I now think, have been like Molière's bourgeois gentilhomme, who was astonished to find he had been talking prose all his life. Our theory has been implicit and unlabelled, and therefore it has never been systematically examined.

If this is true, the second deficiency is open to question. Only after a theory is set forth can we judge if experiments with different methods have all tested the same part of it. If they did, and if their data supported that part of the theory, then the diverse experiments converged on the same finding. The experiments showed repeatability.

The theory can be stated so briefly that after this rather pretentious build-up it will seem like an anticlimax to you—unless you map out the ways it can be elaborated. In its short form it is like a seed that prescribes a plant's growth, where the seed does not look like the fully grown plant. The theory is, simply, that psi is a psychological function.

Vague though this sounds, it has clear, testable consequences; and this book is written to examine them. If psi ability is a psychological function, then psi responses will be processed as other psychological responses are. Variables that affect how other abilities are used will also affect how psi ability is used. Psychological findings about what facilitates or inhibits effective response to other tasks will correspond to parapsychological findings about facilitation or inhibition of psi scoring.

If the theory is valid and is used as a guide in research, the research outcomes will form a coherent pattern. And if the theory is invalid, its implicit acceptance has guided parapsychologists, without their being aware of it, into wasting a great deal of research time by looking in the wrong direction and addressing the wrong research issues.

The theory has been around for over a century. In 1885 a group that included William James followed the model of the (London) Society for Psychical Research and founded the American Society for Psychical Research. They wrote a single purpose into their constitution: "The object of this Society shall be the systematic study of the laws of mental action." In those days psychology meant the study of laws of mental action, thus there could have been no tidier statement of their assumption that psychical research was coherent with research on other psychological processes.

Another statement of the basic idea came from Myers (1903) in his posthumous classic, a compendium of more than 1400 pages that set forth and attempted to integrate what information had already been garnered in psychical research. Myers wrote of "the general line of inquiry to be pursued in this book—an advance from the analysis of *normal* to the evidence for *supernormal* faculty" (p. xxv). This puts in a nutshell the thesis that understanding other psychological abilities is of a piece with, and therefore will lead to, an understanding of psi.

(It is odd, and historically interesting, that Myers downplays the point. He embeds what I quoted in a sentence that raises another issue, and even that sentence is only one item of a long list. It is as if he himself did not recognize its importance, and yet the theme permeates the creative ideas in his two volume work.)

That this implicit theory continued after 1885 and 1903 is shown by the change in nomenclature that J.B. Rhine introduced in the 1930s. When he searched for a substitute for the phrase "psychical research," the word he chose was "parapsychology." This is a clear sign that Rhine, like Myers and the founders of the American Society for Psychical Research, expected a close relation between research findings in psychology and in psi.

A host of other historical examples are available to show that, beginning in the nineteenth century and continuing thereafter, parapsychology has indeed had "a" theory. The theory is that normal and paranormal functions are so similar that learning about psychological processes will give useful information about parapsychological ones.

If this contention is right, why was the theory not made explicit before? Only one explanation occurs to me. It is that assumptions which are basic to our thinking can be so taken for granted that we leave them unstated. The neatest way to put it is a line that I learned from a social psychologist, E.M.

Hartley: "If you asked a fish to describe his environment, the last thing he would mention would be water."

Return now to the theory, and especially to what it does not say. It says that psi findings will show some relation to psychological findings, but it does not say that there will be a one-to-one relation between them. Here are a couple of examples which may clarify the distinction. Take Miller's frequently quoted argument (1956) that seven, plus or minus two, is a magic number for the span of attention, so that on average, for example, we can remember a list of seven digits if we hear it only once. To the extent that this claim is supported for sensory materials, it should lead us to expect that some number is comparably appropriate for our attention to ESP or PK targets—but it should not lead us to expect that seven will necessarily be the magic number for psi. Or take another example. If full focal attention aids in solving arithmetic problems, we can expect a relation between focal attention and psi success—but we should initially have no expectation about whether focal attention will help psi or will hinder it. Myers' wording was careful: one analysis can "advance" to the other. The first does not necessarily describe the direction or details that the second analysis will find. My "relates to" is similarly vague. It leaves open the specifics of the expected relationship.

Can there be any value in so vague a statement of theory? Yes, there are three ways in which it might be useful. First, it can stimulate and guide research; Hall & Lindzey (1957) called this "perhaps the most important" function of a theory. Second, if it is at least partly right, research can build up a body of data within which we find (a) some topics where psychological and parapsychological processes are parallel and march side by side, (b) some where they are parallel but opposite, like mirror images, and (c) some where the theory does not apply. Should this patterning appear, it could be highly informative. It might, for example, give neurological clues about particular brain processes that underlie psi facilitation and inhibition.

The theory could also be useful in a third way, one that examines the same problems as the second, but puts them at a broader conceptual level. The patterns of psi data might let us segregate the "para" from the psychological. On topics where the theory is supported we could assimilate ESP and PK data into the general body of conventional psychology. But on topics where the theory does not hold, we would need either to assimilate the data into some other science or, if attempts to do so have failed, infer that we have isolated a core which is unique to psi.

Where does this bring us with respect to that first major criticism of parapsychology, its lack of a theory? I think it advances us to the demand that the criticism be restated. Parapsychology has long had "a" theory. What it needs is more theory to supplement this one; it needs a grand, all-embracing explanatory concept. But this is not surprising; all other sciences have the same need. Physicists have searched for years for the theory that will reconcile general relativity with quantum mechanics. Psychologists who are exceptionally daring may try to reconcile cognitive with psychoanalytic theory and both with conditioning and with neuropsychology, but no attempt has been generally accepted. Within every discipline there are minitheories that deal with subsets of data. Bigger theories are needed for combinations of subsets; and for every science the data that do not fit into known subsets are expected to give rise eventually to some broader theory.

In short, it would be appropriate to level at parapsychology a criticism like this:

> Parapsychology does not have a theory that includes all its findings.

That revised, sophisticated criticism is justified, but it does not carry the sting of the earlier one. It applies to all the sciences; it tells us that there is more work to be done.

Overview

A theory of psi has been held for over a hundred years: the theory that psi is a psychological process. The theory has not previously been made explicit and therefore has not been formally examined. Evaluating the research which tests predictions from this theory can let us judge whether those psi findings are repeatable and form a coherent body of information, and whether the theory has been supported or disconfirmed.

3. Repeatability and Experiments

It is often said that no one can step twice into the same river: different water is flowing at that second step. In a strict sense, similarly, no experiment in psychology or parapsychology is repeatable. The analogy to the river is obvious when the experimenter and subjects are different. But even when they are the same, other changes are inevitable. Now the task is a familiar one; before it was novel. It is a different day or different time of the same day; body conditions and recent experiences have altered. Everyone recognizes this; everyone bows to it semantically by using the looser term "replication" instead of the strict "repetition." When we speak of repeatable research, we mean that replications of the research have shown similar outcomes.

How much looser than a repetition can a replication be?

This has been a troublesome issue for psychology, but by now so many have written so wisely about it that we know what the problems are and can make a distinction that helps to clarify them. It is the distinction between a direct—or simple or concrete—replication (which tries to duplicate the method of an earlier experiment) and an indirect—or systematic or conceptual—replication (which uses a different method to study the same problem as the earlier experiment). The two kinds of replication need separate analysis.

Direct Replication

A direct replication follows faithfully the method of some earlier experiment to find if the same results will appear. This sounds simple and straightforward but is far more difficult than it seems. Some of its problems are listed here, followed by some ways of coping with them. Chapter 5 includes further discussion.

Subjects

The subjects in a direct replication should come from the same population as those of the original study, and the sample should be drawn in a similar way. The problem here is that descriptions are seldom specific enough to ensure this can be done. They may be as vague as "Males aged 18 to 55," and this leaves a lot of leeway in drawing the sample. Even when they are more specific, like "College sophomores in the introductory psychology class," we need to know at least what kind of college it was. Urban or rural? Religious or nondenominational? With high or low academic standards? Sophomores in an evening class at an urban college where almost all students are members of the same minority will differ in many ways from those at Yale or at a small, rural, religious college. Some of the differences can affect their responses to a particular procedure.

Were the subjects volunteers or conscripts? Research has shown differences that might affect their responses to instructions. Volunteers tend to be more sociable than conscripts, more tolerant of ambiguity, and perhaps younger and higher on intelligence test scores.

If subjects volunteered, what introduction persuaded them to come? This is seldom stated, but is likely to affect the attitude they bring to the research. If they are conscripts, perhaps fulfilling a course requirement, how well do they like the course and its instructor? Reluctant participants often give only surface compliance instead of the serious effort necessary for meaningful results and they sometimes make mischievous, absurd responses.

Experimenters

Although research has shown that experimenter differences can affect the results, reports seldom give adequate descriptions of experimenters. Age, sex, and status can often be inferred but behavior usually cannot. The way an experimenter smiles and leans toward them may predispose subjects to participate freely; a cold, impersonal manner may predispose them to give only guarded, withdrawn responses. Conventional appearance can encourage courteous attention; unkempt hair and sloppy dress might encourage flippancy. In giving instructions, changes of speed or emphasis can highlight some parts but imply that others do not deserve much attention.

Enthusiasm is an experimenter variable that is almost sure to differ between original research and replications. It is usually high for the first tests of one's own idea, but seldom as lively on a second go-round, or for redoing someone else's method. And enthusiasm—or the lack of it—is likely to show through. If a bored experimenter doing a replication unconsciously conveys the impression that all this is a dreary routine, subjects are likely to put less effort into responding than those of the original research.

Procedure

It is astonishing how often procedural details are omitted. Verbatim instructions are seldom included, though small differences in wording can affect how subjects approach a task, for example whether they emphasize speed or accuracy. The material used is often described only by a general category, such as "a set of syllogisms" or "a list of abstract words." Two lists of syllogisms or of abstractions can differ in difficulty and the interest they arouse. Some descriptions are even vaguer, like "We constructed a questionnaire to measure. . . ." Rest intervals and timing may not be stated, but they can be crucial to performance. (My students and I have often written to authors to inquire about such omissions. Sometimes we received a full reply but sometimes there was no answer.)

Setting

Although apparatus is usually well described, setting is usually omitted. It can be important. One experiment found that even the difference between a tidy and a cluttered experimental cubicle influenced the effort that subjects put into their task. And the same test can rouse different levels of anxiety and thus yield different results if they are conducted by a white-coated experimenter in a medical building or by a casually dressed experimenter in a comfortably familiar building.

Courtesy

Did the experimenter go through the usual courteous preliminaries of a face to face meeting? For example, was there provision for disposing of outer clothing, umbrella, books, etc.? Was there a short chat before the formal procedure began? Absence of these could affect a subject's readiness to cooperate.

Promptness

When subjects answered a questionnaire about what was annoying or disturbing in psychology experiments, a good many of their responses were unexpected, especially the item they rated as the most annoying. It was being kept waiting. No report that I can remember has said if the experimenter was on time for appointments. Thus a variable that could affect the subject's cooperation seems uniformly to be left unstated.

Interruptions

Knocks on the door or other interruptions distract the experimenter and can disturb the subject's mood. Were there any? An occasional report mentions this; most do not. Some experimenters routinely discard data if a session was interrupted; others routinely continue and use the data.

Outside Events

Events not directly related to the procedure can affect responses. After they have heard good news, or even after they have seen a lighthearted movie with a happy ending, subjects give different responses (e.g., to appeals for charity) from those who heard distressing news or watched a depressing movie. Ordinarily such prior events are disregarded in research (though it might make the data cleaner if there were a quick preliminary question about them). But occasionally there is an outside event that is likely to affect all or most of the subjects, and in this case it can distort the results of research.

Within parapsychology, two studies were perhaps affected by such events. One (unpublished) came when an experimenter planned to replicate his own successful method and scheduled all subjects for a particular day. That morning the American bombing of Cambodia was announced. Subjects were too indignant at the news to take any interest in their ESP tests, and their ESP scores were null. The second case is reported by van Busschbach (1961). Here the precipitating event was a heavy snowfall that necessitated closing the schools. To compensate for the lost days, Saturdays and what should have been the Easter holiday were added to the school schedule. Children tested during those extra days made significantly lower ESP scores than those tested during normal school hours.

Communicating the Results

All too often, the problems of a direct replication are swept under the rug. The replicating experimenter guesses about what is not specified in the original report and goes on from there. If the same details are omitted in reporting the replication, no one knows if the second method was or was not like the first one.

It also often happens that an experimenter starts a direct replication, finds that the first several subjects fail to respond as expected, and drops that project. If others also try and then drop a replication, the grapevine may carry news of it; but not everyone taps into the grapevine.

Editors, especially of the more prestigious journals, are likely to reject any manuscript describing only a direct replication. It is not novel; they often choose to allot journal space to what is new.

Coping with the Problems

One excellent method of ensuring that replications are truly direct is the apprenticeship system. An experienced experimenter trains students, who learn to follow their role model in experimental arrangements, subject selection, and their own behavior. Thus almost all problems of direct replication are solved for work conducted in one laboratory, or in a group of laboratories headed by experimenters with the same training.

Experimenters occasionally visit each other and observe experiments in progress. This is useful, but all too rare.

In a few subareas of psychology, experimenter training is standardized. The best example is the administration of individual intelligence tests. Examiners are trained to postpone testing until rambunctious children are calmed or timid ones reassured. They also learn a distinctive tone of voice and gestural pattern, and use uniform wording to encourage continued effort after success and other uniform wording after failure.

The problem of communicating one's results can be overcome in several ways. One is to submit the report to a journal that receives few manuscripts. Another is to embed the results in an article with a theoretical slant. A third is to follow the direct replication with a systematic replication, then to include the first data as a preliminary series in an article which describes the other work.

SYSTEMATIC (INDIRECT) REPLICATION

Suppose an experiment on pigeons finds a particular learning pattern. A direct replication with pigeons of the same breed can show if the finding is robust, but this might seem worthwhile only to someone intensely interested in pigeons. Anyone interested in the learning process, however, might think it well worthwhile to find if the same pattern will show up in rats, or apes, or human children and adults, i.e., to make a deliberate change in the original method. This would not be a direct replication; it is an example of an indirect one.

The decision to make a single change will often entail a whole chain of other changes. A shift from pigeons to children demands a different size and type of apparatus, probably different stimuli, different rewards, different timing. But if the same pattern reappears, a great deal has been learned. Not only has the first finding been replicated, but its generality and thus its importance has been affirmed.

In that example, the investigator wanted to make one change but found others necessary. Another type of systematic or indirect replication deliberately makes a radical shift of method to find if the same general conclusion will emerge. An example from parapsychology came after Scherer (1948) suggested that spontaneity was conducive to high ESP scores. He had built a "marble machine," an attractive gadget that showed marbles of five colors mixed in a transparent globe, and below it a slot where one marble would come out. Could ESP tell what the next color would be? Scherer put the machine in a staff room but told the staff they could play the machine only when they felt a strong hunch about the outcome, and that they could never make more than two guesses in the same day. Guesses and outcomes were recorded. Scores of the spontaneous ESP calls made under these conditions were much higher than scores on the same machine when subjects had a long, uninterrupted series of ESP calls.

Ross decided to test the general suggestion about spontaneity without the special conditions of a marble machine (Ross, Murphy, & Schmeidler, 1952). Because he was interested in children, he used children as subjects. Each child took tests for spontaneity and then a separate ESP test with ESP cards. The data showed higher ESP scores for children with high spontaneity ratings than for those with low. Here the subjects, the measure of spontaneity, and the measure of ESP had all been changed, but the general conclusion from Scherer's work still seemed to hold true.

Systematic and Direct Replication Compared

When we compare the two kinds of replication, we can see advantages for each. Here are some examples.

Advantages of Direct Replication

In a direct replication, a model is available for what you want to do; this makes life easier. Further, you often do not know when you followed the model incorrectly; this adds to peace of mind.

Any outcome of a direct replication is worth obtaining. Affirmative results have given support to the original statement; negative or null results cast doubt on it. Either is a contribution to knowledge. Null results from a systematic replication, in contrast, are almost meaningless. You do not know whether the original finding was only a fluke and not worth further study, or whether your own attempt to generalize from that finding was badly conceived, or whether your method was inappropriate.

Advantages of Systematic Replication

Because a systematic replication is an original research project, you must decide what issue you want to test and then think through a number of procedural problems. This is intellectually stimulating; it is a pleasure.

A paradoxical advantage for systematic replications is that they are more likely than direct ones to control the effect of the experimenter's attitude. Because they are creative work, experimenter enthusiasm is likely to be as high as it presumably was in the original study.

Even with a null or negative outcome, the new conditions you are using may give results that offer you a serendipitous, post hoc insight. There is a better chance than with direct replications for some unanticipated pattern to emerge. Systematic replications are more likely to turn into pilot studies for new research.

When the results are affirmative, they make a substantial rather than a minor contribution to knowledge. Your new information not only supports the prior findings, it also generalizes those findings. You are helping build the interwoven body of facts that can constitute a theory, and that are needed to make up the body of a science.

WHAT IS AN EXPERIMENT?

Although there are many good scientific methods, the call that is usually heard from critics of parapsychology and from critical parapsychologists is for a repeatable experiment. What do they mean by "experiment"?

Definitions have changed, at least in psychology. The early, broadest one includes all research where responses are recorded under prearranged, controlled conditions (Warren, 1934). An example might be the determination of the faintest sound that a subject can hear in a room that is otherwise soundless. This is the type of research done in Wundt's laboratory in the 1880s, when experimental psychology was founded.

All psychologists, I think, accept this definition when they are speaking historically. Many of the most rigorous, such as those who work in psychophysics or who use Skinnerian techniques, still accept it. By this definition, parapsychological research would be considered an experiment if a series of well controlled ESP trials was given to a single subject, and scores were evaluated against mean chance expectation.

A more demanding definition was in use by the 1950s. Munn (1956), for example, required "variation of environmental, physiological or attitudinal factors." To be an experiment, research had to compare two or more conditions. If one person were tested, there would need to be a difference between one set of calls and another set before the research could be called an experiment.

Since the 1950s, in psychology, there have been two further requirements. They were generally accepted because of a persuasive argument by Cronbach (1957), which made a sharp distinction between what he considered experimental research (which produced or manipulated the conditions to be compared) and other legitimate but nonexperimental scientific research (which compared conditions that were already present). The two new requirements for what psychologists now call an experiment are that the investigator must manipulate the experimental condition(s) and that conditions must be randomly assigned.

The requirement of manipulation is restrictive. It means, for example, that no experiment can study differences between males and females because the experimenter did not manipulate the subjects' sex. There cannot be an (ethical) experiment to compare the differences in child rearing that might cause psychosis, or to compare blind human beings with sighted ones, or introverts with extraverts. The investigator found the variable already present, rather than manipulating it.

By this definition, research on large classes of important questions is no longer to be called experimentation, even though it consists of prearranged, well controlled observations and comparisons. This is inconsistent with the terminology of other sciences, such as biology and geology, and to my mind it does psychology a disservice. But modern usage cannot be ignored. I will bow to it, occasionally, by identifying research projects which meet or approximate the current criteria for an experiment.

What Is a Repeatable Experiment?

If we use the strict, current definition of experiment, and also use a strict definition of random assignment, the number of experiments in parapsychology is small—and the number of experimenters is much smaller. Few of them have tried to replicate each others' work. Thus if we call an experiment repeatable only when it has been successfully replicated in different laboratories, the number of parapsychological experiments to be considered is almost at the vanishing point. There is not enough material to evaluate.

If instead (as I plan to do) we revert to the older definition of experiment, the next question is what we mean by repeatable. Do we mean that every direct replication gives the same outcome? No, that ideal was derived from classical research in the hard sciences and is too high a standard. Even physicists, now, often interpret "the same" statistically. What we mean by repeatable is that the preponderance of evidence from replications weighs so heavily toward one set of results that any reasonable person will (tentatively) accept those results.

Two methods are in common use, in psychology, for evaluating whether the overall results of replications are clear and strong enough to be called repeatable. Both methods itemize the relevant research. One method then finds their "batting average," the proportion that shows the anticipated relationship. The other method determines how consistent they are by the statistical technique of meta-analysis. The first is less formal than the second, but either of them lets us judge whether support for the original finding was so frequent and so strong that the results cannot reasonably be attributed to chance.

Even for direct replications, however, both methods demand that several preliminary questions be answered. Examples are: How many null or nonsupportive results were never published? How competently was each of the projects performed? Should research with minor flaws be included, or omitted, or classed separately and given a lower weighting? With an informal evaluation, how should a nonsignificant trend be handled? Do we class it as null, or give it a partial weight? With meta-analysis, which of the several formulas should be used?

For systematic replications, after the same questions are answered, we can go further. We can look for clusters among the changed conditions. Sometimes it is possible to extract a pattern that looks meaningful because it shows that some methods give supportive and others nonsupportive results. But of course, if we think we have gained one of these fine new insights, the only way to judge its validity is the same as for any other idea: to test it by seeing if the findings replicate.

Judgments of repeatability thus depend on prior decisions of which research projects should be grouped together, of the method of evaluation, and especially of which work was so well conducted that it deserves full weighting, and which is marginal and should either be given low weighting or be excluded. There is room for legitimate differences of opinion about some of these decisions, and therefore about the final judgment.

OVERVIEW

In a strict sense, no experiment can be exactly repeated. Attempts to repeat are called replications and fall into two types. Direct replications try to duplicate the original method; systematic replications use a different method to study the same problem as the original experiment. There are advantages and disadvantages to both types.

A narrow definition of experiment excludes research on some important issues. This book examines both research which meets the narrow definition and also other careful, well controlled investigations.

Judgment about whether a research finding is repeatable depends first on deciding which studies with different methods should be grouped together, then on deciding whether those studies yielded similar results. There are a number of considerations that enter into the first decision, and good methods for making the second.

4. Method of Examining the Theory

Chapter 2 sets forth a theory. This chapter describes my attempts to learn how good a theory it is.

If it had been a new theory, the first questions to be answered would deal with the new predictions it made. Were the predictions confirmed by new research designed to test them? If it met that criterion a flock of other questions would have followed: about its parsimony, for example, and its breadth of coverage, and how well it conformed with prior findings—though this last has little meaning because older work presumably helped to form its ideas.

But it is not a new theory, even if it is newly being made explicit. Its single parsimonious thesis, that psychological findings are relevant to psi, has been a part of psychical research since before 1900. The base for evaluating it should therefore be a full survey of research in parapsychology.

An Initial Attempt and Its Failure

My first attempt at making a survey failed, and honesty demands that you know of it. It tried to be orderly and thorough by starting with conventional psychological categories and listing all psi research under them, to find if there was a fit between psi and psychological findings.

Its first step was to put together a large set of blank pages headed by topics and subtopics of experimental psychology. (Cognition, for example, included a batch of pages for perception, classical and operant conditioning, other learning, memory, language, intelligence, thinking, decision making, creativity, and cognitive styles.)

Its next step was to search through parapsychological publications, starting at the present and going backwards, and to summarize each research report on the appropriate page, perhaps with cross references to other pages.

Almost immediately a new step was needed: adding a page for psi research that could not be classed under a conventional psychological topic (e.g., comparison of psi scores with random versus pseudorandom targets). This ended any hope of surveying all psi research in relation to the theory.

But by the time my survey had gone back to the 1960s, the whole project came to a dead stop. The lists shouted at me that this was not the way to go. For one thing, items within the lists were noncomparable. They were disparate in the conditions they controlled or even specified, in the number of subjects they tested, in the way they analyzed and reported the data. Some projects were careful and deserved serious attention; others seemed to deserve none at all. This meant that even for psi reports relevant to psychology, some should be omitted. Any reasonably critical summary of findings had to be selective rather than complete.

Another clear reason for stopping was empty pages. Lists were absurdly uneven: no reports or only a very few on some pages, dozens on others. Many major psychological topics could not be examined because they did not have enough well conducted psi research.

It was time to abandon the hope of a full examination of the theory for either psi or psychology. This was discouraging. It made me wonder if the theory was worth the substantial effort demanded by even an incomplete examination. Laziness pulled me toward stopping then and there. But a strong pull came in the opposite direction too, because my research and readings had so often shown psychological tie-ins for psi. This argued that the theory deserved some examination.

How strong was the argument? I found two reasons for thinking it weak. One was that often only a post hoc analysis of my own work or that of others had shown a psychological pattern, and post hoc analyses are suspect. The other reason was the remote possibility that my own long, strong inclination toward the theory had made me somehow encourage psi success when the theory predicted it but discourage success at other times. If so, any evidence from my own data might show only my own (unconscious) influence.

If I ruled out my research and my post hoc conclusions from the research of others, did any argument remain for keeping on with the work? One possibility occurred to me. If there was some topic where I had made predictions but had never tried to check them out, and if later research supported those predictions, it would imply that further tests were worthwhile. I would then overcome my laziness and make as good a survey as I could.

A Test Case

This left me with the question of what in parapsychology had seriously interested me enough to make some predictions about it, and had been studied by others but not by me.

It took a little thinking back, but I found a topic that met these requirements for a test case: subliminal perception. Neither I nor any student under my direction had studied its relation to psi, but some years before 1971

I had made three predictions about it, predictions that were based on theory and were not post hoc.

I therefore decided to let the data from psi research on subliminal perception be my guide for what to do. If research from 1971 to now ("now" was 1983) showed that my predictions from the general theory were headed in the right direction, I would feel the theory deserved further study and would make as systematic a review as possible of psi research on other psychological topics. If the predictions were wrong, I wouldn't.

The history of those predictions begins in the early 1960s. One of the doctoral courses I taught, Personality and Perception, needed a unit on subliminal perception. Twice, as I did the background reading, the results startled me because they seemed so relevant to ESP. One shock of recognition came from a list of personality variables associated with subliminal sensitivity; they looked just like the variables associated with ESP success. The other came when a neat, predicted reversal in subliminal scores was explained by a theory similar to one I had developed for the reversal between psi-hitting and psi-missing. The topic also seemed similar to ESP because back in the 1960s, evidence for subliminal perception was stronger with free responses than with forced choices, and in that same period strong psi effects were found with the free responses in dream reports (see Ullman, Krippner, & Vaughan, 1973).

After I had begun thinking along these lines, Eisenbud (1965) published a careful direct comparison of subliminal and ESP scores, and reported there was no relation between them. A little later Johnson & Kanthamani (1967) made an indirect comparison, with positive results. Eisenbud's research carried more weight in my mind because of its directness: he had used the same test method for both variables. My hypotheses about subliminal-ESP relations still seemed plausible to me, but I felt I was holding them in spite of, not because of the data.

There were three of these hypothesees: (1) ESP success will show a positive relation to success in perceiving weak or faint subliminal stimuli, far below the threshold. (2) ESP success will show a negative relation to success in perceiving strong subliminal stimuli, near the threshold. (3) The positive relation for weak stimuli will be clearer if tested by free response than if tested by forced choice.

A conservative date (Schmeidler, 1972) could be set for all three. In 1971 I had publicly stated the first and third, although I reluctantly left out the second. The reason for omitting it was that the occasion was a formal address limited to one hour. It covered many other topics, and that second hypothesis would have taken too long to explain and justify. My notes, however, show the second hypothesis was clear in my mind from the mid-1960s on.

The outcome of the survey (Schmeidler, 1986) is summarized in Chapter 10. As you can see by the fact that this book exists, the predictions stood up well enough to make me think that duty lay with forging ahead. The first two predictions, with their nonobvious statement of a reversal, were both significantly supported. The third came out so-so; not confirmed but not clearly refuted.

During my review of the later work, a new worry began to trouble me. I had read the post-1971 reports when they were published. Was it an unconscious memory of support for the theory that had made me choose this as the test case? Fortuitously, that doubt was resolved. Some reports had not described the strength of the subliminal stimuli. The reports included two that showed strong positive relations between subliminal and ESP responses and one with a significant negative relation. I wrote to the authors to inquire. When the answers came back, each was in line with my predictions. The two with a positive relation had used weak subliminal stimuli and the one with a negative relation had used strong subliminal stimuli. Obviously I had not known this when deciding to make a test case of subliminal perception. It was only a small sample but it reassured me, and I went to work. The results are reported in Section II.

Method of Examining the Theory

Instead of trying to cover all major psychological topics, the examination was restricted to psychological topics with a substantial amount of psi research. (Some topics clearly met this criterion, but there were borderline cases where psi research was scant. In general these are omitted or discussed only briefly—except for a few of special interest to me, like perception, where even the scanty material seemed worth examining in full.) Thus, although Section II is only a series of spot checks on the general theory, it includes all the checks that it seemed possible to make.

Instead of trying to cite all relevant psi reports, a report was omitted if its method seemed to me so inadequate that its data were meaningless. (Of course, however, no report was omitted because its data were null or because its findings conflicted with my expectations.)

This left for coverage the whole range from excellent, careful research to research that was only marginally adequate. I used two methods of summarizing the outcomes. Sometimes there was no allowance for differences in quality but instead a simple count of significant versus insignificant results or of positive versus null versus negative trends. (These counts, I think, include all usable reports—but I hope that whenever you find me writing that there were only so or so many reports on a topic, you will read it to mean "only so many that I could find.") Sometimes, however, the evaluative summaries weight more heavily the research that seems to me to be especially well conducted. Occasionally this evaluation is different from what the simple counting would give.

Within a topic, none of the long lists of reports and few of the short ones are itemized one by one. Instead I refer to a survey where one is available, bring the survey up to date if necessary, and perhaps give some examples of methods and findings before attempting to summarize the body of research as a whole.

Instead of making the distinction that is conventional in parapsychology between scores of gifted and unselected subjects, the summaries usually combine their data. This has the advantage of making the summaries more complete, but its major reason is my impression, growing stronger over the years, that no sharp qualitative break divides the gifted from the nongifted. My working hypothesis is that psi is an erratic and widespread ability which shows (or approximates) a skewed normal distribution. In a few, psi ability is outstandingly strong and somewhat less erratic; in a good many others it is moderately strong; in most it is weak. (Whether it tails off to zero or to just above zero is anyone's guess.) It follows from this hypothesis that statistical evidence of extrachance results obtained by testing many unselected subjects can be as relevant to theory as the extrachance results from special subjects with strong psi ability.

Another conventional distinction is also usually disregarded. Data from PK and the various modes of ESP are intermingled, and most of the summaries do not specify which is which. This avoids the necessity of splitting the data into absurdly small subcategories, but the major reason for it is a working hypothesis (explained in Chapter 15) which leads me to treat all the methods as tests of psi.

ADDITIONAL COMMENTS

I need to apologize here to many parapsychologists whose good work is not specifically mentioned. Because this is not a historical approach, some innovative, important research is not singled out. Because its aim is to test one theory, it omits important work which seems irrelevant to that particular theory. And because it is an empirical approach, it does not identify many wise discussions that have helped to guide and sharpen later thinking.

For me, making the survey has been instructive. On a couple of topics, results were more consistent than I had realized. On others where I had thought the data were consistent, they were not.

My hope is that the review will be useful to others, too. If my evaluations are wrong or inadequate and thereby provoke someone else into making a better survey, they will have served a good purpose. And if the evaluations are right, you will find some instances where parapsychology has demonstrated the repeatable research that everyone agrees it needs. As for the theory, you will see that (if the evaluations are right) in some areas parapsychological and psychological findings are so similar as to seem identical but in other areas the findings seem unrelated. Although the theory passed some tests with flying colors, it failed abysmally on others.

Overview

In order to evaluate the theory that psi is a psychological process, the chapters in Section II review the psi research which relates to psychological findings. They necessarily omit both psychological topics that have had little or no psi research and also psi research on problems that psychologists have not studied.

For the topics that are examined, the reviews include all relevant psi research.

II. Examining the Theory

5. The Experimenter Effect

The phrase "experimenter effect" sounds as if it means something sadly familiar: that a careless or inexperienced experimenter seldom finds the same orderly data as a careful one. But the term has taken on a technical meaning. It now refers specifically to the thesis that even a careful, experienced experimenter's attitudes and feelings, for example expectations about high or low scores, can influence the subjects' responses.

Although at first glance this may seem only a minor extension of the nontechnical meaning, its implications are shocking. It contradicts what we teach our young. We tell them that the data of an experiment give a factual answer to the question that the experiment studied. The experimenter effect tells us instead that the data, the answers from an experiment, can depend on which experimenter asked the question. It says that one of the variables to be controlled or measured is the internal state of the investigator.

This offends against the proprieties. The conventional and thus the proper view of science is that it is impersonal. Scientific reports should therefore use an impersonal style. Yet the experimenter effect tells us the opposite. It says a complete report needs to include intimate, personal self-analysis of one's expectations about the outcome of the testing and other associated feelings.

To show that this demand is justified, the next unit will review briefly the evidence for the experimenter effect and the following unit will try to put those findings in perspective. Only then will come the survey of psi research on the topic, toward which the chapter is heading.

But that survey will not be the last mention of the experimenter effect. Since it seems to influence psi results, it needs to be taken into account in other examinations of psi research, and a glance at the index will show how often the topic recurs. Further, if we think more broadly, the experimenter is only one part of the social situation in an experiment. Other persons can have effects, too. From this point of view, social psychology (Chapter 6) could be considered an extension of this chapter, and its unit on teacher and pupil attitudes seems especially close.

Psychological Research

Early ingenious experiments by Rosenthal (1966) are probably still the clearest demonstrations of the experimenter effect. One, for example, analyzed data from several experimenters, all of whom conscientiously used the same materials and instructions. Their subjects were asked to judge, from photographs of men's faces, each man's success in life. Half the experimenters were told confidentially that the men were business executives who earned over $100,000 a year; half were told confidentially that the men were mental defectives in a state hospital. Experimenters naturally withheld this information from their subjects—and yet subjects' judgments of success were strikingly higher for experimenters who thought the men successful than for those who thought them failures.

Once we know the results, it is easy to guess what happened. We guess that experimenters responded more warmly to judgments that seemed right than to any that seemed mistaken. We guess that subjects noticed those pleased or pained reactions, and guided themselves accordingly. Later research confirms the guess. It recorded experimenter behavior by cameras or blind (i.e., uninformed) observers. Experimenters often give such unconscious, nonverbal cues.

By now a slew of nonverbal indicators of positive or negative reactions have been identified. There are so many that probably none of us can be fully conscious of all of them. Examples are smiling, leaning toward or away from the subject, forehead constriction, relaxation or tension, vocal intonation, abruptness of movement or speech. And just as we often unconsciously indicate our mood, others are likely to respond to it without being aware of what gave them a positive or negative impression. In short, Rosenthal's experiment with photographs is almost a classic example of conditioning, where cues from the experimenters shaped the subjects' responses.

Even with nonhuman subjects a similar effect can distort the data. In another project, student experimenters ran rats in mazes. All rats were of the same genetic strain but Rosenthal told half the students that their rats had been bred for high intelligence, and told the other half their rats had been bred for low intelligence. The rats thought to be stupid learned the maze more slowly than the others. What was happening here? Observation showed that students who thought their rats were bright were likely to handle them gently and slowly in the transition from living cages to mazes, but students who thought their rats were stupid were more likely to handle them roughly and abruptly. This, too, is consistent with learning theory: the adverse effects of unpleasant handling interfered with subsequent learning.

These and other early experiments attracted interest for several reasons. One was that the results were understandable in terms of learning theory. Another was Rosenthal's catchy phrase, "experimenter effect." But probably the biggest reason was that the research formalized what many had observed informally: that one investigator's self-consistent results differed from the equally self-consistent results of another investigator. In addition, later research brought out practical applications such as showing how a teacher's expectation of a pupil's success could make that pupil learn more effectively in the schoolroom.

The early research was followed by direct and systematic replications from many laboratories; results were usually but not always confirmatory. Recently Harris & Rosenthal (1985) made a formal examination of 135 experiments on the experimenter effect, using meta-analysis. The results show clearly that, overall, the experimenter effect occurs. In addition the meta-analysis supports the plausible theory that two major factors contribute to the experimenter effect. Each can be identified objectively. One factor is the warm or cold emotional climate that the experimenter conveys. The other factor is the positive or negative expectation of the experimenter.

Perspective: Research Context

Now that the experimenter effect is recognized as a variable that can limit the generality of a research finding, it should be put into context. It is only one of several such variables. All apply to psychological research, and some to research in other sciences. I have grouped them under three headings.

Environmental Complexity

A good experiment controls conditions. Although this is necessary, it is artificial; it can make the results almost irrelevant to a natural setting. We can take an example from physics: Galileo would not have given a clear demonstration of how objects fall if he had dropped a balloon from the tower of Pisa during a high wind.

There are many examples in psychology, especially in the simplest, neatest kind of experiment, where one condition is varied and others are held constant. Subjects who respond accurately to small variations in that condition may neglect them outside of the laboratory where many other conditions are changing too.

Brunswik (1944) has made this point most strongly. Subjects were asked to judge how far away an object was. Like previous workers, he found that when the size of the object's retinal image varied, subjects' judgments corresponded to size of retinal image. With a large retinal image subjects said the object was near, with a small one they said it was far, and so on.

However when an experimenter followed a subject on a round of daily activities and, every so often, asked for a judgment of the distance of some object, retinal size was almost disregarded. The response might depend on the object's relation to a known landmark, or on how clear it looked in spite of the haze in the air, or on a dozen other cues. Brunswik argued that the artificial constraints of controlled research were like the oversimplification and stereotyping of a Grade B movie. He called laboratory work "Hollywoodish" and an inferior research method.

His findings are sound, but the consensus among psychologists is that his broad condemnation is not justified. We can make an analogy to biochemistry. Test tube research is useful, even though the way a chemical acts in a test tube is often different from the way it acts in the body. In psychology, similarly, experimental data or scores on formal tests can be useful even though they do not necessarily show how a person will behave in any particular situation. They are a point of departure. Like test tube research, they help to tease out the factors that can influence behavior in natural settings.

From this point of view, can we trust the findings of well controlled experiments? Yes and no. Yes, because they tell us what factors need to be examined. No, because they do not tell us how any of those factors should be weighted, or even whether interaction with some other condition will reverse the factor's usual effect.

Subject Variables

Another argument against accepting laboratory data emphasizes the formality of an experiment. Its most extreme form, which I have heard from some humanists, is that what a subject does in the laboratory has nothing to do with real life. But this extreme form neglects the fact that subjects really are alive in the laboratory. Some may feel frightened because the setting is formidable, others may be flippant, others may be casually interested as if they were on a sightseeing tour, but everyone brings some attitude to the laboratory and then maintains or modifies it as the experiment is going on. Their reactions may differ: some may be on their best behavior and others may rudely assert themselves rather than letting the experimenter take control, but while the experiment is happening it is a part of their real life. We can forget the extreme statement.

A more moderate statement is generally accepted: that an experiment is a social situation. The participants interact with each other. As in any other social situation, their responses are influenced by the social roles they choose to assume. The experimenter's role is ordinarily that of an authority figure, who is in charge and gives instructions. What is the subject's role? Orne

(1962), in a widely quoted article, describes four common ones and advises the experimenter what to do about them.

The role that every experimenter wants is that of the "faithful" subject, who puts aside preconceptions, listens attentively to instructions, and tries to do what the instructions say. The experimenter should use the data of faithful subjects to test the hypothesis of the research.

But an all too common reaction is anxiety about how well one will do in the laboratory and what the results will show about oneself. Orne calls this the role of the apprehensive subject. Apprehension can create such strong self-consciousness and tension that it keeps a person from following instructions or even from hearing them correctly. An experimenter should be alert for signs of apprehension and should take as much time as necessary to allay it. The experiment should not begin until the apprehensive subject has become a faithful subject.

Some subjects take on an antagonistic role, and from resentment or mischief try to give silly or false answers. They deliberately do things wrong. An experimenter should identify antagonistic subjects either during an experiment or in the debriefing that follows. Debriefing should include questions to find if antagonism was present. The experimenter should segregate the data of antagonistic subjects, and not use them to test a hypothesis.

Worse even than the role of an antagonistic subject, Orne tells us, is the role of a "good" subject. The "good" subject tries to figure out what the experimenter really wants and then do it, no matter what the instructions said. Although this may sound farfetched, it is not; it has plagued Orne's own research on hypnosis. Suppose, for instance, that the hypnotist wants to find whether or not hypnosis affects memory. If "good" subjects guess that the experimenter wants to show that memory is better with hypnosis and try to help this along, they will do less than their best when not hypnotized. Orne recommends that the debriefing identify such "good" subjects. Questions should find what the subject thought the experimenter's hypothesis was, and if the subject tried to conform to it. Data of "good" subjects should be segregated, like the data of antagonistic subjects.

Other subject roles have been described; these four are only a sample. And not only roles, but other subject variables can put noise into the data. Even with subjects who try to be faithful, responses will be unrepresentative if they are ill, or deeply depressed, or so elated by recent news that nothing else gets full attention. The general argument is that data are trustworthy only when proper allowance is made for individual differences in attitude or other subject characteristics. Without that allowance we are all too likely to use irrelevant responses when we try to test a hypothesis.

From this second point of view, can we generalize from laboratory results? Yes and no. Yes, if subjects were faithful and their other relevant characteristics are adequately considered. No, if we are ignorant of important variables that are likely to affect responses.

Experimenter Variables

For the experimenter too, the experiment is a social situation. Experimenters' behavior can be influenced by the subjects: young male experimenters, for example, sometimes act differently with attractive young women and aggressive young men. Further, experimenters differ among themselves in such traits as friendliness, assertiveness, insecurity. Often they vary from session to session because of fatigue, time pressure, or some other mood change. Any such differences can affect how subjects respond, just as the subjects' appearance, initial comments, etc., can affect how an experimenter responds. Interactions may be so subtle that even conscientious experimenters are not aware of them and therefore cannot report them; thus variables that can influence the results are often unknown. By now, to go back to where we came in, two of those variables have been identified: warmth and expectation.

Can these complicating personal relations be eliminated? Yes, but research shows that eliminating them can introduce a new contaminant. Experiments have compared responses of subjects tested by experimenters and of subjects who come for their appointments only to find an empty room and instructions telling them what to do. Usually the latter group has inferior test scores, indicating that their behavior was disrupted by the absence of another human being. A "no-experimenter" effect is not zero; it is one type of experimenter effect.

If we ask from this third point of view whether we can trust laboratory results, we find the same answer. Yes and no. Yes, if the experimenter variable is examined and perhaps if the experimenter is "blind" or if a well trained experimenter always acts appropriately. But no, we cannot generalize from the results of an otherwise well conducted experiment if the experimenter effect is not examined.

Summary

The findings of an experiment depend not only on its materials and procedure, but also on other conditions which are seldom described. Some relate to the general situation and setting. Others which deserve separate mention are the experimenter's expectations and the atmosphere the experimenter creates. These influence another set: the subjects' feelings and attitudes, which can modulate the use they make of their abilities.

If information about these conditions is lacking, we do not know how far to generalize from an experiment's findings, nor do we know whether an attempt at direct replication is so different from the original study that it is actually a systematic replication.

Parapsychological Research on the Experimenter Effect

In parapsychology, I have found eight research projects explicitly designed to study one of the factors that Harris & Rosenthal identified (see page 31 above). Two experiments manipulated the emotional climate; one experiment manipulated both positive and negative expectations; five other projects also studied expectation. They will be summarized in this unit. Later units will describe or survey many other reports on experimenter differences. They are omitted here for various reasons, e.g. because they used disparate conditions or groups of subjects, or used uncalibrated targets (Solfvin, 1982), or because their comments on an experimenter effect were post hoc, or because their research design did not conform to the standard psychological one.

Experimental Climate

Honorton, Ramsey, & Cabibbo (1975) compared the effects of a warm and cold social climate on ESP scores. All of their 36 subjects had the same instructions and the same long ESP task with its intrasession breaks. For 18 subjects there was a friendly, informal conversation with the experimenter for a quarter of an hour before the orientation began, and the experimenter made encouraging remarks during the breaks. The other 18 subjects were treated formally and rather abruptly. Their experimenter began the orientation immediately and also made discouraging remarks during the breaks. Results clearly confirmed the hypothesis. ESP scores of subjects treated warmly were significantly higher than mean chance expectation; scores of subjects treated coldly were significantly below mean chance expectation.

Crandall (1985) had for years been giving ESP tests to volunteers from his classes, and had always made introductory comments that conveyed his sympathetic interest in ESP. Although mean ESP scores were near chance, he consistently found a particular displacement effect (psi-missers scored significantly high on targets preceding and following the correct one). The displacement effect became the focus of his research. He performed an experiment to find if emotional climate affected the displacements.

Fifty volunteers from one section of an introductory psychology class met with him, heard his standard introduction, and took his standard test. Fifty volunteers from another and fully comparable section of the course were met by a man who announced that he was filling in for someone else and didn't know much about "this stuff," and who behaved in as unfriendly a way as he could, within the limits of college etiquette. He administrered Crandall's standard instructions and ESP test. As before, ESP scores in each group were near chance (though they were insignificantly higher in the cold setting than in the warm one). As before, also, the displacement effect which Crandall was investigating was present in the volunteers he tested. In the group treated coldly, the displacement effect did not appear. The difference in displacement between the two groups was significant.

Experimenters' Expectations

Taddonio (1976) followed Rosenthal's classic design in an experiment with two series. Her experimenters were six undergraduates with previous practice in conducting psychological experiments. All felt neutral toward ESP but agreed to help her when she told them that a particular ESP method needed checking out. Three were told that prior findings with this method could not fail. The other three were told that Taddonio's colleagues were worried because the method seemed to elicit only psi-missing. All experimenters used the same materials and method.

Both in the first series and in the second, subjects of experimenters with high expectations made ESP scores above chance and subjects of experimenters with low expectations made ESP scores below chance. In each series, the difference was significant.

Crumbaugh (1958) reported briefly on 16 student experimenters whom he selected on the basis of their belief or disbelief in ESP and their high or low self-confidence. All tested ESP subjects. A first series found significant differences between their subjects' ESP scores, in the predicted direction. In a second series the results were at chance, and they were at chance when the two series were pooled.

Parker (1975), like Crumbaugh, first determined the attitude toward ESP of his student experimenters. He then told the three with a bias toward belief that the method they would use had proved that ESP occurs, but he told the three with a bias toward disbelief that prior research on ESP had been flawed and that the method they would use should obtain results close to chance. All used the same method to test all the other members of their class. (The order in which students with a favorable and unfavorable bias tested the subjects is not reported.) Results showed higher ESP scores from the favorably disposed experimenters than from the unfavorably disposed, with a difference that was significant if evaluated by a one-tailed *p*. Parker adds that the difference was due almost entirely to scores from two of the experimenters, one favorably and the other unfavorably disposed.

Layton & Turnbull (1975) simulated experimenter expectation. They preceded their ESP tests with a lecture which presented either a favorable or a negative appraisal of whether ESP occurs. (One wonders what the lecturer's own appraisal was, and whether it showed through the presentation.) In their first series, ESP scores were significantly higher after the favorable lecture than after the unfavorable. In their second series there was an insignificant difference in the opposite direction; and the pooled results were at chance.

Taddonio (1975) also manipulated a simulated expectation and also had two series. Each series tested two hypotheses. One was the conventional experimenter effect, and the other was that the effect would be stronger for subjects with no firm prior conviction than for those with a firm one.

The procedure began with a questionnaire. Answers divided the subjects into three groups: believers in ESP, indecisives, and disbelievers. Half of each subgroup was then randomly assigned to favorable and half to unfavorable written instructions. Instructions stated either that this test was a good one for eliciting ESP and previous subjects had shown ESP with it, or else that this was not a particularly good test for ESP and previous subjects had scored at chance with it. The tests, of course, were the same. Both for the 20 subjects in her first series and for the 40 in her second, ESP scores were significantly higher with instructions for positive expectation than for negative. In both series, also, the difference between scores for the two expectations was more pronounced for indecisives than for the others.

An elaborate experiment by Jacobs, Michels, & Verbraak (1978) used nine experimenters to administer PK tests to 324 subjects: 108 aged five or younger, 108 aged 15 to 35, and 108 who were 65 or older. There were approximately equal numbers of males and females in the two younger age groups, but relatively few aged men. The three authors formed the positive expectancy group; a negative expectancy was induced in the six other experimenters.

Analysis of variance for expectancy, age, and sex found no significant main effects or two-way interactions, but a highly significant three-way interaction. (Scores were highest for adult females tested by the nonauthors and aged females tested by the authors; they were lowest for aged males tested by the authors.) This implies some relation between PK scores and experimenter variables, but a relation that is inconsistent and is modulated by other variables.

RESEARCH TO FIND IF EXPERIMENTERS ARE SELF-CONSISTENT

An early experiment (Pratt & Price, 1938) seems in everything except wording to fit into the unit above. It was triggered by the two authors' attempt to test children's ESP: Pratt, a male, tested boys and Price, a female, tested girls. They report that early in their work, Price asked Pratt what was wrong with his subjects. Pratt was taken aback, told her that they took their tests properly and nothing seemed wrong with them, then asked what she meant by the question.

She said she had noticed his subjects did not talk to him; they did not open up. When the first batch of data showed that Price's girls scored significantly above chance but Pratt's boys scored at chance, they decided that Price's observation deserved a well controlled follow-up.

They then began a new experiment. Each tested about equal numbers of boys and girls. They ensured that their formal procedure was the same by acting as each other's research assistant and observer. Again the data showed that Pratt's subjects scored near chance, but Price's subjects scored significantly high.

Although the experiment took place years before Rosenthal stated his theory of emotional climate, it obviously examines and supports that hypothesis. Pratt's disciplined, no-nonsense manner encouraged discipline and restraint; for children this is a cold emotional climate. Price's outgoing friendliness encouraged her subjects to be outgoing and friendly; the climate she produced was warm.

On the heels of this experiment came a study (MacFarland, 1938) which used a different method to test whether two experimenters would be self-consistent. One had previously found high ESP scores in his subjects; the other had not. During the ESP sessions the two sat side by side but had different sets of targets. On some runs each looked at his own set of targets; on other runs neither saw the targets. Subjects were in a distant room, knew that both experimenters were present, and filled out a single set of responses for each run. Responses were scored against each experimenter's target list. Scores showed only a chance relation to the targets of the previously unsuccessful experimenter, but a high and significant correspondence to the targets of the previously successful experimenter.

How can we interpret this apparent selection by ESP of one person's targets rather than another's? It does not fit easily into Harris & Rosenthal's categories. It was not experimental climate in the usual sense, unless each man set up his own paranormal microclimate. If we think in terms of experimenters' expectations, we must specify them as paranormally transmitted, selective expectations.

Perhaps more reasonable is another possibility: that the complex of target-cards-plus-this-person-and-setting attracted the subjects' ESP while the complex of target-cards-plus-that-person-and-setting did not. (The latter possibility exemplifies Murphy's field theory, which is discussed in Chapter 6.)

The MacFarland report is almost forgotten, but what might be considered a systematic replication of it is often cited. West & Fisk (1953) did a large scale, careful experiment to test an extraordinary hypothesis derived from their prior observations: that ESP scores would be higher if Fisk prepared targets than if West did.

West, a psychiatrist, had consistently found null ESP scores in subjects he tested; Fisk, an engineer, had repeatedly found significantly high ESP scores. The two worked together in an ESP experiment conducted by mail. Fisk wrote all the letters and all responses were mailed to him. Subjects were not aware of West's participation.

Targets were determined by following the order of a table of random numbers. Fisk prepared half the target decks; West the other half. Each deck was in a sealed packet. Each subject received 32 of these packets, with 16 prepared by West randomly mixed among 16 prepared by Fisk. When targets and responses were returned, seals had not been broken. Responses showed significant correspondence to Fisk's targets but only chance correspondence to West's, and the difference in scores was significant. The experimenters not only checked the ESP scoring but also checked each other's preparation from the random number table, and found it accurate. The results seem more striking than in the MacFarland experiment because subjects were not informed that a second experimenter was involved.

Two other experiments were designed to study the same question, but it seems to me that neither did so because neither identified successful experimenters to compare with unsuccesful ones. Parker, Millar, & Beloff (1977) each tested eight subjects, then each tested the subjects of the other two. Millar and Beloff considered themselves unsuccessful. Parker reports having had "some previous success," but this apparently was for psi research with gerbils. (His prior publications describe, for human subjects, a mix of high, null, and low scores.) Results showed null scores for all three experimenters.

Broughton, Millar, Beloff, & Wilson (1978) pretested their 16 experimenters by having them act as subjects in a test like the one they were to conduct. None scored significantly and, remarkably, only two of the 16 scored positively (a result to be expected by chance less than one time in 50). The authors do not vouch for the previous success of the experimenters, describing them only as "keen parapsychologists . . . some of whom claim to have obtained positive psi-effects in their published work." No experimenter's subjects had significant results.

OTHER PSI FINDINGS INDICATIVE OF AN EXPERIMENTER EFFECT

Many additional reports are cited in the reviews of the experimenter effect by Kennedy & Taddonio (1976), Thouless (1976), and White (1976b, 1977). They take somewhat different samples of prior publications, but all conclude that an experimenter effect seemed to influence psi scores.

Most of the reports they review are post hoc comparisons of experimenters who used the same formal method but found a significant difference between their subjects' scores. Interpretations, which of course are also post hoc, usually expatiate on the greater confidence or the pleasanter personality or the past successes of the experimenter whose subjects had higher scores.

An interesting subset of the material describes mood changes either in the experimenter or in someone closely related to the conduct of the research. Sometimes the coincidence of mood and score is striking, as when an assistant was miserably depressed while preparing certain targets and scores on those targets were exceptionally low (Price, 1973). But we must always wonder how much allowance to make for incomplete reporting. How often were other mood changes not mentioned because there was no corresponding change in the scores?

Even when post hoc reporting is complete, there must be a similar reservation. An illustrative example comes from Sondow (1979). She used a lengthy procedure and found in reviewing the data that when she had tested three subjects in a single day, scores were significantly lower than when she had had the comfortable schedule of testing only one or two. But this apparent relation of experimenter's tension or fatigue to subjects' psi scores must be corrected by an unknown amount for selection, because it was only one of many post hoc analyses that she made.

RESEARCH ON EXPERIMENTER PERSONALITY

There have been dozens of comments contrasting psi-conducive with psi-inhibitory experimenters, but only sparse, inadequate research to test the descriptions. The four most recent research reports follow.

Parker (1977) used ratings by three parapsychologists to class 15 psi experimenters as psi-conducive and 14 as psi-inhibitory. He hypothesized that the psi-conducive would score higher on four traits from a personality test (Cattell's 16PF): extraversion; warmth and sociability; confidence adequacy (self-security); tenderness and sensitivity. Not one of these traits showed a significant difference between the two groups and only one of the nonsignificant differences was in the predicted direction. Post hoc examination showed a significant difference in two of the other 14 personality scores, but Parker dismisses them as presumably due to chance and does not name them.

Sargent (1980) examined the same question for experimenters who used the Ganzfeld method (and tells us that the two significant differences in Parker's data were that the psi-conducive were less dominant and less gullible). He used Parker's data for eight experimenters who had worked with the Ganzfeld and added three more, including himself. His new comparison of five psi-conducive and six psi-inhibitory experimenters showed significant differences in the predicted direction for extraversion and for warmth and sociability. Parker (1981) criticized the work and concluded that Sargent's analysis was unacceptable.

Schmeidler & Maher (1981) asked a somewhat different question: how students perceived the experimenter (which may or may not resemble an experimenter's self-reports on a personality test). Videotapes of five psi-conducive and five psi-inhibitory experimenters, addressing a professional audience, were reduced to five-minute segments that included interaction with the audience. The tapes, with words inaudible, were shown to New York students who rated each experimenter on 30 descriptors. Adjectives with higher scores for the psi-conducive were flexible, friendly, free, likable, warm, enthusiastic, playful. Adjectives with higher scores for the psi-inhibitory were rigid, cold, overconfident, tense, irritable, egoistic, unfriendly. Child (1981) criticized the statistical treatment and concluded that none of the differences was significant.

Edge & Farkash (1982) performed a partial replication, showing some of the same segments to students in Florida. Here the psi-conducive were rated more active, nervous, and enthusiastic; the psi-inhibitory were rated more poised, egoistic, cold, and confident. This suggests what common sense suggests too: that the impact of an experimenter's personality may vary from one group of subjects to another.

Evaluation

Does psi research, like psychological research, support the hypothesis of the experimenter effect? At first glance, the answer would seem to be yes. Eight experiments with 12 series studied it and six experiments studied the similar question of whether experimenters were self-consistent. In these 18 series, there were 13 significant differences, and all were in the predicted direction. This is very strong support. In addition, convergent evidence from other psi research also indicates an experimenter effect in psi, and thus supports the conclusion further.

But is this as good as it looks? If a critic tried to deny that the findings are valid, could the denial be defended? As an intellectual exercise, the unit below sets forth the type of attack that a hostile critic might make; the next unit presents a more generous approach; and the next gives my appraisal. This back-and-forth could be added to any other review of research, but it would be tedious to repeat it whenever the findings look strong, and it will not be spelled out so fully in later chapters.

Avoiding Type I Errors

When psychologists evaluate a hypothesis, one message comes loud and clear: Avoid Type I errors!

A Type I error is accepting a false hypothesis, and it is avoided by evaluating conservatively. Specific bits of advice might be: Discard flawed research. Discard research which might be flawed. Discard post hoc analyses because you cannot be sure how much to correct for selection. Make allowance for the file drawer effect (other research with nonsupportive results, that might have been performed and left unpublished in the experimenter's file drawer). If you do not use meta-analysis, discard whatever fails to meet the standard criterion for significance (i.e., consider nonsignificant findings to be nonsupportive, no matter what trend they show).

With this advice ringing in our ears, we start to look at the 14 psi experiments (see pages 35–39 above) that bear most directly on the experimenter effect. Eight were designed to examine the classic experimenter effect by varying experimental climate or experimenter expectations. The other six were designed to test if experimenters are self-consistent. The hypotheses were stated differently. It is therefore improper to pool the latter six with the first eight. The two sets should be examined separately.

Next look to see if the research was well conducted. One requirement is that subjects be randomly assigned to the different conditions. A careful reading of the report by Honorton et al. finds no statement of how subjects were assigned. Although some of us would assume that the point was not mentioned because routinely, as a matter of course, subject assignment was random (as it was—see below), a critic might not make this friendly assumption. Instead the critic might speculate that assignment depended on the experimenter's impression, when the subject entered the laboratory, of how that person would score. If so, the significant results could be taken as evidence on a different and interesting question: the question of whether high and low psi scores can be quickly predicted. The experiment by Honorton et al. will therefore be eliminated.

Does the same objection apply to the other experiments? Not to Parker's; all subjects were tested under both conditions. Not to Crandall's, since he explains that the two groups were equivalent. Not to Taddonio (1975), who specified random assignment. Probably not to the others; though none states that assignment was random, all imply it.

A hypercritical evaluator will surely find still further omission of points that might be important; no procedural description can be complete enough to satisfy everyone. But suppose that the evaluator tentatively accepts the remaining series. The next step in playing the game of "What can I discard?" is to pool the series within an experiment, reducing the outcomes from 11 to seven. This pooling eliminates the significant findings of both Crumbaugh and Layton & Turnbull.

What else can be eliminated? Turn to levels of significance. Crandall mentioned two outcomes, and though the one that concerned him was significant in the predicted direction, the other showed an insignificant trend in the opposite direction. Pool them, and discard the pooled result. Parker's significant finding depended on a one-tailed *p*. Use a two-tailed *p;* call it insignificant.

Only two significant experiments are left, both by Taddonio, while five are now considered nonsignificant and one is considered irrelevant. Clearly two experiments by a single investigator are insufficient to establish the hypothesis.

Now turn to the six experiments on self-consistent experimenters. The critic would probably eliminate the Pratt & Price research. The argument would be that Price established a warm experimental climate and Pratt a cold one; therefore the finding can be attributed to the familiar experimenter effect rather than properly testing this different hypothesis. That leaves five. The Fisk & West replication can be pooled with the West & Fisk report. That reduces the total to four. Of the four, two gave significant results and two did not. Again, this is not enough for conviction.

You will have noticed a bit of razzle-dazzle here. After the evidence for the experimenter effect had been set aside, the Pratt & Price experiment was assigned to that category but the category was not reevaluated. Probably it is unfair of me to imply that a stringent critic would resort to this stratagem. More probably that experiment would be classed in one spot or the other, but with an appeal to the file drawer effect the evidence could still be assessed as not strong enough for acceptance.

Avoiding Type II Errors

The next message psychologists hear when they try to evaluate a hypothesis is also clear but it is usually less emphatic. It is: Avoid Type II errors.

A Type II error is rejecting a valid hypothesis, and there are two supplementary ways of avoiding it. One is to examine not only research directly designed to test its predictions but also research which is indirectly related, and bears on the same general topic. The other is to refrain from rejecting a hypothesis until it has been disconfirmed and its supportive evidence can clearly be assigned to another cause. Specific advice, for example, might be: Do not consider a hypothesis falsified merely because evidence for it is weak. The weakness might be due only to inadequacies of method, such as contaminating variables or not enough subjects.

From this point of view, the hypothesis of a psi experimenter effect is worth holding, tentatively, until it is disconfirmed. It converges on the hypothesis that psi experimenters can be self-consistent in their ability to elicit evidence for psi. The two hypotheses should therefore be examined together.

How should we evaluate the data, if we are to avoid a Type II error? Gently. For example, Crandall was concerned with the displacement effect, and we therefore accept his significant finding for displacement. Because Parker's directional hypothesis was already in place, his data can justifiably be evaluated by a one-tailed *p*. To assume that Honorton et al. made a biased assignment is gratuitous and insulting; their research should be included. Each series in Crumbaugh's or Layton & Turnbull's or Taddonio's work seems to have been planned as a self-contained experiment; each should be considered separately, as should the two reports by Fisk and West. We return to the earlier ratio: out of 18 series, the hypothesis was significantly supported in 13 and significantly disconfirmed in none. It not only should be retained; it should be considered established.

Balancing Type I and Type II Errors

It would be absurd to carrry to an extreme the avoidance of either Type I or Type II errors. If we withhold all opinions until we find flawless research exactly replicated, we will be in limbo, with no opinions at all. On the other hand, it would be gullible to accept every hypothesis that has not been hopelessly disconfirmed. What are reasonable guidelines for avoiding these extremes? And how do they apply to the topic of the psi experimenter effect?

I suggest four general guides for evaluating a body of research. The first is to discard any project with clear major flaws. ("Clear" is a key word. Honorton et al. were unclear about assigning subjects. I wrote to ask; Honorton answered. Each experimenter assigned subjects alternately to the two conditions, and this is appropriately random.) The second guide is judging significance and frequency of the supporting data. The next is significance and frequency of the disconfirming data. The last, and probably most important, is examining the whole topic for convergent evidence. Do systematic replications point in the same direction? (If so, possible loopholes in one but not the other method seem less damaging.) Does the conclusion fit with findings on other topics? (If so, the other topics can also be considered a set of systematic replications.)

All four guidelines suggest an acceptance of the psi experimenter effect. The 12 series designed to test the classical psychological effect seem well conducted. They gave many significant confirmations and no significant disconfirmation. They used different methods, and converge with data indicating that experimenters are self-consistent and with some of the other results reported here (and later chapters will show they converge with other findings as well). The psi experimenter effect seems as well supported as any psychological finding can be, when only a fairly small body of research has investigated it.

What should a reasonable person think about it? In my opinion, the reasonable assessment is that the existence of a psi experimenter effect should be accepted — tentatively. We should not think it has been written in stone. Later research may suggest a different interpretation of the findings. But until there is a reason to think otherwise, we should (tentatively) accept that it occurs.

Overview

Psychological research on the experimenter effect has shown higher scores with a warm than with a cold experimental climate and with an experimenter who expects high rather than low scores. Eight experiments, comprising 12 series, tested for the experimenter effect in psi. Nine of the 12 series had significant results, all in the predicted direction. Six other experiments tested a related hypothesis: that psi experimenters would be self-consistent in obtaining results like their prior ones. Four of these had significant results, all in the predicted direction. Other psi research which bears on the experimenter effect tends also to find results that are consistent with it. Thus both formal psi tests for the experimenter effect and convergent psi findings seem to show that in this area, what was found in psychology is also found for psi.

6. Social Psychology

Social psychology is often said to comprise two major areas: psychological study of groups (including dyads, or groups of two) and study of attitudes, attributions, expectations, etc. The areas overlap, of course; one's attitude toward a group affects behavior while a member of it. They also overlap with other topics: the experimenter effect is a particular type of group study; attitudes are sometimes classed as personality variables.

The first of the four units in this chapter summarizes all the psi research I could find that was designed to study conventional group membership; it then adds a few post hoc analyses. The next unit treats group membership unconventionally, in a way that is unique for psi. (Because psi apparently is not limited by space or time, the psi group for a project may perhaps include anyone connected with any stage of the project.) Research related to this definition of a group has no clear analogue in psychology and therefore is not fully reviewed, but some mention of it seems a necessary preliminary to the third unit: a short statement of four theories of psi experimenter or group effects. The last unit returns to conventional social psychology. It summarizes psi research on three attitudes as well as the scanty psi work on attributions and values.

Group Membership

Membership in the Dominant Subgroup

Between 1964 and 1970, Dean & Mihalasky collected a huge and unique data set (Dean, Mihalasky, Ostrander, & Schroeder, 1974). Their work is a period piece. It was appropriate only at an early stage of the burgeoning women's movement, and at a time when computers (using punch cards) seemed strange and formidable to many.

The data were gathered after either Dean or Mihalasky (both males) had lectured on ESP at business conventions, community gatherings, etc. Their 102 groups included 41 that were all male, 14 that were all female, and 47 of mixed sex: a total of almost 5,000 subjects. The lecture emphasized that precognition would be useful in making decisions. It was followed by a precognition test in which targets were selected and responses scored by computer.

Although they had begun with two different hypotheses, Dean and Mihalasky discarded them and formulated two new testable predictions. These were that when groups were of mixed sex, precognition scores would be high (a) for dynamic males who were in a male-dominated group and (b) for dynamic females who were in a female-dominated group. The terms were carefully defined. Choice of preferred item on a short list determined whether a subject was classed as dynamic or nondynamic. The decision about male or female dominance was made before data were collected. It was determined, not by counting noses, but by whether males or females had officially arranged the lecture.

Now for their procedure. After the lecture, envelopes with identical contents were distributed. They held three color-coded punch cards, along with the stylus and other equipment needed for punching. But, in those chauvinist days, envelopes were different for men and for women. The men's were plain manila; the women's were white and were tied with an orange ribbon ending in a pretty bow. Clearly, in mixed groups, the conspicuous difference between packets would accentuate whatever sex-consciousness already was present.

Subjects were instructed to punch one hole to designate sex; in the next column to punch one hole to show one of five attitudes about ESP (data from this scale are not reported); in the next column to punch one hole to choose the best metaphor for time out of a list of five metaphors; and then in each of the next 100 columns to select one of 10 digits as a precognition response. A computer was programmed to select a separate list of pseudorandom targets for each subject. It printed out the sex, presumably printed the attitude choice, designated the subject as dynamic if either of two predesignated metaphors had been selected, and printed the ESP score.

Total scores were null for the single sex groups and for nondynamic subjects. But in the groups of mixed sex, both hypotheses were supported. For the 21 groups which were male-dominated, ESP scores of the 534 dynamic males were significantly high, and in the 26 female-dominated groups, ESP scores of the 334 dynamic females were significantly high.

What seems to me especially interesting is an unpredicted mirror image effect for the scores of dynamic subjects in mixed groups. (The authors had not examined it but it showed up recently when I reanalyzed their data.) The 146 dynamic males in female-dominated groups scored significantly below chance; the 270 dynamic females in male-dominated groups scored (nonsignificantly) below chance; pooled male and female scores were significantly low. There was thus an interaction between dynamic tendencies and subgroup status. The mirror image effect, I think, converges with the major findings and thus supports them.

In general, considering the culture of the period, the findings seem to make sense psychologically. In the 1960s, women in a male-dominated group (typically, here, wives who attended the banquet at a convention of executives) seldom asserted themselves. Beribboned envelopes were distributed to them but not to their husbands. The implication was that the fair sex was different from the businesslike one, and it probably dampened the women's enthusiasm for making 100 punches to show their precognitive skill. But if the women were at a lecture that they themselves had arranged (for example a PTA meeting to which some brought their husbands) the same dainty implication might have spurred the more dynamic to think, in effect, "I'll show that man who's good at precognition." For dynamic men at their own meeting, the difference in envelopes might have put them on their mettle; at their wives' meeting it would seem more likely to make them feel even more detached from the whole procedure.

Nowadays, I think, the envelopes with orange bows would look only comical and old fashioned; they would diminish the importance of whatever came next in the procedure. But even if a direct replication is impossible now, Dean & Mihalasky's finding can be explored with a modified method. The general thesis is that awareness of being in a dominant subgroup will activate pleasantly the livelier (dynamic) members of that subgroup and therefore be psi-conducive. Dominance could be defined by any of a number of criteria: sex, of course, or race, or age, or others.

I know of no attempted replication, but one post hoc analysis supports the thesis. It comes from research by Friedman (Friedman, Schmeidler, & Dean, 1976). Of the 11 college classes that Friedman tested, six had a marked sex imbalance. In those classes the 325 members of the more numerous sex tended to psi-hit; the 29 members of the less numerous sex scored significantly below chance; and the difference between their ESP scores was significant.

Unreplicated research by Kanthamani (1966) is relevant here; it studies intragroup dominance with a different method. Subjects were pairs of same-sex friends, junior high school students. Kanthamani administered a pretest and recorded her judgment of which was the dominant member of the pair. The friends than played a competitive ESP game. She found, as predicted, that ESP scores were significantly higher for dominant subjects. They psi-hit; the submissive subjects psi-missed.

Mood and Group Membership

Anyone who teaches two or more sections of the same course will probably agree that, once the classes have settled in, they often have remarkably different group atmospheres. One may be dull and heavy, another eager and lively, another disputatious. Groups that differ in their typical mood may also differ in the mood that facilitates their performance. I therefore include here five research reports that investigate psi-conducive moods for differing groups. All used a variant of Nowlis's Mood Adjective Checklist to measure mood, and all used pretests to form a hypothesis about which moods would be psi-conducive, then a posttest to check the hypothesis.

The first was a study of gifted children enrolled in an optional parapsychology course (Schmeidler, 1971). Their instructor administered a mood checklist, a sheep-goat scale, and a test of clairvoyance, then mailed me the records without having scored them. I scored them, and correlated ESP scores with various combinations of mood and sheep-goat responses. The fishing expedition found a high correlation with the sum of scores for concentration, social affection, and surgency (playfulness). I then stated as a formal hypothesis that the same correlation would again be high when the group was retested. The instructor, blind to my hypothesis, administered the same tests again (but of course with different ESP targets) and mailed them to me. Many of the children had different moods (and ESP scores) on retest. As predicted, the correlation was high and significant.

Schmeidler & Craig (1972) attempted a replication. A colleague offered to test three groups for us (but one of the three was unusable because the pretest came when it first met, before a group atmosphere had developed). There were two changes in method: groups were small and the ESP was precognitive. The posttest correlation for one group was large but not significant; for the other group it was significant only by a one-tailed p.

This was disappointing, but after data analysis was complete it was gratifying to learn their instructor's descriptions of the groups. She said one was composed of lonely housewives and bored males; and here the pretest had shown a correlation of ESP scores with the algebraic sum of vigor minus fatigue, egotism, and anxiety. She said the other group was made up of competitive, energetic, upwardly mobile young men; here the pretest had shown that high ESP scores correlated with the algebraic sum of egotism minus anxiety and aggression. (Note that egotism correlated negatively to ESP scores in the passive group, but correlated positively in the active one.) My perhaps biased judgment is that differences in the mood patterns have a fair amount of face validity. My unbiased judgment is that, statistically, this project gave only weak support to the finding of the first.

A cleaner method was devised by Friedman and Dean in the research cited earlier. Friedman borrowed classes taught by others, and had a single session with each. His pretest came from the scores of his first 532 subjects. A computer was programmed to select separate pseudorandom targets for each subject, score the ESP responses, and compute a canonical correlation between ESP scores and mood scores. (This statistic shows how each mood should be weighted to show the strength of its relation to ESP scores.) For the posttest, on his later 568 subjects, the computer selected ESP targets and scored the responses as before, but it also weighted each subject's mood responses according to what the canonical correlation had shown and used those weighted mood scores to predict each subject's ESP score. The correlation of predicted with actual scores was positive and highly significant. Friedman's method thus successfully predicted ESP scores on the basis of mood.

What was the mood pattern here? Look first at how Friedman, a stranger to the classes, handled the test. His introductory remarks were short, and emphasized the value of precognition for business decisions. He implied that the test might be undesirable by excusing any who chose to leave. He then distributed mark-sense cards, showing that he, personally, would not be involved in the scoring. Cards would be fed into a computer. He instructed the students briefly but clearly how to mark the cards. With this cold procedure, the best mood predictors for ESP were low scores for aggression and for social affection.

Research by Carpenter (1983a) is striking: he made opposite predictions for two groups: subjects who were students in his own classes and all other subjects. His other predictor variables were mood, sheep-goat responses, and authoritarianism. His combination of variables repeatedly gave the significant results he had predicted. A replication (Carpenter, 1983b) reports 100 percent accuracy from redundant information about binary targets. A bit of information was obtained by the difference in responses between those predicted to psi-miss and to psi-hit. Twelve bits were obtained and all were correct. The 12 bits spelled out, in Morse code, the dots and dashes of a target word.

In summary, the many significant findings imply that groups vary in the mood which is psi-conducive for them.

Groups That Facilitate Psi

Later chapters include a number of other group comparisons, but they appeared post hoc and it seems appropriate to list them under the topic which the research was designed to test. The only other experiment of which I am aware that was formally designed to examine group differences is Condey's doctoral dissertation (1976). His subjects volunteered to come for an ESP test; he compared larger with small groups and sets of friends with sets of strangers. In each set, one was the percipient and the others acted together as agents. He predicted higher GESP scores for friends than for strangers, and also higher scores for larger groups of agents than for smaller ones. Neither prediction was significantly supported. But when Condey reexamined the large groups of friends, he found they split neatly into two subgroups. Some had met only socially; others had worked together, e.g., in a repertory theater or a commune. The GESP scores of those who had worked together were significantly high; the others were not.

Interaction Within the Group

A somewhat different problem deals with interrelations among individuals within a group. These can override relations to the group leader. An example that many of us may remember from our school days is listening to what a neighbor whispered even if it meant neglecting what the teacher said. The analogy, in a group ESP test, is to make null scores on the designated target but to respond by GESP to someone else's response.

Warcollier (1948) described this sort of cross-talk in groups of psychics, and called it "mental contagion." His records show case after case where psychics' responses were remarkably similar to each other but bore at most a remote relation to the official target. It is possible, however, to explain this away on any of three grounds. The resemblances are post hoc with no allowance for selection; an external cue may have triggered similar responses; and the similar responses may have been common ones. But even if his data do not prove his point, they give strong enough evidence to warrant examining it.

Intragroup patterning is difficult to analyze, as many of us have found (see, e.g., Schmeidler & Goldberg, 1974), but I can cite one careful analysis of it. Wiesinger (1973) tested 325 German and Swiss schoolboys. He found the children had null ESP scores on the designated targets. He then compared their responses with each other (omitting responses from children in neighboring seats). There was a significant overall correspondence among the responses. His next analysis is interesting: he made a cut-through according to popularity. He took the responses of the least popular child in a class as if they were the targets, and scored other responses against them. Scores were significantly lower than chance, as if the others avoided the responses that the unpopular child had made. On the other hand, when he took the responses of the most popular child as targets, scores were significantly higher than chance. This suggests that intragroup effects in psi can follow the pattern expected of intragroup effects in other forms of behavior.

Perhaps relevant to this topic is a type of research initiated by Humphrey (1947) where a subject tries to make a PK call while another person hopes either for the same outcome or a different one. Most such studies show higher scores with attempts to help than to hinder. This can be interpreted as social facilitation or inhibition of the subject's psi, but it can just as well be interpreted as a direct PK effect from the second person, bypassing the nominal subject.

Humphrey's experiment studied the minimal group: the dyad, or group of two. Many reports of dyadic interaction are scattered through these pages (see, e.g., Dean 1962, in Chapter 12; Kanthamani, 1966, in this chapter; Feather & Rhine, 1969, Chapter 8). I will add here only one example: an unreplicated study of mine. It was the last of three series that examined dyadic relations when one subject tried to send the other telepathic messages for success, or for failure, or for specific ESP cards (Schmeidler, 1961).

Students in my classes eagerly agreed to take a personality test (the Rorschach) and act as ESP subjects. On the basis of their Rorschachs, I paired students from different classes who were available for the same hour of ESP testing, and whom I had never seen together, so that each pair was predicted either to be congenial when they met, or else to be uncongenial, i.e., hostile or reserved. All pairs then went through the same procedure.

They were introduced; they were told that one would be the percipient and the other the agent for ESP; that there would be four ESP runs; and that the percipient would set the timing by sounding a buzzer when ready for the next message. The agent then went with me to a distant room, and was given the target deck and instructions for that run.

My instructions to the agent differed from one run to the next. On two runs (not in succession) the agent was to look at each card and try to send a telepathic message about it. On one run the agent could not see the cards, but was to hope the other person would get them right, like cheering for one's side at a baseball game. And on another run the agent could not see the cards, but was to hope the other person would get them all wrong, like hoping the opposing team would strike out. The percipient did not know about the different instructions.

As predicted from their Rorschachs, when agents tried to send a message about each card the ESP scores were significantly different for the two personality groupings (a little above chance for pairs expected to be congenial; significantly below chance for the pairs expected to be hostile or reserved). This was pleasant, but no great surprise. More interesting was a significant negative correlation between those scores and scores in the "hope for failure" condition. When the congenial agents hoped for failure, percipients scored very slightly below the chance level. When the uncongenial agents hoped for failure, percipients scored significantly better than chance. It was like the effect of a double negative. When uncongenial persons said "Fail!" the subjects significantly succeeded.

The experiment thus seems to show (as do many others) that psi interactions occur between members of a dyad, and that the interactions involve both the specifics of the situation (in this case, a message of failure versus a message about the target) and the social relation between the individuals.

Others Who Are Present

Many anecdotes and post hoc reports tell of marked changes in psi scores if visitors or others are introduced into the procedure. (See W.G. Braud & L.W. Braud, 1973, for an example and White, 1976a, for a review.) Such changes are to be expected on the basis of psychological research, but I know of no psi experiment designed to test for them.

Possible Psi-Extended Groups

Observing the Outcome

If time and space do not limit psi, the group of a psi experiment can include anyone involved in it, from the assistant who prepared the targets to those who know the experiment is going on and to whoever does the scoring and thinks about it later. So far as I know, only West and Fisk (Chapter 5) designed research to study target preparation, and no one has studied bystanders, but recently a sizable number of studies examined the effect of scoring (when there are no scoring errors) or of merely observing the results.

Although some earlier research indicated that the person who did the scoring could affect psi success, this received little attention until physicists' theories derived from quantum mechanics emphasized the point (see Chapter 14). The general line of reasoning is called observational theory, and it leads to the statement that the individual who first observes the psi event may determine its outcome. In some variants of observational theory, even a second or later observer may have an effect upon the outcome.

A research question to test the theory asks whether, all other things being equal, data are different with different first (or later) observers. Some researches found null results (e.g. Houtkooper, Andrews, Ganzevles, & Van der Sijde, 1980, where no finding is significant when corrected for selection); many found significant results—especially when a gifted subject was one of the observers (e.g., Schmidt, 1986). I will describe here only one recent experiment.

Weiner & Zingrone (1986) gave subjects four runs of calls on ESP cards, but told them that only two of the runs would be scored by their experimenter; the other two would be scored by some unnamed other person. Subjects guessed which two of their runs their own experimenter would score. Two runs were later randomly assigned for scoring by the experimenter; the other two were scored by the coauthor. In the first series, with 15 subjects, the scorers knew the subjects' guesses about the scorer. In the second series, with 52 subjects, each scorer had this information for one of the runs guessed to be scored by the experimenter and for one of the runs guessed to be scored by the stranger, but they were blind for the other two runs. Data were carefully examined to ensure against scoring errors.

Where the scorer knew the subject's guess, each series showed significantly lower ESP scores for runs correctly guessed to be scored by the stranger than for runs correctly guessed to be scored by the experimenter. Where scorers were blind, in the second series, there was no difference. The authors suggest that this tends to support the observational theory, since the scorers could make a complete observation only when they were not blind.

Possible Transfer of Psi Ability

Sporadic observations and anecdotes converge to suggest that individuals with strong psi ability can sometimes, temporarily, transfer that ability to others. Alvarado (1980) cites a number of such cases with appropriate cautions. The best known and best supported describe D.D. Home, a man frequently observed under excellent conditions to do a variety of psychic feats such as making a table levitate (once with no less a person than Sir Francis Galton crawling underneath to make sure that nothing supported it). One of Home's common demonstrations was to hold a burning coal in his hand without having the hand burn. Sometimes, according to well witnessed reports, Home designated an onlooker and that person was then able to hold the coal, still burning, without pain or injury. There are somewhat similar but unpublished reports about another gifted psychic, B.D. (see Chapter 10), and many accounts from anthropology or folklore of a master who can temporarily confer psychic powers upon a disciple.

There has been no research on transfer of psychic ability, but perhaps the closest approach came in an incident that I know at first hand (Schmeidler, 1970). A student told me that a swami wanted to visit one of my classes to show them ESP. A graduate class in experimental psychology agreed to let him try, and he visited them. The class first made an ESP run under my supervision; their scores were at chance. They then listened courteously but skeptically while the swami discoursed on chakras and such, and took them through a brief period of meditation and breathing. He then sat benignly at the side of the room while they made another ESP run. To the class's astonishment and mine, scores on that run were significantly higher than chance. It might have been only a coincidence, but it was not inconsistent with the swami's having kept his promise and shown them ESP.

Four Theories of Psi Group (or Experimenter) Effects

Four theories follow. We can think of them as lying on a continuum from rejecting the occurrence of experimenter or other interpersonal psi effects to making such effects basic in psi research.

At one extreme is a theory as short and simple as the classic one-sentence chapter about snakes in Ireland. It says only: There are no interpersonal psi effects. It attributes to other causes or to chance any findings that seem to show group effects. The unit in Chapter 5 about avoiding Type I errors shows the debating technique by which this theory can be defended. Some flaw is assigned to almost every research report (and since no human effort is likely to be perfect, some flaw can almost always be assigned). Any reports that remain are considered too few to support a conclusion.

Move now to the other extreme. This theory states that all psi effects are due either to a gifted subject or to a gifted experimenter; it was seriously stated by Millar (1979). It argues that psi ability is either absent or strong. If one of the rare gifted subjects who have this ability is tested, psi can be demonstrated. If neither a subject nor the experimenter is gifted, scores will be null. But if the experimenter is gifted, he or she can use PK to make subjects score high in whatever condition the hypothesis demands, and also to make subjects score low where the hypothesis demands it. The apparent evidence for a hypothesis shows only that a gifted experimenter used PK to produce that evidence. In effect, this theory takes the sporadic accounts which imply that a gifted psychic can transfer ability, and makes them the overarching explanation of other data. It seems to me to be one of those exasperating speculations that have little to support it but that cannot be tested and therefore cannot be falsified.

Now for the two intermediate theories. The simple psychological one is that psi scores will be like other psychological scores, e.g., higher in a warm experimental climate or with high expectations from the experimenter than in a cold climate or with low expectations. The experiments which try to test this theory seem to me, on the whole, to give strong support to it (Chapter 5). When the theory is extended in this chapter to cover group relations not determined by the experimenter, it also seems to account rather readily for the significant findings. It leaves unexplained, however, other effects without analogues to psychology, such as differences in score depending on who prepared the targets or who checked the results.

A broader concept was proposed by Murphy (e.g., 1970). His field theory for interpersonal relations, put briefly, proposes that we can convey good will, or withdrawal, or other feelings by our words, by our nonverbal behavior, or by psi. The social situation of an experiment thus has its climate determined by any or all of these modes of communication. The social nexus is a subtle and complex one. In addition to subject and experimenter it includes others who are part of the total situation and who thus contribute to the interpersonal field. It is a richer psychological theory than the one I have been stating and for me, though perhaps not for others, Murphy's arguments are persuasive.

ATTITUDES, ATTRIBUTIONS, VALUES

This unit surveys a fairly extensive body of psi research on attitudes, then moves to a single experiment on attributions and a few studies of values. (Values are discussed here because, by the standard definition, they are components of attitudes. Attitudes are evaluative; they include favorable or unfavorable feelings about their objects.)

Sheep-Goat Effects

Let me apologize for the peculiar pair of words which head this unit, and then explain them. They come from my first ESP research. It was preceded by preliminary ESP tests of anyone who came along, to find if they showed some pattern that looked as if it might be worth formal investigation. Most of those initial subjects were interested in ESP in a vague, tentative way and their scores tended to average a little better than chance. Then in rapid succession came two with a markedly different attitude. Both were convinced that ESP did not occur and both acted as subjects only to help me finish the project quickly so that I could be free to work on something else. Both scored strikingly lower than mean chance expectation.

Their low scores, combined with their strong opinions, suggested that unconsciously they had used ESP to avoid the targets and thus to fail in a test where they expected and wanted failure. If so, they were showing a familiar psychological effect, like Freudian slips, or the forgetting of unpleasant experiences, or selective inattention. It seemed a reasonable topic to investigate. I stopped the preliminary work, stated a formal hypothesis, and began testing it.

The hypothesis was that subjects who were convinced that ESP could not occur under the conditions of the experiment (whether or not they thought it might occur under other conditions) would have lower ESP scores than other subjects (even if those others thought they themselves could not show ESP, or if they thought ESP very unlikely but stopped short of thinking it impossible). Thus one group was rigorously defined; the other was defined by exclusion. Later, when I wrote a report of the research for the journal of a society with many lay members (Schmeidler, 1943) I tried to make it readable. I referred only briefly to the cumbersome definitions, which would be so heavy and dull when often repeated, and instead tried to add a little sparkle by designating the exclusion process briefly as separating the sheep from the goats. "Goats" were those who thought ESP success impossible under the experimental conditions; "sheep" were all others.

The terms caught on better than my definitions did, and have since been used in a good many different ways. Some, for example, define sheep as those who believe in ESP and define goats as those who think ESP somewhat improbable. Thus a person who believes in telepathy between those who love each other would be called a sheep, even if that person is sure ESP cannot occur under the test conditions, where no loved person is present and no one knows the targets. This usage differs radically from mine; others differ only a little.

A useful and meaningful additional category was added by Beloff & Bate (1970): super-sheep, for sheep who are sure they themselves will show ESP under the experimental conditions.

Now turn from nomenclature to research findings. Each of my first three series, with individual testing, showed significantly higher ESP scores for sheep than for goats. After that, to do something meaningful and to prevent my own boredom, I added other measures to the sheep-goat inquiry. By mid-1951 I had run seven individual series with a total of 151 subjects and also, during 14 semesters, had accumulated group tests on 1157 subjects. The predicted sheep-goat difference was significant overall in group tests as well as individual ones, although the mean difference was small. There were many reversals, where sheep scored low and goats scored high (Schmeidler & McConnell, 1958).

Palmer (1971) reviewed the topic, along with replications by others and by me. He reports that of the 15 other sheep-goat studies with a procedure comparable to mine, 11 had shown a trend supporting the hypothesis and 6 of those 11 had found a significant difference in the predicted direction; 4 showed an insignificant opposite trend; none gave a significant opposite score. Further, the distribution of mean sheep-goat differences in those 15 later studies was just about what would be predicted statistically from the distribution of means in my group series. His more recent review of replications (Palmer, 1982) concludes that the status of the hypothesis is unchanged. The sheep-goat effect is seldom a strong one, but overall it is well supported.

By now my own feeling is that the coarse division into two categories is uninteresting: good only as a first approximation. It pools too many qualitative differences. Some sheep think ESP occurs but are terrified of it; they should not be expected to make high scores. Some feel a fear of success after they learn of their initial good scores; for them the prediction should be that after feedback of high scores, their scores will be at or below chance. Some have a "What of it?" attitude; they think that ESP occurs but do not care. Some who tend toward mysticism disapprove heartily of laboratory attempts to formalize psi. Some dislike and want to frustrate the experimenter. Some super-sheep feel it so personally important to score high that they become overanxious. It is unreasonable to lump all these together into a single group predicted to have high scores.

Goats also show interesting and potentially important differences among themselves. Here are two examples. Some make the public disavowal of ESP that they think is intellectually correct, but have a sneaking suspicion that they are lucky. They take an ESP test eagerly in the hope that a high score will confirm their happy suspicion. Others, like my preliminary two subjects with low scores, hope their scores will demonstrate that ESP does not occur—but they have heard of the prior findings and know that if they score low it will be interpreted as evidence for ESP. For them, the sheep-goat prediction has become a self-disproving hypothesis.

Further, social factors can contaminate the response. For a good many subjects, the answer to the sheep-goat question will change with the circumstances and with who asks it. A person of high prestige with a clear pro-ESP bias is likely to find a higher proportion of sheep than one with a clear anti-ESP bias. An extreme example comes from Crandall (1985). With samples drawn from the same population, he reports that after a sympathetic introduction to an ESP test, 14 percent of the subjects were goats; after an unsympathetic introduction, 72 percent were goats. Findings of this type, along with subjects' introspective reports, show than even when the question is clear, the response is cloudier than it seems. It is likely to be less a response to the wording of the question than a response to the total situation. (But this may be why replications have so often been successful. The sheep-goat question taps not belief alone but also a general readiness to accept or to reject the instructions as a whole.)

Two loose ends in the research reports seem especially promising to me, and worth further study. One is an apparent tendency of super-sheep to score either very low or very high; by now I expect the variance of their scores to be higher than the theoretical variance. The other is that strong sheep-goat differences seem likely to be found in a culture or subculture that is highly polarized between the traditional and modern. If traditional beliefs include psi but modernism is taken to mean both materialism and a contempt for old beliefs, members of such groups are more likely than others to have thought through their sheep-goat attitudes and to care about the conclusion they reached.

Goal-Oriented and Process-Oriented Attitudes

In early PK research, subjects typically hoped that tumbling dice would come to rest with a particular face uppermost. Significant success under well controlled conditions indicated that their hopes somehow acted upon the dice, but many of us wondered about the mechanics of it. The dice moved so rapidly that there was no time for the subject to judge whether success would come if a die took one more turn or if it stayed where it was. When and how did the subject act?

The question was not answered, but the problem was clarified after Schmidt (1969) devised what he called a random number generator (RNG). In parapsychological research, RNGs are instruments that use a random source to select a psi target and that record both the number of trials and the number of successes. Often they are called random event generators (REGs). They are now in wide use because of their convenience and their flexibility.

An example of how they can be used to study what a subject does in making a psi response comes from Schmidt & Pantas (1972). They compared psi scores from two RNGs with different circuitry, one designed to test PK and the other precognition (although the authors comment that the distinction between PK and precognition is unclear). There was a single display panel to which each RNG was attached when in use. Scores were significantly high with each RNG, both with blind subjects and when Pantas, nonblind, made the calls. High scores from the blind subjects suggest that knowledge of the mechanism involved in psi success is irrelevant to the success.

Schmidt (1974) used a well controlled procedure to follow up on this suggestion. Again there were two RNGs. One had simple circuitry and its choice of target was determined by random emissions from radioactive decay. The other had complex circuitry and its choice of target was determined by the random output of an electronic noise generator. As before, either could be attached to the subject's display; but here both subjects and experimenter were blind as to which was attached. For each call, a selector switch followed a sequence of prerecorded random numbers to attach one or the other. There was an insignificant difference between scores with the two instruments, and the scores were significantly high with each.

How were those high scores obtained? Did subjects try to intervene, perhaps choosing which part of which instrument to act upon and then changing radioactive emission or electronic noise or some other component process? The report gives no hint of such rapid, accurate responding. Instead it implies that subjects relaxed, and merely hoped for the correct outcome. This does not answer the question of how psi operates and it tells us nothing about the physics of the psi process, but it has an important implication for the psychological pattern in psi success. It implies that our psi can give us the outcome we want even if we do not know how the outcome is reached.

That implication is consistent with the finding, both in physiology and psychology, that a desirable end result can be reached through different means. Sherrington (1906), for example, reports that a decorticate animal placed in different positions will achieve the same balanced posture even though achieving that posture demanded flexing and relaxing different muscles. He summarizes the importance of ends as opposed to means with a pleasant phrase: that the spinal cord thinks in movements, not in muscles.

Well replicated data in psychology lead to a similar conclusion: that the means of achieving a goal can be readily interchanged. If a rat learns to run through a maze and then the maze is flooded, the rat will swim along the correct path. If the right forefinger is conditioned to withdraw from an electrode at the sound of a buzzer and then the subject's left forefinger is placed on the electrode, the left forefinger will withdraw when the buzzer sounds. And examples from everyday life are common. We can walk on an uneven path without attention to its irregularities. We can detour around obstructions. We express an idea in different words to different listeners. We vary the means by which we reach a goal, and often we do it unconsciously.

A well controlled psi experiment examined this point by comparing goal-orientation with process-orientation (Morris, Nanko, & Phillips, 1982). An RNG gave continuous feedback: it displayed a light moving clockwise or counterclockwise, randomly. Subjects were to try to influence its direction. The 16 subjects of the first series were told they would use two strategies. Half began with the process-oriented one: they visualized energy built up in their own bodies, then flowing out to assist the light's progress in the specified direction. The other half began with the goal-oriented: pointing to where they hoped the next illumination would be. The goal-oriented strategy gave significant positive results; results with the process-oriented strategy were null.

The second series had 20 subjects and two sessions. Its first session replicated the earlier series and also found significantly higher scores for the goal-oriented strategy. Between sessions, subjects tried to practice at home. In the second session they used whichever strategy they preferred. Eight preferred the goal-oriented strategy and had significantly high scores. Scores of those who preferred the process-oriented strategy had a nonsignificant trend toward psi-missing.

The Morris, Nanko, & Phillips experiment had been conducted in the late 1970s, and it had two follow-ups. Both used only goal-oriented instructions. Nanko (1981) retested high scoring subjects from the first experiment and found significant psi-hitting. Morris & Reilly (1980) used a different display on the RNG and thus a modified set of instructions. Their 24 subjects had PK scores only insignificantly above chance.

In an elegantly planned experiment on this topic, Levi (1979) used a $3 \times 2 \times 2$ design, and an RNG that displayed number of hits. Of the 51 subjects, one-third were randomly assigned to goal-oriented instructions: imagining a high display number. One-third were randomly assigned to process orientation: imagining those workings of the machine that would lead to high numbers. The other third, in a control condition, heard a tape about RNGs and chance. The other two variables were feedback versus no feedback and having the subject or the experimenter push the control button for the RNG. Analysis of variance showed no main effect but a significant interaction. For goal-oriented subjects, scores were above chance with feedback but below without it. For process-oriented subjects, scores were below chance with feedback but above without it. Thus Levi's data with feedback replicate the finding of Morris, Nanko, & Phillips, but Levi's data for the condition without feedback keep us from drawing any simple conclusion from the replication.

Here, then, are two careful experiments from different laboratories comparing goal-orientation with process-orientation. Their three series found that, with feedback, goal-orientation was more psi-conducive. Is this a general finding? We do not know. I have searched the indexes of the journals that carry most psi research reports, and found many references to goal orientation and process orientation but no other clear data. Other studies that compare the two attitudes have, I think, confounding factors, such as passivity with one attitude but activity with the other. Although the consensus among parapsychologists is that goal-orientation is the more psi-conducive, good research evidence for that opinion seems limited to these two experiments, and the interaction with feedback has been studied only by Levi.

Teacher and Pupil Attitudes

One rather large body of research is always categorized as a study of attitudes and I therefore list it here, although it perhaps belongs with intragroup or experimenter effects. It was initiated by Anderson & White (1956) and their careful procedure was replicated by themselves and many others. The hypothesis they tested is that when a teacher administers an ESP test, pupils who like the teacher and whom the teacher likes will psi-hit, but that where teacher-pupil attitudes are mutually unfavorable, pupils will psi-miss.

Pupils' attitudes were tested by a seven-item questionnaire, asking, for example, whether they would choose the same teacher or some other for another course. (The teacher assured the pupils that responses would be confidential; each pupil put the response sheet into an envelope, then sealed it.) Since it was expected that good teachers would be reluctant to report an unfavorable attitude toward a pupil, a subtler question was put to them: "If you could form your ideal group for this class, would you include this student?" After the pupils' questionnaire responses were sealed, the teacher read standard, clear, and lively instructions for the ESP test. (The teacher had been asked to read the instructions as if they were personally important.) Each student had separate targets; the teacher was ignorant of the targets.

The first experiment, in which seven teachers each chose one of their classes for testing, gave strikingly consistent results in the predicted directions, and so did the next two. After 20 replications, however, White & Angstadt (1965) reported that the findings were mixed. Pooled results from high school pupils strongly supported the hypothesis (largely because of data collected by Anderson and White); pooled results from grade school pupils did not; and neither of the two studies with college students was supportive. Overall there seemed to be a tendency for high or low ESP scores to be better predicted by the pupils' questionnaires than by the teachers'.

Several of us have speculated about why a procedure that so often gave strong results has often given weak ones, and the speculations center around Anderson's recruitment of teachers and her instructions to them. She was an experienced teacher; she recruited teachers she thought were "good"; and she showed in various other activities that she had a gift for evoking enthusiastic cooperation in what concerned her. She may have been better able than some others to persuade teachers to read the standard instructions effectively. And a post hoc finding suggests that recruitment was important too. In one of the college studies with null results, the mean ESP scores of the four classes varied directly with their four professors' readiness to accept ESP.

My own inclination is to think of the research as a meta-experiment (where the chief experimenter is the person who recruits teachers and gives them instructions) and to think of the teacher's attitude toward the project as an important but unspecified variable. From a purely statistical point of view, the bottom line is that data from grade school and college are null, but that the pooled data of high school pupils significantly support the hypothesis that in high school, mutually favorable attitudes between teacher and pupil will be associated with higher ESP scores than will mutually unfavorable attitudes.

Attributions

A single experiment manipulated the subjects' attributions for ESP calls. Lovitts (1981) obtained 40 subjects by advertising a paid experiment on subliminal perception. She assigned subjects randomly (as far as possible) to two conditions. In what she called the Prove-ESP condition, instructions stated that ESP targets were interspersed among the subliminal stimuli, advised subjects to relax, and gave mildly positive suggestions for ESP success. In what she called the Disprove-ESP condition, instructions stated that evidence for ESP had come from sloppy experiments which had not fully eliminated sensory cues, that success in perceiving the subliminal stimuli in the present experiment would show that this was a viable hypothesis and success would therefore disprove ESP. This was followed by brief advice to relax.

All subjects went through the same procedure. First came a sheep-goat questionnaire (to which the experimenter remained blind), then a short practice to familiarize subjects with the apparatus, then the test. The test period for all subjects consisted of 125 ESP trials. On every trial the same complicated figure was exposed subliminally: a figure that consisted of all five ESP symbols, superimposed. Subjects responded with whatever one of the five symbols they "saw" on that trial.

The hypothesis was that ESP scores would show an interaction between attribution of success and sheep-goat attitude. Analysis of variance significantly supported the prediction, and each of the four subgroups of subjects scored in the predicted direction. For the Prove-ESP condition, sheep scores were above chance and goat scores were below; for the Disprove-ESP condition, sheep scores were below chance and goats' above.

This neat manipulation of the meaning of hitting and missing ESP targets has not been replicated, but is clearly consistent with both the sheep-goat hypothesis and the manipulations described in Chapter 5 for experimenter expectations. A brief earlier report by Waldron (1959) roughs out a somewhat similar but less tidy method with somewhat similar results: a change in ESP scoring when subjects were led to believe that an ESP test was a test for acuity of vision.

Values

Only four psi studies, so far as I know, were designed to investigate values. All used the Allport-Vernon or the equivalent Allport-Vernon-Lindzey scale, where scores show the relative importance of six values: economic, esthetic, political (power-oriented), religious, social, theoretical.

When I first administered this test to my classes (Schmeidler, 1952b) scores showed a positive relation between theoretical values and ESP success. I had not predicted this but it seemed eminently reasonable to me; in discussing ESP, my emphasis was always on its theoretical implications.

Not one of the three replications showed the pattern of my data. Nash (1958) found a significant positive relation between ESP scores and religious values. Buzby (1963) reported briefly that he had tested for Nash's correlation but found it nonsignificant; he does not describe correlations with other values. Collymore (1978) replicated neither Nash's finding nor mine. His subjects' ESP scores showed a significant positive relation with social values and significant negative relations with economic and esthetic ones.

Such diverse significant results demand clarification. I suggest two possibilities. One, implausible but not impossible, is that each significant finding is a statistical accident. The other is that a type of experimenter effect was operative. It seems likely to me that in the classroom atmosphere I generated, students with high theoretical values would be most responsive to whatever was going on. Did Nash have high religious values? Did Collymore emphasize that ESP could provide close personal relations but comment that concern with ESP was not an asset in the job market?

Checking out this second interpretation demands an experimenter whom the subjects know so well that they have developed an understanding of him or her, and an appropriate modern test for values that is taken by both experimenter and subjects. (The Allport-Vernon-Lindzey scale now seems outdated.) The prediction to be tested is that students' ESP scores will correlate with their scores on the predominant value (or value pattern) of the experimenter: correlate positively if the experimenter's attitude toward ESP is favorable and negatively if it is unfavorable. (Any students with unshakable sheep or goat attitudes should perhaps be excluded.) Until suitable tests are made, those of us who want to avoid Type II errors will hold open the possibility of a relation between values and ESP scoring; but all of us who want to avoid Type I errors must say that no relation between values and ESP has been established.

OVERVIEW

Psi research on the effect of group membership is sparse and seldom replicated but the trend of the findings fits psychological expectations, e.g. showing higher ESP scores for those more comfortable in a group, or scores that reflect how well the group members like each other or work together.

Several studies successfully predicted psi scores on the basis of mood. They converge to show that groups differ predictably in the mood which is psi-conducive for them.

Considerable scattered evidence implies that, for psi, interpersonal relations extend beyond the group as it is conventionally defined, and that the psi group can include distant or unknown persons concerned with the research.

Two attitudes seem conducive to psi success: acceptance rather than rejection of the task, and (with feedback) goal orientation rather than process orientation.

Research on values has given contradictory data, perhaps because experimenters' values were unmeasured.

7. Personality

We differ from each other. This is a banal statement but is too often forgotten; it deserves attention whenever we plan psychological or psi research or examine its outcome.

Over the years it has been hammered home to me that personality differences are so pervasive and powerful that they can affect responses to any conditions we want to study. This means that they will falsify any simple, precise generalization and that even learning or perception need families of sublaws to show how different individuals respond.

Take learning, and turn again to the example from Chapter 2. Is seven plus or minus two the magic number for memory span? One test is to present a series of random digits at one second intervals and find how many the subjects can recall; I often tried this with introductory classes. On the first go-round the average score is indeed likely to be near seven. But does the rule hold if there are minor changes of procedure? Suppose we repeat the tests. Scores of some students decline with boredom; scores of others increase with practice. Their personality or attitude has affected their memory span; the law must be therefore modified. And what if length of list increases, say to 15? Of the students who were correct for seven out of seven, some—but not all—will remember fewer from a long list. We need to modify the law again.

When even the stripped down, barren, rote learning of digits shows these individual differences, there will obviously be even wider differences when the learning has a stronger emotional component and is more complex. A host of personality factors enter into the way any of us learn moral values, or learn how to present ourselves favorably in a job interview, or even learn mathematical concepts.

In perception, the impact of individual differences is striking. I learned this slowly, the hard way, while teaching a graduate course on perception. My first naive emphasis was on what Gordon Allport called nomothetic processes: the general laws that hold true for any normal adult (as opposed to idiosyncratic processes, the special patterns of a particular person). But for nearly every topic, my readings showed the single law was incomplete.

Take afterimages, sometimes called the persistence of vision. If we watch a rotating spiral and the movement stops, we "see" the spiral rotating in the opposite direction. Is this an acceptable law? Not yet. It is stated too crudely; laws should be quantified. We ask how long the afterimage persists for a given stimulus and a given length of rotation. And we find no single answer; we find differences with personality. For extreme introverts the duration is even longer than the original rotation; for extreme extraverts it is much shorter.

Or consider what happens if subjects wear aniseikonic (distorting) lenses. The visual world changes quickly for well adjusted, flexible subjects. At first a table or the walls and floor may seem properly rectangular, but in a few seconds the shapes distort. Flexible subjects see what the lenses show them. But for rigid subjects, whom other tests show to be bigoted or closed-minded, there is little or no effect from the lenses. They continue to see the objects as they know the objects are.

Topic after topic shows similar meaningful, predictable differences in our perception. Susceptibility to visual illusions changes with age; it increases for certain types of illusions and decreases for others. A perceptually deprived, monotonous environment drives some people into a panic but induces in others a pleasantly dreamlike state. My attempt to teach generalities demanded so much class time for the exceptions that it began to look as if the tail was wagging the dog. And even after a new course allowed a whole semester for the topic of how perception relates to personality, lectures had to move fast to include all the material I had put in the syllabus.

What does this mean for the early hope that psychology or parapsychology would find general laws and that we could demonstrate them whenever we set up uniform, controlled conditions? It means, I think, that our goals should be less grandiose. Research aimed at finding average values for learning or perception—or psi—is as defective as research that aims at finding the average weight of fruit, without specifying if it measures grapes or grapefruit, and without control for soil fertility, or drought, or insect depradation. The hope for a single law should be modified to the hope for an orderly pattern of sublaws; the hope that every attempt at demonstration will be effective becomes unrealistic unless a great many factors are specified. Both the sublaws and the possible demonstrations demand that we take into account variables of personality.

THE PERSONALITY VARIABLES TO BE STUDIED

Which personality variables should be examined? Psychology gives a wide choice of where to look: analyses differ from one respected theorist to the next. Further, even when theorists use the same term, they may use it with different meanings. Some, for example, treat introversion as a unitary concept; but Jungians distinguish primary and secondary introversion, and divide each into four subtypes.

Most personality theorists analyze traits: long term tendencies that are present in everyone but that vary in strength from person to person. Examples are affiliation, aggression, anxiety, and the longer lists can continue through the alphabet to zeal and zest.

It is traits that this chapter will examine, to find if any relate to psi scores. Other variables that could come here but do not, are temperament (omitted in spite of the impressive data from Bhadra, 1965, because no other psi research studied it); moods and longer altered states of consciousness (which are in chapters 6, 8, 9); cognitive styles (which come in Chapter 11); and attitudes and values (which came in Chapter 6).

Personality Traits and Psi

Well over 200 studies report on personality traits and psi, but they are a mixed bag. Many give so little detail that the method is unclear. Some measure psi only by uncorroborated claims of psychic experiences. (These are omitted.) Others, I am glad to say, give careful descriptions of well controlled psi tests, and these are the basis of the descriptions that follow.

Besides problems of method, the variables in the studies are so diverse that they made me give up my first attempt to write a survey and write instead a call for multivariate research (Schmeidler, 1983c). I had turned to the index of what was the current volume of *Research in Parapsychology;* it listed 20 personality variables. Then I turned to the preceding volume. Again there were 20 subheads under Personality Variables—but only two of them were on the current list. Although the variety spoke well for parapsychologists' range of interests, it also reminded me of Leacock's man who "flung himself upon his horse and rode madly off in all directions." It left me feeling that it was hard to see where all the effort was heading.

But all was not lost. My recent longer look showed that over the years there had been a good many studies of one trait, extraversion-introversion. It deserves a review. And it now seems to me that two other traits were often tested, although the tests labelled them with different names. For these two I group the studies and list them below as Openness versus Defensive Withdrawal and as Anxiety and Neurotic Tendencies. There will also be a brief mention of traits where research is scant but where what has been done looks promising.

Extraversion-Introversion

Eysenck (1967) surveyed research on extraversion and psi, and found that nearly all reports showed more effective psi for extraverts than for introverts. Recent surveys by Palmer (1978) and Sargent (1981) agree. To the studies they cited I added others done by mid-1986, and compiled 38. Of these 38, 29 show this trend; it is significant for 12 of the 29. The general relation thus seems well established. Extraverts tend to have higher psi scores than introverts.

Does its being well established mean that it is a consistently repeatable finding? Can anyone who wants to demonstrate psi merely administer tests for extraversion and psi and show their positive correlation? No. "Well established" means only that its batting average has been consistently good. It was good in Eysenck's 1967 sample and in later ones; with different investigators and different samples of subjects; even with different tests for extraversion. But other factors interact. Extraverts can be expected to score high only under conditions appropriate for them. To emphasize this point, I describe below two of the exceptional projects that showed a contrary trend.

What are those appropriate conditions for extraverts? Eysenck, a distinguished psychologist who makes the extraversion-introversion pattern basic to his entire theory (see end of Chapter 9) describes several, but I will mention only the two that seem most relevant to the exceptional cases that follow. One is that extraverts tend to respond well to novelty but their performance declines with monotony; another is that they tend to respond better in groups than in individual testing. Introverts show opposite trends.

Now look at one exception to the general finding: a small project which predicted and found higher ESP scores for introverts than extraverts. A student of mine, himself highly introverted, made appointments for an ESP test with 20 friends or acquaintances (Szczygielski & Schmeidler, 1975). They met in either his home or theirs and talked for a while, then he administered a repetitive, dull ESP test and two tests of extraversion. ESP score correlated negatively with extraversion, and this was significant by a one-tailed p.

This is an exception to the trend, but its method was exceptional too. The results were predictable from Eysenck's theory. It could even be argued that with this method, the data converge to support the theory and strengthen the other findings. Part of Eysenck's thesis is that the optimal level of arousal is higher for extraverts than for introverts. Classroom or laboratory conditions are more arousing than a chat at one's home or one's friend's home; extraverts tend to score better at ESP in the former, introverts scored better in the latter. Extraverts do badly with monotony and introverts do better; the test conditions were monotonous. In short, under the test conditions introverts became comfortably relaxed, but extraverts felt little pressure to perform well at their dull task.

The major recent exception to the finding of higher ESP scores for extraverts comes from eight series by Thalbourne and his associates (see Thalbourne & Jungkuntz, 1983). ESP scores were compared with extraversion scores and with scores on a type of sheep-goat inquiry that asked about psi experiences but not about attitudes to this ESP test. The hypothesis throughout was that extraverts classed as sheep would score higher at ESP than introverts classed as goats. The first two series showed a decreasing trend in the direction of the hypothesis, but the next six showed an increasing trend in the opposite direction. By the eighth series, scores were below chance for introverts, extraverts, sheep, and goats. Though the difference between groups was not significant, extravert sheep significantly psi-missed.

The rather steady shift from near-significant support for the hypothesis to near-significant reversal may, of course, be only happenstance; but those of us impressed by the experimenter effect are tempted to speculate about experimenter changes. The first series was performed when Thalbourne was a young man and had just constructed an unusual type of sheep-goat questionnaire. It seems plausible that he was more enthusiastic at first than later; most of us are. This could be adduced post hoc as a reason for decline of scores toward the chance level.

But his groups' scores tend to go past the chance level; they tend to reverse the initial trend. A post hoc interpretation is that the cause might be experimenter negativism. This guess is based on two bits of evidence: one procedural change that Thalbourne made and one that he failed to make. In his seventh series he introduced a new condition, but he selected one that prior research indicated would make ESP scores lower. (The change was a money reward for high scores; and this series gave overall scores significantly lower than chance.) What he failed to change was the type of ESP test. He used one that subjects found uncongenial and that, in other research, gave null results. Thus a highly speculative post hoc interpretation of his discrepant findings is that the dull task, imposed by an experimenter who did not enthusiastically hope for ESP success, tended to depress the ESP scores of extraverts even more than those of introverts.

It is imbalanced to describe in detail two projects that gave deviant results, and none with the usual positive relation between extraversion and ESP success. But since I did, I will use it as the occasion for two generalizations. One is that an apparent exception to a prediction may be an exception only to an oversimplified version of a theory, but still be consistent with the complete (and more complex) basic hypothesis. The other generalization states a riskier thesis: that if a hypothesis about psi is supported under test conditions which led to psi-hitting, opposite results will often be found in conditions which lead to psi-missing. This is what I called a double negative in Chapter 6; it states there is often a multiplicative rather than additive effect of two variables (i.e., a minus times a minus gives a plus).

Openness versus Defensive Withdrawal

While compiling my notes on psi studies of personality, I found myself grouping a study of withdrawal with one on avoiding attention, then adding to the same group other work that used terms like barrier, defensive, compressive. The opposite pole was described by terms like expansive or open. Studies with nine different designations follow. In spite of their different labels and methods of testing, all seem to me to converge on the same trait: openness.

It is a trait that recently has been receiving attention in psychology, as one of the five factors needed to describe personality (McCrae, Costa, & Busch, 1986). (The other factors are neuroticism, extraversion, agreeableness, conscientiousness.) Openness is associated with being imaginative rather than down to earth, preferring variety to routine, being independent rather than conforming, etc. The nine labels under which it has been studied in parapsychology are listed below.

Coartation and Dilation. Early in my ESP testing it began to look as if ESP scores above mean chance expectation were being made by subjects who were lively and outgoing and fun to be with, but lower scores were being made by subjects who acted timid and constrained. At Gardner Murphy's advice I learned and began administering a personality test, the Rorschach, to find if its scores tied in with differences in ESP scores.

Two of Rorschach's classic categories matched neatly with liveliness and constraint. The categories are for extremes, but could be used to test my impressions. One, "dilated ambiequal," is assigned to those who respond to the ink blots with many descriptions of color and lively movement; it is taken to show an inner richness of ideas and an active emotional responsiveness. The other, "coartative," is assigned to those who give few or no movement and color responses; it is taken to show they permit themselves to have only a constricted, narrow range of responses.

Of over a thousand subjects whom I tested in groups from 1943 to 1951, only 40 were dilated ambiequals (23 sheep; 17 goats). As predicted, their ESP scores were significantly above chance (with the goats' scores only slightly lower than the sheep's). There were 63 coartatives (35 sheep, 28 goats). Their ESP scores were near chance (sheep negligibly above, goats suggestively below). The difference between dilated ambiequals and coartatives was significant (Schmeidler & McConnell, 1958). No other psi research has used this particular pair of scores, and we can forget Rorschach's awkward terms.

Withdrawal. But we should not forget the concept. A few years later a better term, "withdrawn," was used to describe the shy, constrained subjects. Shields (1962), a school psychologist, tested children referred to her, using a battery of psychological tests to divide them into diagnostic categories. She also gave the children ESP tests. The ESP scores were above chance in all diagnostic categories except one. In the group she listed as withdrawn, scores were significantly below chance. It was as if those children withdrew from the ESP targets just as they withdrew from parts of their daily life.

Seeking and Avoiding Attention. Some years later Shields & Mulders (1975) used a different test battery but found what seems a similar result. The children they classed as "attention-avoiders" had significantly lower ESP scores than those they classed as "attention-seekers." Again, it was as if the avoiders were avoiding the targets for ESP.

Compressiveness-Expansiveness. Humphrey (1946a, 1946b) used drawings as her ESP targets, and subjects responded with drawings. Responses were scored for ESP and also independently scored on a scale of expansiveness and compressiveness. Criteria were not only area and vigor of stroke but also whether the drawing conveyed the impression of force and boldness or of timidity and conventionality. Subjects rated expansive made significantly higher ESP scores than those rated compressive in a clairvoyance procedure, but compressives' scores were significantly higher in a GESP procedure, when the experimenter tried to send telepathic messages about the targets. The post hoc interpretation was that expansives welcomed the freedom of finding the targets themselves but compressives welcomed close cooperation with the experimenter.

Palmer (1978) lists seven other reports that used Humphrey's criteria for personality ratings, to which I add one report published after he wrote. The eight comprise 16 series. Eleven of the 16 showed the trend Humphrey described and for three the difference was significant; the other 5 found a contrary trend but none was significant. Thus the results of replication are mixed, but tend on the whole to support Humphrey's original statements.

Kanthamani & K.R. Rao (1973) used a different procedure to study expansiveness. Targets were ESP cards; the procedure was clairvoyance. Subjects also made drawings, and the area of the drawings was measured. Subjects were then rated as expansive or compressive according to a median split of the area that the drawings covered. The data significantly support the relevant part of the other findings: the 53 expansives had ESP scores slightly above chance but the 57 compressives had ESP scores far below, and the difference in ESP scores was significant.

Two questions might be raised here. One is whether a measure taken from drawings is likely to be fairly stable (and thus indicative of a personality trait) or likely to be so variable that it indicates only mood. Psychological research has answered this already: drawings tend to be stable. They vary somewhat with mood and also with what is being drawn, but on the whole those from a single person resemble each other closely. Like most other measures, however, this one is noisy when categories are determined by a median split instead of by taking only extremes. Especially at the center of the distribution, a good many subjects are likely to be misclassified.

The other question is whether compressiveness is merely another term for introversion and expansiveness for extraversion. Eysenck's theory suggests that the categories overlap but are not the same, and this is what Kanthamani & Rao's data imply. A standard test for extraversion classed about two-thirds of their compressives as introverts, but only about half of their expansives as extraverts.

The two cross-cuts gave four subgroups, two with consistent scores (expansive extraverts and compressive introverts) and two with mixed scores. The mixed groups had ESP scores near chance, but scores of the self-consistent groups were more extreme. Expansive extraverts had significantly higher ESP scores than compressive introverts. Using two personality measures gave cleaner psi results than either personality measure alone.

Rigidity. A single study compared scores on Schaie's Test of Behavioral Rigidity with scores on an ESP test. Mythili & P.V.K. Rao (1980) found that the scale as a whole, and also each of its three subscales, all gave correlations in the predicted direction: lower ESP scores for the more rigid subjects. All the correlations were insignificant.

Barrier and Penetration. Again, a single study. Schmeidler & LeShan (1970) arranged that old Rorschachs in my files be scored blind for a new pair of measures: barrier and penetration. (Responses like a coat of armor or a closed door symbolize barrier; responses like a harbor entrance or a sword going into flesh symbolize penetration. Barriers imply a self-protective distancing from events; penetration implies an openness which may or may not be injurious.)

Our procedure reversed the usual one: we divided subjects according to their ESP scores to see if the ESP scores would predict the personality scores. ESP means and variances were listed. Rorschachs were then pulled from the files for all sheep who had both high means and high variances and all sheep who had both chance means and chance variances. Names were taped over to ensure confidentiality. The Rorschachs were arranged randomly with some others and then sent off. The blind scoring assigned significantly lower barrier scores and also significantly lower scores for barrier minus penetration to the group with high ESP means and variances than to the group with scores at the chance level.

Defensiveness. There are a good many studies here. All but one used a well validated measure, the Defense Mechanism Test (described in Chapter 10). A quick summary is that nine of the ten series with this test showed lower ESP scores for more defensive subjects; three were significant by a two-tailed *p* and two others by a one-tailed *p*. The finding seems strong.

A unique behavioral measure of defensiveness was used by Stanford & Schroeter (1978): the subject's choice of adjusting the experimental chair to a fully reclining (nondefensive) position. ESP scores of the 40 subjects with a nondefensive choice were significantly high, and were suggestively higher than scores of the 27 more defensive subjects. Again, nondefensiveness seems psi-conducive.

The work on defensiveness not only shows a high level of replication, but also converges on a good many other findings, especially where the setting might be expected to make subjects feel defensive. An example is the lower ESP scores of members of nondominant subgroups (Chapter 6). Another example is the lower ESP scores of subjects tested in a cold emotional climate (Chapter 5).

Inhibition versus Impulsivity. Stanford (1964) asked subjects to describe themselves on an adjective scale, and also asked them to use the same scale to describe what their ideal self would be. (Psychologists make the unkind assumption that we all fall short of our ideal. Thus when a person reports a close similarity between the self and the ideal self, it is taken to show repression or inhibition, but a sizable discrepancy between self and ideal self is taken to show openness.) As predicted, sheep with a high disparity made higher ESP scores than sheep with a low disparity. Stanford (1965) replicated this finding.

Years later, Stanford (1973) retested the interpretation with a different method, i.e., he performed a systematic replication. His ESP test was the choice of the (randomly assigned) right word in a word association task. His measure of impulsivity or inhibition was the speed with which the subject gave associations. Speed had a significant positive correlation with ESP success. (This surprised me because often, though erratically, I had noticed that slow ESP responses were associated with high scores. But different measures, different findings. . .) Stanford & Schroeter (1978) modified the method slightly and in this systematic replication there was an insignificant negative correlation between speed of response and ESP success. (This is the project which tested defensiveness by chair-tilt; the authors do not report combining the inhibition and defensiveness scores.)

Openness. L. [Williams] Braud (1976) developed an 88-item questionnaire to study openness, including a subscale for extraversion. In the original report and in her two replications (L.W. Braud, 1977; Williams & Duke, 1980) she found nonsignificant trends toward a positive relation between openness and ESP success. Bellis & Morris (1980) also report a nonsignificant trend in the same direction with this questionnaire. Both L. Braud (1976) and Bellis & Morris found that the extraversion subscale showed a significant positive correlation with ESP scores.

A sidelight on this project is too pretty to omit. Sondow, L.W. Braud, & Barker (1982) report that they could not appropriately use the openness questionnaire because all their subjects were open. But with openness in mind, they examined not the subjects but the 40 targets of their Ganzfeld study. Targets were ranked, before data were collected, on how threatening they seemed. In their responses to the three most threatening targets, subjects mentioned fences 13 times, while responses to the other 37 possible targets had only 13 mentions of fences. Fences prevent openness; fences are defensive barriers; threatening ESP targets apparently elicited barrier responses. It was a post hoc finding and thus carries no statistical weight, but it gives a pleasant metaphor for defensiveness or non-openness and suggests an interesting direction for further research.

Summary. This has been an unconventional unit, because it argues that a variety of methods and terms all examine the same trait. It suggests that coartation, withdrawal, attention-avoidance, compressiveness, rigidity, barriers, defensiveness, inhibition, and non-openness all overlap to describe one end of a continuum, and that the opposite end is described by such terms as liveliness, expansiveness, openness. Preponderantly, results have been showing higher psi scores for those at the open than at the withdrawn end.

Will the results replicate? We cannot be certain. Probably multiple measures, like the pair used by Kanthamani & Rao, or a test battery like that used by Shields, will give cleaner data than a single measure. Almost surely such factors as attitude, mood, and the experimenter effect will modulate the pattern. Nevertheless, it seems to me that the convergence of the results from the methods listed here indicates that they rough out a personality variable highly relevant to psi success.

Anxiety and Neurotic Tendencies

Anxiety may be specific to a situation and stop when the situation changes, while neurotic tendencies are long-lasting; but Palmer (1978, 1982) surveys them together and I follow his lead. His articles review 48 reports on ESP and anxiety or neurosis. (My supplementary review of PK and of later reports adds ten more to the list; these ten support his conclusion.) His evaluative summary is that, especially for individual rather than group testing, there is a clear trend toward higher ESP scores for better adjusted or less anxious than for more neurotic or more anxious subjects.

Palmer's examination was careful; his conclusion should be respected. His wording was careful, too. Let me state at once three things that he did not say, then elaborate on each. One: his conclusion applies to scores obtained in research, not to anecdotes about possible psi experiences. Two: he makes no statement about highly gifted psi subjects. Three: he does not state that all investigations support the general trend.

Scores versus anecdotes: When a person claims to have had many psi experiences, does this mean the person is a gifted psychic? Perhaps. But it also could mean that the person credulously attributes normal experiences to psi; it could mean distortions of memory, or neurotic fears and wishes, or psychotic fantasies. Until the claims are checked out, we do not know what they mean. A glance at statistical findings about those who claim psi experiences indicates that many score high on neuroticism scales. This need not be relevant to data from psi scores obtained under well controlled conditions.

Gifted subjects: What Palmer evaluated was statistical trends, and they tell us little about exceptional individuals. Case studies of gifted psychics indicate they can be found anywhere on the range from an outstandingly successful social adjustment to a very poor one. No generalization is justified, but two lines of a priori reasoning suggest that some maladjustment might often be present. One is that anyone with exceptional ability is "different" and psi ability, unlike muscular skill, is not always esteemed in our society. A child who displays psi might be teased or rebuked; a child who keeps it secret is under an unusual strain; either choice can lead to anxiety or difficulties in adjustment. The other line of reasoning is more speculative. It is that good social adjustment as usually defined often represents overcontrol, an inhibition not only of maladaptive behavior but also of creativity (and perhaps of psi). Creative individuals often show both neurotic tendencies and also the ego strength that permits coping with those tendencies. Gifted psychics may similarly show both of this balanced pair of tendencies.

Exceptions: Research findings differ. This is no great surprise for anxiety or neurosis scales, which often measure different tendencies. An example is that few measure separately the moderate levels of anxiety which can be facilitative. (Many a lecturer has found that if there was no anxiety beforehand, the lecture bored the audience and fell with a dull thud, but with tension—anxiety—beforehand the presentation was livelier and well received.) Another problem comes when scores on a scale of repression-sensitization are compared with anxiety scores. We ordinarily rate repression as bad and sensitivity as good; but repression and low anxiety seem to relate to each other. A third issue is the distinction between social and personal adjustment. It has often been argued that in our society with its many inequities, anyone with extremely high social adjustment must be either blind or callous, and therefore psychologically unhealthy.

In short, labels of high anxiety or neurosis versus low anxiety or good adjustment sound clear, but what the labels represent is not. I describe in some detail below three of the psi projects that use these labels, so that we can examine the complexities and at least guess at other factors that interact with them and therefore need to be controlled in later research.

The first was one of the crosscuts I made with the Rorschachs from my early ESP subjects. A scale of social adjustment for the Rorschach was available. Its ratings for my first group of 58 subjects with Rorschachs showed that sheep with good adjustment had higher ESP scores than other sheep; goats with good adjustment had lower ESP scores than other goats. Blind ratings of Rorschachs for all following subjects significantly supported this pattern of an interaction between attitude and adjustment (Schmeidler, 1960).

It seemed to me to make sense. Well adjusted subjects tended to score in line with their expectations and desires; poorly adjusted ones were less predictable. But did it mean that poor adjustment was associated with low ESP scores? No, just the opposite for the goats. They rejected the possibility of ESP success, and it was those with good adjustment who made the low scores consistent with their expectations. And how did it fit in with the other prediction about liveliness and constraint? Not very well. The overconstrained almost always scored low on social adjustment and on average had chance ESP scores. This fit. But the liveliest ones with an unusually high number of color and movement responses often had low social adjustment scores too, and their ESP scores were high. More was going on here than any single score or pair of scores could show.

The second example comes from Palmer and his coworkers. Palmer had found many studies with significantly better ESP scores for the better adjusted and less anxious. He also found many studies that were null, but only a single report with significant findings opposite to the general trend (Haight, Kanthamani, & Kennedy, 1978).

This exception interested him, naturally, and Palmer, Ader, & Mikova (1981) replicated the work, examining two conditions to see if they were important. One was comfort: Haight et al. had left subjects alone during the ESP test. Palmer et al. interpreted this as perhaps making anxious subjects less self-conscious and more at ease. The other condition was feedback. Each subject had had trial-by-trial feedback for half their calls but feedback only at the end of the run for the other half of their calls. The better scores of anxious subjects came only in the latter condition.

The replication was direct for feedback, but found no effect from it. For comfort it could not be direct because subjects were high school students and regulations forbade leaving them alone during testing. Instead Palmer et al. arranged a comfortable condition for half their subjects by having their own teacher act as experimenter, and a less comfortable one for the other half by having a teacher who was a stranger conduct the experiment. In the more comfortable situation, the anxiety-ESP correlation was nonsignificantly positive, thus tending to support the finding from Haight et al., but in the less comfortable condition the correlation was nonsignificantly negative, thus tending to support the general trend of other findings. The implication is consistent with both common sense and psychological research: a tendency toward anxiety may disrupt performance if other conditions cause additional anxiety and the person becomes overanxious, but it may facilitate performance when other conditions are not anxiety-provoking and the total anxiety during the task is only moderate. (See also Chapter 8 for a similar finding by Mischo & Weis, 1973.)

The last example of interacting variables comes from Broughton & Perlstrom (1985, 1986). I report it in oversimplified form. In each of their three series, subjects used an RNG to play a PK game, and took tests of anxiety. The first series was a competitive PK tournament among members of the laboratory staff and their friends; scores of the 16 subjects showed a significant negative correlation with anxiety. The second series falsely told 50 subjects that they would use the RNG to compete against a distant, unseen person. Subjects also were given a ten page questionnaire and asked to fill it out at home, then return it. The anxiety-PK correlation was negative but insignificant for the 50 subjects—but post hoc examination showed the negative correlation was significant for the 23 who cared enough about participation to return the questionnaire. The third series replicated the second and its finding replicated too. For the 28 out of 50 subjects who returned the questionnaire, there was a significant negative correlation between anxiety and PK score.

The implication is clear. It is only when subjects care about what they are doing that their tendency toward anxiety is likely to relate to their psi performance.

Other Possible Variables

Many other possibilities seem worth attention. I mention a sample.

Self-confidence: Perhaps self-confidence is one opposite of anxiety, but I list it separately because it is usually measured by a different scale or method. A handful of findings suggests a positive correlation between self-confidence and psi success—but surely here the optimum is not the maximum. Extreme confidence is often unjustified; it can be a sign of poor adjustment. For the extremely confident super-sheep, scores are often low. Further, results vary when confidence is measured in respect to particular calls or series of calls. (When subjects check individual calls on which they feel confident, data are mixed and interesting but I omit them because they do not describe a general personality trait.) One other report may be relevant, and it will amuse you. It deals with lizards. G.K. Watkins (1972) found that lizards who were dominant in their home cages, and whom I therefore infer to be the more confident lizards, had higher PK scores than their submissive cagemates.

Lability: Psychologists seldom study lability as a personality trait, but its potential relevance to psi has interested me ever since an informal study in the 1940s. Bruno Klopfer, a preeminent Rorschach analyst, studied the Rorschachs of several gifted psi subjects to find if they had anything in common. No conventional scoring category showed anything unusual, he told me, but they shared a characteristic that he had not seen in other protocols: the fluid way in which their thinking moved from one concept to another. When two concepts are contradictory, subjects ordinarily comment that they are ending one and starting the next. These subjects accepted without comment, as if it was natural, that one concept flowed into and became something different. This sensitive interpretation from a man with a wealth of experience in judging Rorschachs seemed of major importance to me, though of course a rigid critic would dismiss it because Klopfer's scoring was not blind.

Another speculation along these lines was that perhaps spontaneity, as measured by Scherer (Chapter 3), might be an instance of a fluid or labile episode in a person for whom fluidity was not habitual. Perhaps also the "open track" or "in-between states" described by Murphy (e.g., 1962) as conducive to spontaneous experiences (i.e., moments when a person is waiting with a blanked mind or else has stopped one activity but not yet started the next) offer an opening for a labile response.

The only research I have found which tried to examine this pattern was by W.G. Braud, Shafer, & Mulgrew (1983). Braud had previously found a labile PK target more psi-conducive than a more stable one. Now the investigation was extended to differences in lability between subjects. Each heard a tape on which a single word was continuously repeated for 16 minutes. (Everyone, with this method, sooner or later hears different sounds.) Subjects were asked to report any change they heard, and the number of changes was taken as a measure of lability. With 19 subjects, the number of changes correlated with ESP score at a level that was significant if tested by a one-tailed p. A systematic replication, however, gave only a nonsignificant positive correlation. (I consider the second method unfortunate: it measured lability by reversals of a rectangular ambiguous figure, but rectangular figures reverse at different rates from others.) The study thus gives a hint of research support to Klopfer's observation.

Absorption: The tendency to become absorbed in one's own thoughts or activities is at least superficially the opposite of lability, though perhaps a deeper analysis can find a similarity between them. Absorption, as measured by the Tellegen scale, was found by Stanford & Angelini (1984) to correlate positively and significantly with sensitivity to psi in the Ganzfeld. It seems a promising possibility as a psi-conducive personality variable, perhaps especially for the Ganzfeld. Other work indicates that absorption scores are also high for many who believe, perhaps falsely, that they have had spontaneous psi experiences.

Multiple Predictors

Many useful personality tests include several scales. Everyone agrees, I think, that a score on a single one of these scales is less meaningful than the profile or pattern of the test as a whole. An example was already cited: the combination of high ego strength and high neurotic signs might show a dynamic, creative person whereas the neurotic signs without the ego strength probably indicate an ineffective, maladjusted one. So far as I know, profiles of subjects from conventional multivariate scales have not been used in psi research. Single scores from these scales often give a significant value which fails to replicate.

A different method of using multiple predictors in diagnosis of character structure was used by Hudesman, a clinical psychologist (Hudesman & Schmeidler, 1976). We examined 24 sets of records from a single subject. Each set consisted of ESP calls and a mood scale, taken just before a psychoanalytic session and retaken just after the session.

Hudesman describes the patient as going through a period of negative transference (dislike and disapproval of the therapist) and as employing defenses associated with an obsessive personality. Mood scores show that when social affection toward the therapist decreased, there was increase in skepticism, impatience and aggression—all directed at the therapist (who was not aware of the ESP test). And for this obsessive and defensive person, though surely not for everyone, his ESP scores showed a significant negative correlation with social affection, and significant positive correlations with aggression, impatience, and skepticism. (There was also a significant negative correlation between psi scores and depression, but this may be a more common finding.) This unreplicated study thus strongly suggests that multiple measures may lead to valid but idiosyncratic predictors of how a particular person will score at psi.

Overview

Research on many individuals gives strong support for the generalization that on the whole, by and large, psi scores relate positively to three traits: extraversion (opposed to introversion); openness (opposed to withdrawal); good adjustment and low anxiety (opposed to neurotic tendencies and high anxiety). Careful research has indicated many interacting factors that modulate and can even reverse these general relationships. Studies of other personality variables and of particular individuals are not adequately replicated but often seem promising.

8. Moods

Moods relate to personality variables in much the same way as short-term weather forecasts relate to the climate. Though our long-lasting traits and attitudes describe how we typically behave, they are weak predictors of what we will do at any one time. A situation may rouse two traits that pull in opposite ways, like friendliness and shyness, or rouse two conflicting attitudes like tolerance and disapproval. When this happens, and with us humans it happens often, our short term mood, our feeling or "affect," can be pivotal in determining which trait or attitude we bring to the fore.

Research would be simpler if moods could be disregarded. The experimenter who wanted to examine any ability would have a straightforward directive. Find what motivates your subject appropriately; establish a situation with that motivation; repeat it as often as necessary to study all the questions that interest you. It is a research formula that works well with laboratory-reared rats or trained pigeons.

But we all know better than to expect it to work with humans. When a single motivating situation is repeated it becomes a different situation. We may grow less (or more) self-conscious about what we are doing, and therefore do it differently. We may grow bored and find our minds drifting to something else. We may try out a new way of responding just to see what happens. We may even become suspicious that we are being manipulated and then begin to work against rather than with the experimenter. Seldom do we stay so consistent that we behave the same way in test after test after test.

Changes in mood can influence even strong and well established skills like figure skating. They will naturally have more of an effect when a skill is not well established and is therefore unstable. This makes mood potentially important in studies of psi, because psi for almost everyone is a weak, untrained ability. Mood can be expected to determine whether, instead of hoping our responses will show psi, we let ourselves attend to other interests, for example esthetic preference for one target or another. With changed attention, psi might not emerge at all. Mood can also be expected to determine whether, if psi emerges, it will be used for the psi-hitting that the experimenter asked for or misused (from the experimenter's point of view) for psi-missing or displacement.

Are these expectations justified? This chapter addresses the question of whether moods affect psi scores. My first plan for it was to have three units: one on recent major psychological findings on mood; the next on two models that these findings suggest for psi; the last a review of psi research to see if the findings fit either model. It was to be a set of straightforward descriptions.

But writing it made me uneasy, because it was shaping up like a critique instead of a survey. I kept claiming reports were incomplete. This forced me to recognize that for years I had thought of moods in terms of a different model, and my model gave me a bias about how mood research should be conducted. Biases need to be stated. I therefore insert a first unit on my model, along with a sample of the anecdotes that formed it. That should clear the air; you will know what allowance to make for any lack of objectivity in the units that follow.

Anecdotes and a Model They Created

Anecdotes about A.

Among my early ESP subjects was A., a charming young woman, eagerly interested, animated, friendly. Her ESP scores were far below chance—so low that they seemed worth exploring further. I asked her to come for another session. In the second session she scored as far above chance as she had been below it earlier. She told me that the previous time she had been worried about an exam she was to take; this time she was not worried. Both of us were interested in her change in scores and she agreed to come again if it wouldn't be boring. We cast about for ways to prevent boredom, and settled on having her fingerpaint while she told me her ESP calls. Since I was blind to the targets, I could record her calls.

Consistently, in the next several sessions, her paintings were pretty designs in bright colors and her ESP scores were high. Then one day her first color choice was black; her painting (she told me) was of dark clouds under water; her ESP score was below chance. Her second painting was also of dark clouds under water but with a reddish mass at the bottom; ESP again showed psi-missing. The reddish mass was meant to be coral; her association was "Full fathom five thy father lies; of his bones are coral made." She stopped to think about what she had said. Was it a death wish against her father? Yes, A. was angry at him—but no, she was not *that* angry. And her next painting, after the hostility had surfaced and been thought through, was unique in her series: bright colors again, but this time so free that it went beyond the paper onto the desk. Her ESP scores were high.

One sequence like this is of course not proof of anything, but it looked meaningful. It looked as if the color shift from dark to bright symbolized a mood shift from negative to positive, and as if the ESP shift from low to high followed from the mood change. It also looked as if the large sweep of her third painting symbolized release after catharsis.

I wanted, naturally, to see if others showed a similar pattern but have never found a good technique to test it. Fingerpainting was out of the question for the young adults available as subjects; they would think it silly and childish; it would make them self-conscious. Instead I turned to a projective technique they would accept: telling stories to a provocative series of pictures (the TAT). But a pilot study fizzled. Once the subjects grew engrossed in their stories they forgot about making the ESP calls. If I reminded them they resented the interruption and made only perfunctory, meaningless responses. A. had integrated the ESP calls into the flow of her feelings; they did not.

(What caused the difference? Without further research we can only speculate. One possibility would assign the primary cause to motivation and perhaps rapport; another would assign it to A.'s use of a visual-motor task and the later subjects' use of a verbal one.)

Post hoc observations are quasianecdotal: unplanned, one-shot events. I add one here. It fit, some years later, the interpretation that with hostility, psi socres will be low but after hostility is released, scores will be high.

Eilbert, a graduate student doing research for his M.A. thesis, arranged for subjects to visit him at his home to be tested (Eilbert & Schmeidler, 1950). Reaching his home demanded a long, tedious trip. His subjects were polite about the inconvenience—except for his friends, who were outspoken in telling him what they thought of him for taking so much time out of their weekends. After expressing their feelings loud and clear they calmed down and did the experiment. ESP scores were low for the polite subjects who had shown no resentment; but for the friends who had fully expressed their resentment, ESP scores were high.

Anecdotes about B.

B., a graduate student with an office near mine, was also one of my early subjects. She made a rather low ESP score and felt mildly disappointed. A few weeks later she came to the office in a boiling rage. She was just back from a psychoanalytic session in which her analyst had forbidden her to do the dissertation project she wanted. She ordered rather than asked me to give her another ESP test, took it while she was still angry, and scored exceptionally high.

This impressed me. It looked like the opposite of A.'s pattern; it looked as if B.'s anger released her ESP. Later conversation with her suggested why.

B. thought ESP was wrongly rejected by authority. She thought her research plan had been wrongly rejected by authority. She said to herself, more or less, "I'll show them!" High scores meant that ESP occurred and that authority was wrong. Making a high score served her hostile need.

What do we infer about hostility from these two or three instances? Nothing, if we are conservative, because each was a single case. But if we are willing to take an intellectual risk we infer that for A., both fingerpainting and ESP were pleasant ways of exploring her potentials; both were outlets for her feelings. For B., affirming ESP meant rebelling against authority. The affirmation and the rebellion were important to her when authority had frustrated her. They were not important in her normal, pleasant state.

This leads to two generalizations, which rough out the general shape that I think a model of mood should take, and thus constitute my bias. One is that mood is an important determinant of psi scoring. The other is that merely specifying a mood, such as hostility, does not tell what the accompanying psi score will be. The direction of the hostility, and what psi means in relation to that direction, interact with mood. The specifics of the situation and the person's attitudes and personality dynamics determine how mood will affect behavior.

Anecdote about C.

C. was a reserved, meticulously careful woman who was writing a novel. She was interested in psychical research, and early in the morning would make a run of ESP calls, hoping the body of data she accumulated could become useful. On some days her writing went smoothly; on others it blocked. She told me that when she checked on the two activities together, she found that on the days when her ESP score was high, the writing flowed; on the days when it was low, the writing was blocked. She inferred (and because I had learned to respect her, I accepted her inference) that moods of which she herself was unaware had either facilitated both the writing and ESP or had inhibited them both. For her, creative ability and psi waxed and waned together.

Andecdote about D.

A gifted artist, winner of many awards, agreed to be interviewed for a project on creativity and psi (Murphy, 1963, 1966). She said that in some periods of her life, each lasting for weeks or months, she had had many correct ESP impressions. These were always periods when her personal life was unhappy and she had a work block. When she was happy and working well, she never had ESP impressions. And she added: "Why should I? I didn't need them."

Anecdote about E.

E., a distinguished scientist, repeatedly took ESP tests and scored near chance. A few times in her life, however, when she was ill or overworked or miserable for some other reason, she had extraordinarily accurate ESP impressions. In one memorable example she desperately needed to get in touch with someone but could learn only that he was traveling and was somewhere in an area of hundreds of square miles. She prepared to telephone the long list of hotels in that large area, chose one at random, and found him on her first call.

Summary

A. and B. come to you secondhand; C., D., and E. at third hand. If you choose to accept them, as I do, you find two different patterns. For A. and C., psi is effective when all goes well. For B., D., and E., psi is mobilized under conditions of frustration and helps to compensate for it. If indeed this is true, is it an anomaly? No; it has parallels in other skills and other forms of behavior. For one example, some people do their best work in an encouraging atmosphere. Others do mediocre or even careless work when all goes well but rise to the occasion when there is a challenge; they do their best when there is difficulty. We need to know what is sometimes called a person's character structure to predict what the person's behavior will be.

PSYCHOLOGICAL RESEARCH ON MOODS

Everyone agrees that moods are hard to measure. The common methods of measurement are physiological responses, behavioral change, test scores, and self-reports. I will go down the list briefly, emphasizing the problems of each.

There are three major problems with physiological responses. Their data are noisy, confounded by nonmood variables. They show individual differences, so that the most sensitive physiological indicator for one person can be almost irrelevant for the next. They yield at best only crude, nonqualitative measures, such as arousal, which do not adequately specify particular moods. (The lie detector is a notorious example here. The heightened arousal it shows may be caused by guilt or awareness of lying, but it may be caused in an honest person by anxiety about an unrelated personal association or by fear that the test will be misinterpreted.)

Behavioral changes, as in posture and facial expression, have different meanings in different cultures, in different contexts, and for different individuals. Global judgments about them are therefore often in error. Careful, detailed analysis of muscular changes is time consuming and some authorities consider it overly rigid.

Self-reports or scores on psychological tests demand that a person shift attention from whatever created a mood to introspecting about it or to making some other response. A self-report may itself change a mood. It thus can confound the data if it comes early in the session. If it comes at the end of the session, it may reflect relief at having finished the experimental task. Further, self-reports are often influenced by wanting to put oneself in a favorable light or by response biases.

Each measure has weaknesses, but each can give useful information. When findings from them converge and replicate, results seem strong. Just such strong results are reported by Watson & Tellegen (1985). They review dozens of research projects and show that, overall, self-reports converge with behavioral measures and with results from formal tests to demonstrate that there are two major dimensions for affect. One is the range from positive to negative (equivalent to happy versus unhappy or to pleasant versus unpleasant). The other dimension is the range from high to low arousal (equivalent to activity versus passivity).

Watson & Tellegen then present a diagram that locates many moods in a two-dimensional pattern. Elated and enthusiastic are at the positive, high arousal extreme; dull and sluggish are the negative, low arousal opposite extreme. Dozens of other mood descriptors are placed between them, on either the active or the passive side.

All this is good. It gives us structure. But at the same time it seems to me to be incomplete: only a beginning for the analysis of moods. Here is one of many possible examples. On the diagram, lonely and sad are placed together; both are unpleasant moods with moderately low arousal. The moods exactly opposite to them include warmhearted and content; pleasant moods with moderately high arousal. I suggest that to predict behavior we need another distinction for those four moods: whether they are person-oriented, like lonely and warmhearted, or are not, like sad and content. A person who feels lonely would be expected to give a warmhearted reception to a telephone call from an acquaintance; but someone who is sad would be expected to give a sluggish, indifferent response to it. There are of course many further distinctions like this one. Two dimensions do not give a full mood structure.

Nevertheless, even if they need supplementation, the two dimensions that Watson & Tellegen describe are a sound, conservative base from which to analyze mood research. I will use them below.

Three Models for Mood and Psi

The Watson & Tellegen schema immediately suggests two models for psi, one vague and one specific. I list them, then add the more complicated model I think necessary.

Model 1. Since two major dimensions of mood are positive/negative affect and high/low arousal, either affect or arousal, or both, will relate to psi scores.

Model 2. Psi is often measured by a mean score showing positive or negative level of success in relation to mean chance expectaton; it also is sometimes measured by the variance of the scores. It seems intuitively plausible that these fit the two major dimensions of mood. Model 2 therefore predicts that average score will correlate with affect: there will be psi-hitting in pleasant moods and psi-missing in unpleasant ones. It also predicts that variance will correlate with arousal: there will be higher variance with higher arousal.

Model 3. This model takes as a premise that no simple, tidy rule of human behavior is true to life. It therefore predicts that psi scores and mood will be related, but will interact with personality and situational variables. Specific predictions can be made only after appropriate pretests, or after appropriate measures of personality and situational variables.

Psi Research on Moods

In 1956 appeared two major articles on mood and psi, which I think were the first formal investigations of the topic. My review begins with them, and surveys more than fifty later reports. It omits studies of traits like anxiety (Chapter 7) which may in some cases be examining a state rather then a trait; and it omits long-term changes in state of consciousness (which come in Chapter 9). It also omits research on psi targets expected to elicit some mood if the experimenter did not check on whether the expected mood had been elicited.

Fisk & West (1956) report a project conducted by mail in 1954 and 1955. Subjects were asked to make a short set of ESP calls whenever they chose during the day, to do this for 64 or more days, and for each set to check off their mood on a 5-point scale (exaltation, pleasure, neutral, un-pleasure, depression). Over a period of 56 weeks, 162 subjects had sent in responses for at least

32 days; these responses were the data base. So few had marked either exaltation or depression that the scale was collapsed to three categories: pleasurable, neutral, un-pleasurable. Data were consistent with Model 2: significant psi-hitting in pleasurable moods and significant psi-missing in neutral moods or in neutral and un-pleasurable moods.

Nielsen (1956), who knew of this research, modified the method. She recruited seven eagerly interested subjects (including herself). On 10 days in Series 1 and another 10 days in Series 2, at times of their own choice, they made five precognitive ESP runs and checked off an elaborate mood scale. Nielsen divided her scale in two ways: pleasant versus unpleasant moods and extreme moods versus mixed. All seven subjects showed overall psi-hitting. Scores for wholly pleasant moods were significantly high in each series. Scores for wholly unpleasant moods were slightly below chance in Series 1 but significantly above in Series 2. Scores for mixed but pleasant moods were insignificantly above chance; for mixed but unpleasant moods, insignificantly below. These data partly support but partly disconfirm Model 2. Nielsen suggests that the cleanest cut-through comes from pooling extreme moods and comparing them with the others. This pooling shows higher ESP scores with higher arousal, not predicted by Model 2. No measure of variance is given.

After these two provocative studies came what Sherlock Holmes might have called a curious incident, like the incident of the dog that did not bark in the night. There were no mood studies for a decade (except for one brief report from a student of mine). The next large scale study of mood did not refer back to these earlier ones.

Rogers (1966) used himself as a subject for 20 sessons of 10 ESP runs each: 10 sessions while he was in a positive mood and 10 while in a negative one. He reported the variance of the scores but not their means. The happy moods showed chance variance (i.e., the scatter of scores was about would be expected theoretically, if psi did not function). In unhappy moods, however, variance was significantly low (i.e., there were fewer extreme scores than expected by chance) and the difference in variance between happy and unhappy moods was significant.

(Although it interrupts the account of mood studies, I cannot resist a comment on this finding. Rogers was the first to center attention on a significantly low variance, but many others have observed it since. The effect seems associated with feelings of withdrawal or constriction, as in Rogers' negative, non-outgoing mood. Statistically it is clear: scores hover around the center of the distribution; they do not scatter as expected by chance. But isn't it extraordinary? Along with a conscious effort to make high scores, in this mood there is apparently an unconscious tendency to avoid not only extremely high scores but also extremely low ones. It has no psychological parallel that I can think of. It is one example of the interesting questions in parapsychology which are almost entirely omitted from this section of the book, because of my being unable to find a psychological category into which they fit.)

The next year Rogers (1967a) reported further on this study: an analysis of the hits while he was in a negative mood. Scores on the first 20 calls per run were significantly high; scores on the last five calls per run were significantly low. He also (Rogers, 1967b) replicated his first study with five other subjects, who had from one to five pairs of sessions in negative and positive moods. The variance of scores in negative moods was again significantly lower than in positive ones. The data support Model 1 but not Model 2.

Data disconfirming both models came in the next report. Mussig & Dean (1967) had six subjects take ESP tests for 32 consecutive days, and each day report their mood on a 5-point scale from elation to depression. There was no significant relation between mood and ESP mean.

Carpenter (1968) asked the 12 subjects of his first series to have five sessions, and the 11 subjects of his second series to have four. In each session they made a series of ESP runs and filled out a variant of the Nowlis Mood Adjective Checklist. Carpenter reported only the ESP variance, which in each series was nonsignificantly higher in positive than in negative moods. He then divided the mood scores into extreme or moderate, i.e., high or lower arousal. In Series 1 ESP variance was highest for moderate pleasant moods and lowest for moderate unpleasant moods; differences were not significant. In Series 2 variance of moderate pleasant moods was again the highest and was significantly above mean chance expectation; variance of extreme pleasant moods was lowest. A replication with 48 subjects who had one session each (Carpenter, 1969) gave no significant results, but again the highest variance was in the moderate pleasant moods. The data disconfirm Model 2. His most recent findings on mood (Chapter 7; Carpenter 1983a, 1983b) are also inconsistent with Model 2.

Other studies of pleasant or unpleasant moods have used one or another unusual method, seldom replicated even by the original experimenter and very seldom by others. Instead of trying to evaluate this research I will show its diversity by adding eight more examples to the mood studies already cited in Chapter 6 (Carpenter, 1983a; 1983b; Friedman, Schmeidler & Dean, 1976; Schmeidler 1971; Schmeidler & Craig, 1972) and in Chapter 7 (Hudesman & Schmeidler, 1976) and will then move on to the more coherent body of findings on arousal.

Feather & L.E. Rhine (1969), a daughter and mother, made PK trials at the same time. Dice faces were the targets; an automatic dice machine cast the dice. Targets were preset so that on half the calls both hoped for the same die face; on half the trials they hoped for different faces. When the daughter's mood was pleasant, mean scores were lower and score variances were higher for the same-target condition than for the different-target condition. When the daughter's mood was unpleasant, each of these relations reversed. The interaction between mood and same versus different hopes is perhaps understandable post hoc, but it was not anticipated. It is not consistent with Model 2.

Osis and his coworkers conducted a series of elaborate projects using several indicators of ESP. A summary of mood findings (Osis & Carlson, 1972) shows that in one series elation correlated significantly but negatively with calls scored against the target following the intended target. In another series elation did not show this but it correlated significantly and positively with missing the target that followed the intended one. In a third series it did not correlate significantly with anything. Other mood correlations were similarly inconsistent.

Nielsen resumed research with her mood scale, and her colleague Freeman sometimes used it. A series of abstracts report varied methods, with the findings often significant when mood was examined in relation to some other variable like extraversion or intragroup changes. (See, e.g., Nielsen, 1972).

Mischo & Weis (1973) examined the interaction of an unpleasant mood, frustration, with personality traits. Subjects made PK trials in a normal mood and while frustrated. The PK scores were lower after frustration for subjects shown by other tests to be more depressed, neurotic, or inhibited, but PK scores were higher after frustration for subjects shown by other tests to be calmer and more sociable. Thus for one personality type the data support Model 2; for another they disconfirm it.

Here, briefly, are two more early reports and two of the more recent. Bickman (1963) found higher mean ESP scores for bored goats than for interested sheep. This disconfirmed his own hypothesis (and disconfirms Model 2) but if we follow some psychologists and take boredom to be a state of high arousal it is perhaps consistent with what Nielsen found. Hudesman's single subject (Chapter 7) showed the significant negative correlation between depression and ESP score that Model 2 predicts, but neither anxiety nor surgency (a happy state of high arousal) correlated with ESP. This not only is inconsistent with Model 2 but also warns us that mood ratings are not so simple as they look.

L.W. Braud, Ackles, & Kyles (1984) tested 10 subjects in the Ganzfeld. Eight psi-hit; the two who psi-missed were depressed introverts. Milton (1985) studied 20 Ganzfeld percipients and found significantly higher ESP for bad than for good mood and also for unpleasant rather than pleasant Ganzfeld experience. If her subjects were extraverts the finding is consonant with Braud et al. (just above); if they were introverts it is discrepant. Extraversion was not examined.

We come at last to a large body of research that examines relaxation, a state of low arousal. Impetus for these studies came after W.G. Braud &

L.W. Braud (1973) used Jacobsen's progressive relaxation technique to help prepare subjects for an ESP test. Targets were pictures; ESP scores were high. Stanford & Mayer (1974) replicated both the method and the findings. Many other studies with this method followed, most also indicating that relaxation is conducive to ESP success.

What was apparently strong support for this pattern came when W.G. Braud (1981) reviewed the psi studies that had used physiological measures of arousal. There were 13, and 10 had found significantly higher ESP means with low arousal than with high. Braud then, however, reports his own further research, which leads him to impose a restriction on the general thesis. His revised conclusion is that ESP success is associated with moderately low arousal but is not associated with either extremely low arousal or with high.

This conclusion has a familiar ring to psychologists. It restates the Yerkes-Dodson law, the finding that performance is typically better at a moderate level of arousal than when arousal is either extremely low or extremely high. Until there have been more psi studies throughout the range of arousal, however, the conclusion can be only tentative. Later, W.G. Braud (1985) suggested a further restriction for the general thesis: that it applies to ESP but not to PK. His survey of gifted subjects indicates that for PK the optimal condition may be tension rather than moderate relaxation (but see also Chapter 14).

In summary, research strongly supports the conclusion that moderate relaxation is associated with better ESP scores than is tension. A relation between ESP success and level of arousal seems well established.

EVALUATION OF THE THREE MODELS

Model 1 predicted only that psi would relate to positive and negative moods and to arousal. Of the 46 studies I found where moods could be characterized as positive or negative, 18 report one or another significant relation between this mood dimension and some psi score, either hits or variance. If we make no allowance for selection or for the variety of the relationships, this implies that psi relates to affect. A substantial proportion of psi studies show significant relationships with arousal; thus the second part of the model seems well supported. The model, however, is too vague to be satisfactory; it is useful only for initial analyses.

Model 2 does not fare well. Its prediction of a positive relation between arousal and variance cannot be properly tested because few articles report on both; but it is not supported by those few. Its prediction of a positive relation between hits and pleasantness of mood can be examined in 41 reports. Most have mixed or null findings; in three, psi scores are significantly higher for pleasant than unpleasant moods; in two the psi scores are significantly lower. Model 2, I think, is disconfirmed.

Model 3 predicted interactions between mood and other variables, but so few studies are designed to study such interactions that it cannot be properly evaluated. Seven articles report significant or suggestive interactions of the type it predicts. This implies support for it, but the picture is cloudy. We do not know what allowance to make for the file drawer effect. Further, different projects describe different (but not contrary) interactions. No one, so far as I know, has tried to replicate an interaction that was reported from a different laboratory. Thus support for Model 3 is weak, but is frequent enough to be provocative.

Other Moods

It is tempting to latch onto some combination of an unusual mood associated with a fairly unusual set of psi scores and speculate that the mood caused the scores. Many of us have done this; none of our hunches have been neatly confirmed; but some of them still look promising. I will give only one example of these inconclusive lines of research: the one I have worked on most, which still tantalizes me. It is the possibility that impatient but cooperative subjects will direct their psi to targets that are later in the series than the ones they should be trying for; that they will unconsciously aim ahead of themselves, and will psi-hit on targets ahead of the designated ones.

The idea seemed plausible, post hoc, to explain scores on psi tests given during the final exam period. The students were friendly and eager to score well, but also eager to finish quickly and go back to their course reviews. And their responses showed significant hitting, not on the target, but—as if they were hurrying—on the item that came after the target (Schmeidler, Friedenberg, & Males, 1966). Two follow-ups supported the idea: both Heyman & Schmeidler (1967) and Goldberg, Sondow, & Schmeidler (1976) predicted and found similar scoring-one-ahead-of-the-target in subjects whom a personality test classed as Dynamic-Hasty and who were being forced to respond slowly. The pattern was also consistent with a good many post hoc analyses of other research, but when recently I tried a large scale test for it, with a cover story to explain the need for responding slowly, it did not show up at all (Schmeidler, 1985).

What should we make of this? My guess now is that my recent cover story was too persuasive; it kept the hasty subjects from feeling impatient at their slow response rate. They were too cooperative to show an impatience effect. I'd also guess that if the cover story had not been persuasive enough the subjects would have resented the whole procedure, turned negativistic, and psi-missed. This means that if the impatience effect is valid (and I suspect it is) it can be demonstrated only with a delicate mood balance: feeling cooperative about the procedure as a whole but at the same time feeling uncooperative about some delay in the procedure. It is balanced on a narrow knife edge of moods; it will be a hard hypothesis to confirm.

OVERVIEW

Some investigators found no relation between the moods they examined and psi scores, but many others reported a significant relationship. Analysis of the data in terms of two dimensions of mood shows no consistent relation of psi scores to positive versus negative mood, but strong evidence that arousal relates to psi. Moderate relaxation has repeatedly been found to be associated with higher ESP scores and tension with lower ones. In addition, a scattering of significant findings, many with face validity, indicates that mood and psi scores interact with personality traits, attitudes, and the experimental situation.

9. The Longer Altered States of Consciousness

Turn now to what have been called altered states of consciousness ever since Tart (1969) published a book with that title. They include intense mystical experiences like "cosmic consciousness" or "the rapture of the deep"; self-induced states like meditation or trance; externally induced states like hypnosis or the Ganzfeld experience; and physiologically induced states like drunkenness, or those due to psychedelic drugs or to body injury in the near death experience. Dreaming is sometimes classed with them, as is psychosis; the list is elastic. Although they differ among themselves, each is so different from the normal range of moderate mood shifts that it has become customary to group them as if they constituted a single topic.

But thinking of them as a group becomes theoretically embarrassing. It raises at least three questions which do not have satisfactory answers. The basic one is: What is an unaltered state of consciousness? The next: Is there any sharp, qualitative break between each altered state and some (unspecified) unaltered state of consciousness, or is there instead a continuum of gradual changes? And the third question is: Is there enough similarity among these states to have them truly constitute a group, or are they so different that each needs to be considered separately?

The first question is the most difficult. A person who struggles to answer it will immediately recognize that the struggle itself is not a normal state; it involves more concentrated effort than normal. But neither is relaxation the normal state, nor boredom, nor any other particular mood. We are forced back to something like William James's continually altering stream of consciousness, within which we can identify some specific but transitory states.

For the second question, the conservative answer—which may or may not be the final one—is that each altered state has intermediate gradations between it and the normal flow. In prayer, for example, many feel something which partakes of but is not quite a mystical experience; and many feel a somewhat similar rapture through music or other forms of art. Both EEG records and introspections show that meditation can merge into drowsiness. Hypnosis is not unlike the uncritical acceptance of what an authority tells us. And small amounts of alcohol or of other drugs obviously produce gradations of change.

If these states merge into the normal range of experiences at the low end, what of the high end? Are common characteristics shared by the deepest hypnotic trance and the state following high drug dosage and a fulfilling meditation and religious ecstasy? The answers from research are mixed. The issue is tantalizing, but for the present it is surely safer to consider the states separately.

A half dozen states where there has been psi research are discussed briefly below: trance because of the qualitative research with gifted subjects; hypnosis, meditation, dreams, and the Ganzfeld because of the quantitative research with them. To these I add another, not ordinarily classed with them. It is the state induced by remote viewing, and is included because the comparison seems instructive. The scanty research on drug induced states is mentioned in Chapter 12.

TRANCE

Within parapsychology, history demands that we study trance. Especially in the period before J.B. Rhine's first major quantitative analyses (1934), it was the striking, inexplicable ESP or PK from entranced mediums that made psychical research of intense interest to many. There is space for only a few examples, and I cite two which are rather similar, then two that seem remarkably different from them.

Mrs. Piper, according to William James and other investigators, seemed a commonplace housewife in her ordinary condition, but in trance gave information that she could not have learned normally and that was remarkably accurate. Once, for instance, a stranger visited her for the first time. She went into trance and described his dead father, saying among other correct details that there was a bald spot where men are not usually bald, on the right side of the head. She pointed to the place, and the man tells us that an accident had indeed made his father bald, asymmetrically, at just that spot. She also told the man many other accurate and uncommon details, such as the pet name which only his father had used for him, and the tragic, lonely way in which his half-brother had died (Hodgson, 1892).

Mrs. Leonard, in trance and only then, described accurately both events known to others and also facts known to no living person. When a widow visited her, for example, Mrs. Leonard said that the dead husband had had a dark leather book. She gestured to show its size, then said that on page 12 or 13 was a diagram or table of Arabian or Semitic languages, and gave a jumble of language names. The widow recorded the early part of this but not the later part because the whole message was meaningless to her; she thought there was no such book. After reaching home she looked for it, and to her astonishment found on a top shelf of her husband's study a book that matched the description. On page 13 of the book was pasted a diagram labeled General Table of the Aryan and Indo-European Languages, a table with many terms that sounded like the gibberish she remembered Mrs. Leonard saying (Sidgwick, 1921).

Mrs. Piper and Mrs. Leonard were called "mental mediums"; it was the accurate information they gave that was impressive. When they shifted from a normal to a trance state there were typically changes in breathing, twitches or other minor movements, and a longish period of body quietude. They were often investigated to check on their honesty, and no evidence of trickery was ever found. Eusapia Palladino differed in all three respects. She was called a "physical medium"; she produced PK changes. Her entry into trance involved not only breathing changes but lively, writhing body activity. She often used the writhing to release a leg or an arm from restraint so that she could move objects normally while pretending to move them paranormally. When she shrewdly judged that trickery would be ineffective she entered what was an apparently authentic trance and showed clearly paranormal ability, such as making a table rise in the air while the scientists with her checked that no one touched it above, below, or at the sides (Feilding, Baggally, & Carrington, 1909).

This might imply, as W.G. Braud suggested (Chapter 8), that relaxing body functions is conducive to ESP, while intense activity is conducive to PK, especially since many other cases fit the generalization. But before we rest content with it, consider this report. An anthropologist, Laubscher (1938), decided to test a South African diviner reputed to have marvelous abilities. Laubscher intelligently arranged a test procedure that was culturally appropriate. He went to a deserted place, checked that no one was within eyeshot, took a purse wrapped in brown paper, buried it, put a brown stone above it and a gray stone above that, then immediately drove as fast as he could some 60 miles to where the diviner lived. He asked the diviner to tell what he had done. The diviner did not, like Mrs. Piper or Mrs. Leonard, sit down and relax in order to go into trance. Instead he began a seance dance. After a long period of this lively ritual he described the purse, the brown paper it was wrapped in, and minute, accurate details of both the brown stone and the gray one. Here intense activity apparently helped ESP.

And now consider another set of observations. Apparently trance, induced either by quiet or by activity, was a necessary precondition for psychic success in all these persons. Not so for Mrs. Garrett, probably the most gifted and certainly the most tested of modern psychics. She told me that early in her career she needed trance to make best use of psychic ability, but with practice found that trance was unnecessary. She merely needed to shift the way she directed her attention. A young man, B.D., produced over long periods extraordinarily strong statistical evidence of ESP and of PK (Kelly & Kanthamani, 1972); observers consistently describe his quick movements and lively body and verbal activity but never describe a trance state. Accounts of D.D. Home similarly often depict him as being socially active and taking part in conversation while he performed some of his extraordinary feats (Medhurst & Goldney, 1964).

Where does this leave us? Because some of the most impressive instances of psi occur in trance, any theory of psi should include a theory of trance. But trance can be either extreme body quietude or else intense activity. Further, psi can function effectively without trance in some gifted subjects. It is as if we had three loose ends to tie up.

Cultural conditioning may be one way of tying two of the loose ends. Psychics in our own culture do not ordinarily prepare for psi by dancing. Psychic healers in the United States are likely to meditate and to pray. Elsewhere, for example in many parts of Africa, preparation for psychic healing demands a prolonged ritual dance. The !Kung are perhaps the best known example of this (Katz, 1982), and it is also true for many cults of South America, with their admixture of African tradition. Dervishes whirl; yogis sit immobile. The apparent uniformity within a single culture suggests, I think, that part of the preparation for psi is moral reassurance. Making use of unusual abilities carries potential danger and may be evil; but freeing one's own psi may seem proper and justified and the right thing to do if one first complies with religious ritual and cultural expectations.

A second way of tying those same ends together may be to think of both quiet and activity as departures from the usual state. It may be the departing, rather than the direction of departure, which is important. (This is in line with a theory proposed by Fischer, 1971. His research on altered states led him to describe them as a circular continuum, where arousal and tranquillity depart from the normal in opposite directions, but meet at the other extreme in ecstasy.) To put it another way, either intense activity or extreme repose will prevent the normal deployment of attention, just as either darkness or a glaring light will prevent normal vision.

There is one more pair of loose ends: that evidence for unusually strong psi comes both in apparently normal states and in trance. Perhaps we can begin to connect them when we think of the range of normal states as shading into those we call altered. An example is that a light hypnotic trance is difficult or impossible to distinguish from normal consciousness, but lighter trances shade into deeper and deeper ones. I suggest, very tentatively, that two characteristics within the normal range of consciousness may be especially psi-conducive. One is the intense absorption that can make us inattentive to stimuli we usually notice. It is a mild, common form of dissociation that many of us experience while reading, or thinking, or watching a drama. The other is the way we all occasionally find ourselves having an idea or making some movement or gesture which surprises us when it comes. We had not planned the gesture; we had not tried to find the idea. Both in such spontaneity of thought or movement and in the state of absorption there is a departure from our normal reality-oriented, planned activity and thus some resemblance to trance. Possibly some psychics, at some times when they are not in trance, function at the extreme upper level of the normal range of absorption or dissociation.

There has been so little psychological analysis of trance that none of this bears directly on the thesis of this book as a whole. But it has an indirect bearing, because it suggests that psi is most effective in trance and in normal states which share some of the characteristics of trance. If this is true, psi is less likely to be effective when we concentrate upon precision in practical activities. It is more likely to occur when, without concentrating, we "go with the flow" in activities like social interaction or fantasy or creative thinking. In all of these, our own words or ideas or actions sometimes are unexpected; they go beyond what we had been planning. We are seldom able to exercise full control over successful performance. Psychoanalysts speculate that the lack of full conscious control is due to intrusions from the preconscious; it is possible to test the hypothesis that psi sometimes unexpectedly enters in.

Hypnosis

Back in the old days, everything about hypnosis was controversial. Practiticners of mesmerism or hypnotism made extreme claims; critics countered them with slashing denials or accusations of fraud. By now, thanks in large part to the research typified by Barber (1969), there are wide areas of agreement. Controversies remain but they are narrow ones. It is agreed, for example, that not only do hypnotized subjects exert more strength, withstand more pain, and so on, than seems normal, but nonhypnotized subjects also show the same behaviors if properly motivated, e.g. by a persuasive experimenter who urges them to simulate a hypnotized subject. Although the introspective reports of the two groups usually differ, even that difference decreases or disappears if the simulators are asked to respond as they think a hypnotized subject would. In a paradoxical way, this modern research validates many of the early claims about the unusual effects of hypnosis, but it shows that the effects were due largely or wholly to the hypnotists having mobilized the full cooperation of the subjects. It also has become clear that hypnotized subjects accept some suggestions but reject others. Hypnotic suggestions interact with pre-existing attitudes and values rather than wiping them away.

What brought this new understanding? Methodological advances, by which research workers first identified and then avoided the pitfalls of prior research. It is now recognized that in addition to the usual controls of any experiment, such as accurate recording, hypnotic research needs especially to guard against two such pitfalls: the experimenter effect and Orne's "good subject" effect (Chapter 4). Both need elaboration.

Good hypnotists develop special skills, including ways of speech. Tart (1964) demonstrated this neatly. He recruited hypnotists who agreed to have their voices recorded while giving the same instructions to hypnotized subjects and nonhypnotized controls. Blind judges heard the recordings—and accurately sorted them according to whether or not the subject was hypnotized. Apparently the hypnotists, even though they knew they were being recorded and were trying to give identical instructions, could not help speaking more slowly and emphatically to subjects they knew were hypnotized. There have been many similar findings. They show that when a hypnotist instructs both hypnotized and control subjects, test conditions are likely to differ for the two groups unless the experimenter is blind. Differences in outcome may be due to subtle differences in instructions.

There are individual differences in any behavior that is tested, and it might seem that a tidy experimental design should control for this by testing each subject both when hypnotized and when not. Practice could be controlled by testing half first when hypnotized, the other half first in their normal state. But here the "good subjects" contaminate the data. When hypnotized, they cooperate fully. When not hypnotized, they show their friendly cooperation by putting forth only moderate effort. By now the standard procedure to prevent such contamination is to test each subject in only one condition. Subjects are assigned randomly (or else matched, and then assigned randomly within the match) to one condition or the other. The nonhypnotized group is either not informed abut the purpose of the research or else is asked to simulate what a hypnotized subject would do.

With these points in mind, let us examine psi research. An excellent summary by Schechter (1984) analyzes 20 experiments from 1945 to 1979 which compared the ESP scores made with and without hypnotic induction. (I have found no later psi research which makes this comparison.) We can begin with the bottom line. In 16 of the 20 experiments, ESP scores were higher with hypnosis; they were significantly higher in 7 of those 16; they were significantly lower in none of the 20. If we stopped here, the data would look like impressive evidence that hypnosis is psi-conducive.

But we cannot stop without having checked out the experimenter effect and "good subject" effect. How many of the 20 experiments used separate groups of subjects for the hypnosis and the control condition? Only five. Of those five, one found a significant difference and three an insignificant trend toward higher scores with hypnosis; one found an insignificant trend in the opposite direction. The trend is the same as in the other 15 studies (though the significance level is weaker). So far, it still looks good.

Now the next key question: in how many of the experiments was the experimenter blind? The answer is, none. Thus a parsimonious, conservative interpretation of the data could attribute the findings to a strong experimenter effect, perhaps combined in 15 of the studies with the subjects' expectation and cooperation. (It assumes the hypnotist hoped for high scores.)

Where does this leave us? It depends on where we are going. If we are trying to find "proof" of psi (see Chapter 1) or to find psi experiments that replicate, we may have reached our destination. Look at the research where a nonblind experimenter tested the same subjects in a hypnosis and a control condition. For 6 out of 15 experiments, psi scores showed a significant difference in the predicted direction. For 12 of the 15, scores showed a trend in the predicted direction. For the three with a contrary trend, no difference was significant. This is a high level of replication.

If what we are looking for is evidence of either similarity or difference between psi data and data from psychology, I think we have found a similarity that approaches identity. With hypnotists who know when each subject is and is not hypnotized, and with subjects who know their hypnotist wants them to score higher when hypnotized than when not, performance is better in the hypnotic than in the control condition, both for psi scores and for a variety of other responses.

But if we are looking for the effect on psi scores of an altered state of consciousness, we are left very near to where we began. All we have, I think, are two hints. One comes from another set of scores in some of these same projects. A few investigators asked subjects to judge their depth of trance; those studies show better ESP scores accompanying self-reports of deeper trance. If replicated more often, this would be impressive. The other hint is anecdotal and it sends a mixed message. Some subjects in deep trance seemed to stop trying to make psi responses; this is like what I found (Chapter 8) if subjects were too engrossed in their story-telling to care about ESP. The other group of anecdotes tells of psi being markedly enhanced in deep trance. The topic is clearly worth more research. As it stands, we have hints of an effect but no certainty.

Ganzfeld

In 1974 Honorton introduced the Ganzfeld procedure into parapsychology (Honorton & Harper, 1974). (The German word Ganzfeld means that the visual field is a unified whole, i.e., that there is no patterning within it.) The method seemed strongly psi-conducive and quickly became popular.

The procedure resembles but differs from the psychological method of perceptual deprivation. Typically the subject reclines in a comfortable chair, is alone in a sound-shielded room, wears goggles that admit diffuse light but no patterns, and wears earphones that provide meaningless, continuous sound. Meanwhile, ESP material, usually a set of four pictures, has been prepared. After the subject is in the isolated room, one item of the set is randomly chosen as the target. Instructions to the subject are ordinarily to let one's thoughts drift, hope for ESP impressions of the target, and speak whatever thoughts come to mind. What the subject says is recorded. This continues for a half hour or so, then either the subject or blind judges, or both, try to match the subject's impressions to all the pictures in the set. The question is whether the target makes a better match than the other pictures.

The comfortable solitude, the diffuse, unpatterned vision, and the monotonous sound induce in almost everyone a half-drowsy state in which it is difficult or impossible to think coherently. It is an altered state. If it is psi-conducive, this can yield important insights into how psi functions.

Honorton (1983) wrote that he knew of 48 Ganzfeld studies and also stated that over 50 percent of Ganzfeld projects had given significant results. There were three quick consequences. The statements impressed many. They brought him reports of six other Ganzfeld projects with null results. And they provoked Hyman, a sophisticated and careful psychologist, into making a large scale critical assessment of the Ganzfeld work.

Two interesting articles represent the outcome. Hyman (1985) examined critically all the Ganzfeld studies that claimed significant results, and many of the others. His criteria were more stringent than any I have seen used in psychology, and with those criteria he was able to assign a flaw to every project. Some flaws were major, such as a multiple analysis with no correction for selection. Others seem absurd, such as assigning the flaw of inadequate documentation to a GESP study because the report failed to state if agent and percipient were friends. (This would have been important if the agent had been allowed to select the target. Choice of what would appeal to a friend could have helped make a good match between the target and the subject's train of thought. But selection of targets was random, and therefore friendship was irrelevant to documentation for the point at issue: whether the Ganzfeld data show psi.) Hyman considers the evidence too weak to demonstrate psi.

Honorton (1985) responded to Hyman by making his own critical review. It agreed with Hyman's on some flaws, but strongly disagreed on others. Honorton's evaluation, based on a meta-analysis of the appropriate subgroup of studies, was that the Ganzfeld procedure yielded significant evidence for psi in well controlled research.

Hyman and Honorton promise to coauthor an article which shows some areas of agreement between them. But even before this appears, some general comments and an evaluation seem justified.

The general comments deal with scientific method. Generations ago, scientists searched for the "crucial experiment" that could prove some theory was correct and that would admit no counterhypothesis. The quest now seems to us only a happy dream, like the alchemist's quest for a universal solvent. The consensus now is that data can support a theory but cannot "prove" it; someone will surely be ingenious enough to think up another explanation of the data. The search for crucial experiments is out of date.

Hyman's demand for flawless method flawlessly documented seems to me to represent a similar happy but unrealistic dream. A method that meets all criteria for good research at its own time may not control for other variables identified later. And someone can always demand further documentation. (What did the percipient eat for breakfast this morning? What were the atmospheric and geomagnetic conditions at the time? Was the random assignment of the target initiated by a psi-conducive person?) The list of items that some critic could later require but that no reasonable experimenter would have included is probably infinite.

Instead of waiting for unattainable perfection, we can evaluate what evidence there is, then draw tentative and testable conclusions. What the Ganzfeld material adds up to, I think, is that the method is not a sure-fire way of inducing psi in everyone, but by and large, in well conducted research, it tends to be psi-conducive. The ratio of significant findings is high. Further, subsets of the data offer some interesting hints that seem psychologically plausible, for example about the relation of psi success to personality variables and to their interaction with other variables like length of Ganzfeld interval.

Meditation

Meditation is a broad term that includes diverse disciplines. My short comments here will be inadequate—when I tried to prepare students for their own reading about meditation, in a course on altered states of consciousness, the introductory lectures needed six to eight class hours. In general, though, the practice of meditation prescribes repeated periods with both a semirelaxed body position and a mind that is stilled, perhaps by continual attention to a phrase, or an object, or one's own breathing. This is expected to lead to calm, relaxed, but efficient body and mental functioning, feelings of peace, and other desirable states, perhaps culminating in ecstasy. Many disciplines teach that meditation encourages ESP, but that ESP impressions, like sensory ones, are irrelevant and distract from meditation's major goals.

Research on the effects of meditation demands careful controls. The argument against using the same subjects in both experimental and control conditions is as strong as for research on hypnosis. But finding an appropriate set of subjects for the control condition is troublesome. Meditators who know the purpose of the research can be expected to show the "good subject" effect.

Meditators who do not know the purpose are likely to prepare themselves for psi by meditation and thus defeat the purpose of the comparison. And randomly selected subjects from the general population may have attitudes and personalities different from meditators, since meditators are a self-selected group who probably felt a need for some change in their lives, and who then selected and stayed with this particular, demanding practice.

But finding a good control group is not impossible. One method would be to test those who are about to start meditation study, but have not yet begun—and later to discard the data of any who did not stay the course.

Another problem for psi research is that meditators may disapprove of the experiment. Some meditators think that encouraging psi is antithetical to their goals. Many are likely to think that carefully controlled quantitative research is the wrong way to direct one's effort. With either of these attitudes, cooperation cannot be wholehearted; and data from meditators who hold either attitude should be segregated from the other data.

Since few studies use these necessary controls, it is no wonder that psi research on meditation has given mixed results. I found 15 studies of it, done between 1971 and early 1986, and divided almost equally between ESP and PK. Eight have null findings; seven describe a significant difference, often not corrected for selection. On the whole, if taken uncritically at face value, the 15 indicate meditation was psi-conducive. I will describe some examples.

Schmidt & Pantas (1972), in the research reported in Chapter 6, tested unselected subjects on two RNGs and found significant hitting on each instrument. They also report that Pantas, an experienced meditator, independently had significantly high scores on both machines. (Would Pantas have been equally successful if he had never meditated? We do not know.)

Dukhan & K.R. Rao (1973) enlisted the cooperation of a guru who headed an ashram in India. As a result, dozens of his students volunteered to act as subjects. When a comparison was made between novices and experienced meditators, ESP scores showed only minor, erratic differences between them. Each group, however, had significant psi-missing in the premeditation (control) tests and significant psi-hitting in the postmeditation tests.

The psi data are unusually strong, but it is not easy to see what they mean. Consider the juxtaposition of significant psi-missing before meditation and psi-hitting afterwards. This is how Orne's "good subjects" would psi-miss and psi-hit. Do the strikingly strong scores show only the good subject effect? Or do they show in addition that meditation induced unusually high levels of psi for both hitting and missing?

I also wonder whether those strong psi scores imply self-selection. Was it those with a high level of psi who chose to enter the ashram, or to volunteer for the experiment? Or do the scores imply that training in meditation is psi-conducive? If we tentatively opt for the latter, the lack of consistent differences between novices and experienced meditators suggests that, for the forced-choice psi tests that were used here, short training is as psi-conducive as long.

Palmer, Khamashta, & Israelson (1979) tested 20 graduates of Transcendental Meditation, using the Ganzfeld. When subjects rated the targets, scores showed a strong trend toward psi-missing, but when two blind judges used the subjects' comments to rate the targets, scores showed a strong trend toward psi-hitting. The difference between subjects' scores and blind judges' scores was significant. Isn't this odd and interesting? It seems well worth following up. What it implies, to my mind, is that (a) the Ganzfeld was psi-conducive and (b) the free reporting of their impressions was a congenial experience for these meditators, but that (c) the stringent, forced-choice rating afterward was uncongenial to them and they reacted negatively to the 31-point rating scale. It is of course also possible that they resisted seeing the implications of their own earlier free comments.

(Obviously the findings of this project support no firm conclusion. But they resemble a good many other findings in implying that it is necessary to distinguish between ESP impressions and the subject's identification of them. This distinction seems a reasonable working hypothesis. It resembles one that is well recognized in memory research: the difference between learning and the ability to retrieve what was learned.)

W.G. Braud & Hartgrove (1976) used a good between-groups design. They tested ten experienced meditators and a control group of ten subjects recruited after they had attended a lecture on meditation (and who presumably felt favorably interested in meditation). Each of the 20 was asked to influence an RNG during a 20 minute period in which meditators meditated and control subjects rested. In the next five minutes each was asked to keep the mind still so as to receive ESP impressions of a slide.

Hartgrove, an experienced meditator, both tested the subjects and (in part of the test) acted as a subject. She was, of course, blind to the targets. During each of the 20 periods while subjects waited for an ESP impression, Hartgrove meditated and made her own response to the ESP target.

Hartgrove's scores on the 20 ESP targets were significantly high. The ten meditators' ESP scores were somewhat above chance and the ten control subjects' were somewhat below; the difference between these two groups was significant. For PK on the RNG, each group scored slightly below chance, and their pooled scores showed significant psi-missing. We might speculate, post hoc, that meditators found the free ESP responses congenial but that both groups felt it inappropriate, during meditation or rest, to try to influence a machine. This post hoc speculation finds some faint support in responses to a post-session questionnaire. Both groups had lower scores for liking the PK task than for judging the importance of the ESP task.

I have been tempted to pay particular attention, perhaps more attention than it deserves, to a pattern implied by the data of Pantas and Hartgrove. Both were not only experienced meditators but were also interested enough in research to act as experimenters. Their own psi scores, over many sessions, were exceptionally high. Might the combination of a proresearch attitude and long experience in meditation be worth following up to find if it is consistently psi-conducive? An easy way to do it, if the data are available, is to check back on psi subjects who have already been tested as meditators. If any of the subjects were sufficiently research-minded to do an experiment of their own, this speculation postdicts that their earlier psi scores were high.

In summary, these and other significant findings in psi research on meditation suggest that meditation may be psi-conducive; but the multiple analyses, the possibility that other variables enter in, and the large number of null or unanticipated results prevent a firm conclusion. The sprinkling of reports where meditators psi-missed indicates an interaction with attitude. But even if we tentatively accept that meditation is psi-conducive, we still need to learn how much importance to assign to each of four possible reasons for its effect: the personality traits of those who choose to meditate, the discipline of meditation, the attitudes associated with this discipline, or the altered state of consciousness that meditation can induce.

DREAMS

Dreams vary from simple, realistic images to long, bizarre, inchoate sequences accompanied by strong emotion. They are of interest to parapsychology because of the common belief that they give paranormal information. Methods of studying them include collecting dream reports and checking them against other events; comparing dream diaries to records of daily events; and using dream reports as responses to ESP targets—the latter often in conjunction with waking a subject and asking for a dream report when rapid eye movements and EEG records show there has just been a dream.

One careful method of investigating spontaneous cases to find if they showed psi in dreams was used especially by the (London) Society for Psychical Research and the American Society for Psychical Research. It was to check that the dream was reported before its coincidence with some other event was known, to find if the other event occurred and resembled the dream report, and to try to evaluate whether the event could reasonably have been anticipated. Thus a dream of the death of someone known to be ill would have little evidential value. More value would be attributed to a case (Myers, 1903, I, 431–433) where a woman told her husband of a feeling of foreboding accompanying a dream in which two respectably dressed women fell into water and sank, and then their hats rose to the surface. A newspaper clipping was later received in the mail describing the death by drowning of two women, one a distant relative, whose bodies were found only after two hats were seen floating on a lake.

L.E. Rhine (1981) adopted a different method: collecting large numbers of cases, discarding only those that seemed psychotic or fraudulent, and collating the rest. Comparisons of dreams with other cases collected in the same way indicated that the dreams were more likely to be precognitive and to be detailed rather than vague. The finding of more precognition in dreams than in waking experiences is consistent with folklore and also with what was found in other large case collections (see West, 1948).

The best known dream diary (Dunne, 1927) and several others describe many coincidences with later events (these often reported in the same person's diary), coincidences which seem both unforeseeable and out of the dreamer's control. Sondow (1984) suggests, on the basis of her own diaries and the reports of others, that coincidences are more frequent soon after the dream, tailing off rapidly after a day or only a little longer.

But it is hard or impossible to obtain a baseline for chance coincidence against which to evaluate coincidence with a dream. Millions of us have many dreams each night; our days are full of incident; some correspondences will occur by chance. The dream diarist may record the day's incidents selectively. Laboratory research on dreams is usually less dramatic, but its evidence is clearer.

Ullman and Krippner set the model for such laboratory work (Ullman, Krippner, & Vaughan, 1973). In a typical session the subject knew that there would be an ESP target, and was to hope that dreams would describe that target. The subject slept in the laboratory, while an experimenter monitored EEG and eye movement recordings. After the subject was in bed for the night, the person who was to act as telepathic agent went to a file which contained many pictures, each concealed in an envelope; selected one at random; went to a distant room (which had its own lavatory) and stayed there for the night.

After entering the room and before going to sleep, the agent looked at the picture which was the night's target. The experimenter wakened the subject after dream periods and asked for dream reports, and in the morning asked for supplementary recollections of the dreams. Typical scoring, after completing a series of up to ten such sessions, asked blind judges to match the pictures against each night's dream reports. There were several minor variations in method, such as clairvoyant or precognitive sessions or utilizing the agent's associations as part of the target material. The procedure was impeccably blind.

A useful summary of this work by Child (1985) shows that hits exceeded misses for 14 of the 15 series, that seven series were independently significant, and that the work as a whole showed highly significant psi-hitting. The method is expensive, and there have been only three attempts at direct replication elsewhere. None had significant findings. Other dream studies which do not waken the subjects to collect dream reports have fairly often reported significant correspondence between dreams and targets, but Child suggests that with this easier and less expensive method there is more likely to be non-publication of null or negative outcomes.

I will describe only one of these reports, one which had weaker results than several of the others but used an unusual and careful procedure (Markwick & Beloff, 1983). Markwick was in London, Beloff in Edinburgh. They agreed to have 100 trials. For each, Beloff prepared five possible targets and sent the set to Markwick, who kept it sealed. Beloff randomly selected one item as the target. Markwick recorded dreams for one or more nights, and only then looked at the five possible targets. She ranked them according to their correspondence to the dream or dreams, and mailed both dream reports and ranks to Beloff. Data are reported in units of 10. Beloff's practice was to evaluate separately the first and second halves of the data collected in any study, as well as evaluating the whole.

This demanding procedure gave a mixed outcome. Scores for the first 50 targets were high and significant. The trend continued for the next unit of 10 but scores approximated the chance level thereafter. Markwick reports that her father died during the seventh unit and that the nature of her dreams then changed. When the 100 records are pooled, their score is significantly above chance if evaluated by one-tailed p. Does the outcome support the findings of Ullman and Krippner, in spite of the difference in method? The internal pattern and the statistics, especially for the first half, would lead some to say yes, but those who disregard the internal pattern might withhold judgment because the data are not significant with a two-tailed p.

Astonishingly few of the dream studies utilized the one consistent finding from spontaneous reports and dream diaries: that dreams seem especially likely to give precognitive rather than contemporary information. An exception is a set of three series within the work by Ullman et al. (see Krippner, Ullman, & Honorton, 1971) where a brilliantly innovative method gave brilliant results. The subject was Malcolm Bessent, a psychic who had had precognitive experiences. He slept in the laboratory and his dream reports were collected in the usual way. After he woke in the morning, a target was randomly selected. Then, while he dressed and had breakfast, a multisensory setting was prepared to suggest the target. For the target, "parka hood," e.g., Bessent went to a room draped with white sheets, two blue floor fans blew air on him, he saw a picture of an Eskimo with a parka hood, blankets were put around him and a hood made from towels put on his head, ice cubes were suddenly dropped down his back, his hand was plunged into ice water, he was told to smell and taste the ice, Finlandia was played, and a color organ made light patterns supposed to resemble Northern lights. His dreams of the night before had had frequent mentions of white and some of "ice blue"; and the usual blind judges made an excellent match between the preceding night's dreams and the target. Child's summary shows 16 hits and 2 misses for Bessent's 18 sets of precognitive dream reports.

Overall, the high level of significance in the work of Ullman et al. is impressive evidence that psi occurs in dreams. On the one hand the conclusion is somewhat weakened by null results in three replications (although these three are compatible with the null results of many series which Ullman et al. conducted). On the other hand the conclusion is strengthened by frequent significant results from other careful methods of studying psi in dreams.

There is little more to say on this topic. Although spontaneous cases suggest that psi in dreams is more likely to be precognitive and precise in detailed accuracy than is psi while awake, the reports from laboratory and other formal research have identified no distinctive patterns of psi in dreams. Dream reports resemble Ganzfeld reports, with some psi material embedded among much that is not. The lack of distinctive information is perhaps similar to the clinical observation that dreams symbolize the same information as waking fantasy—but that is a null conclusion, of no differences in content. At most it offers some minimal support to the theory that psi resembles other psychological processes.

Remote Viewing

Targ & Puthoff (1977) introduced an interesting ESP procedure which they called remote viewing. It asks subjects to describe a distant scene. Their original procedure demanded two experimenters, an assistant, and a great deal of advance preparation; a description follows.

The target pool consists of a long list of visually distinctive places which can be reached from the laboratory in a half hour. For each session, the subject is welcomed into the laboratory and has a friendly conversation with both experimenters, during which there is gentle encouragement to accept on the basis of prior findings that success in the experiment is possible. The subject then retires with one experimenter into a pleasant, comfortably furnished room, with subdued lighting and decor.

The other experimenter goes to the target pool, where an assistant issues a randomly selected envelope containing a target. He goes to his car, opens the envelope, drives to the designated place, and there experiences the site as fully as possible: swinging on a swing if it is a playground, feeling the spray if there is a fountain, sniffing odors, etc., and also taking pictures from a number of vantage points.

Back in the laboratory, the subject chats with the first experimenter, who encourages relaxation and gently suggests that remote viewing will work best with a mind emptied of one's usual preoccupations, and with a willingness to accept any images that come, no matter how fleeting or odd they are. After a half hour, the subject is asked to describe or draw all impressions as they occur. Responses are recorded. The experimenter encourages some comments, probes for more information after others, but discourages others if he sees fit. For example, if the subject says, "I see something long and white, like a column," the experimenter might discourage the "intellectual overlay" by saying, "If it's *like* a column, it isn't actually a column. Tell me what you see, not what it's like." This continues for about a quarter of an hour. After a series of such sessions, blind judges evaluate the match between the various sites and the subjects' protocols.

Variants of the procedure are numerous. Many simplify it: they do not demand that targets be nearby or that timing be synchronized. Some have a single experimenter and a single subject who makes many trials. Nelson, Jahn, & Dunne (1986) recently used objective scoring: a checklist of 30 binary items that might or might not describe the scene. Each item is weighted on the basis of how frequently it appeared in a pool of over 40,000 previous responses, so that different weight is assigned to a hit or to a miss on an unusual response and on a common one. They report highly significant psi success in 334 trials with the checklist.

Initial reports described almost invariable success in remote viewing. Descriptions often coincided with the site itself, but occasionally with what the distant experimenter had been doing. Statistics were criticized, then revised to meet the criticisms and found to be still significant (Tart, Puthoff, & Targ, 1981). Schlitz & Haight (1984) report that about half the 28 replications showed significant evidence for psi. The method of remote viewing thus seems strongly ESP-conducive.

There is general agreement that remote viewing does not induce an altered state. Why, then, report on it in this chapter? Because the success rate seems to be as high as for the altered state techniques, and because of the conditions it shares with hypnosis, the Ganzfeld, and meditation. Each typically includes a long, leisurely introduction, with strong (though sometimes low keyed) suggestions that the method will elicit psi. Each also includes a rather long period of relaxation while waiting for images or impressions to appear, and reporting them. This naturally raises the question of whether it is these shared conditions that are psi-conducive in altered state research, rather than the altered state itself.

SPECULATION

I suggest five interpretations of the material in this chapter. One is nihilistic. A person intent only on avoiding Type I error could disregard even the successful replication of well controlled and statistically significant reports by finding some flaw in any study, and thus could interpret the whole as inadequate. This disregards the risk of Type II error, but so far as it goes, is legitimate.

A variant of the nihilistic approach dismisses the research because of an ambiguity in the procedure. Most quantitative studies of altered states, as well as a good many other studies, provide interesting targets (qualitatively different pictures or scenes) and ask the subjects to hope to receive impressions of the target. Then the subjects (or blind judges who have access to the subjects' reports of their impressions) match the impressions to items in the target pool. Suppose, as is often the case, that the matches are significantly high and thus give evidence of ESP.

Using qualitatively different targets has two clear advantages. It helps in enlisting the subjects' cooperation and it permits varied exploratory analyses of the ESP process. But it also raises an important and unresolved question. When did the ESP occur? Could it have been at the moment of making the match? Were the blind judges lulled into a psi-conducive state by thinking that it was the subjects, not they, who were on trial? Was their study of the protocols irrelevant except as it helped to induce this feeling? When subjects themselves made the matches, were they similarly nondefensive because of thinking that the ESP part of the procedure had already ended? Whenever research asks for target identification only from those who are not in an altered state, it is possible to argue that psi in altered states has not been studied.

How can the argument be answered? Not by having subjects respond to an objective checklist of items; this bypasses the issue. Not by reference to the selections from subjects' impressions that have been published; selections can be misleading. Ideally, the answer would come by programming a computer to score all of a given protocol against each item in the target pool, but this is impossible as yet, because we do not know what instructions to give the computer (or to give a human judge). There are no rules for how much to weight various possible correspondences or clues (for example, recurrent but vague references to a picture's general theme, or a single clear description of an unusual pictorial detail, or an illogical intrusion as when a subject says, "I don't know why this came into my mind but I've just thought of. . ."). Preliminary research on how to make these judgments offers promise of a solution but has not yet provided one, and perhaps it will need to supply different formulas for subjects and for judges with different cognitive styles.

Although it seems unlikely to me that this nihilistic argument will be supported, it has not been disconfirmed.

A third interpretaton is parsimonious. It accepts—but always tentatively, of course—the evidence that some or all of these altered states are psi-conducive. It then examines them in the framework of other evidence about what is psi-conducive. It considers that an adequate hypothesis to account for the findings from the various altered states is that all involve a readiness to accept psi impressions, a readiness to put aside ordinary response biases (i.e., to "clear the mind"), and either moderate relaxation or some other body state which differs from the usual one. The tentative interpretation here is that, so far as psi is concerned, there is no qualitative difference between a so-called altered state and the normal state which is psi-conducive.

Of the many other possible interpretations, one seems especially promising to me. It was proposed in the early days of psychical research, when striking evidence for psi came not only from trance but also from automatic writing, crystal-gazing, and similar activities called "automatisms." Early in this period, Janet (1886), a highly respected psychiatrist, reported extraordinary telepathic success with hypnosis. Trance, automatisms, and hypnosis were all described as dissociated states; apparently dissociation was psi-conducive. Somewhat later, the concept of dissociation seemed especially appropriate because of the strong psychic ability frequently reported for one of the personalities in cases of multiple personality (see, e.g., Prince, 1915).

In modern psychology the term dissociation is applied to cases of multiple personality, but is seldom used elsewhere. Perhaps one of the reasons is that, when the term is defined broadly, all of us dissociate so much of the time. When our bodies are active in a familiar routine, our thoughts can be busy with something else. When we explain something to a young child we use simple language and concrete examples; we detach—dissociate—ourselves from our abstract ideas and a part of our vocabulary. We are constantly switching on some of our potentials and switching others off (though of course extremes of dissociation, such as multiple personality, are rare).

The fourth interpretation that I propose for the material in this chapter involves using a broad definition of dissociation. It is that psi is more likely to emerge when we switch off or dissociate from our normal reality-orientation. Doing so demands what Batcheldor (1984) calls a suspension of disbelief; and this lack of our usual critical alertness is surely encouraged when we can feel relaxed and comfortable with our situation. A shift from our normal alert reality-orientation would, I think, be encouraged by each of the techniques described in this chapter.

If detachment or dissociation from the ordinary ways in which we have learned to cope with reality is psi-conducive, this fits, as if it was made for it, with Eysenck's theory of extraversion (1957). His thesis (much simplified) is that the extraversion and introversion difference is a difference in readiness for inhibition. Extraverts are better inhibitors. They more readily inhibit (forget, dissociate from) the cautions they have learned; they therefore enter more freely than introverts into what is happening now. And surely trance, hypnotic induction, meditation, and the settings of the Ganzfeld and of remote viewing, all encourage just this detachment from the everyday world and the ordinary patterns of our life. They encourage, temporarily, the freely flowing responses to new impressions that are characteristic of extraversion.

The fifth interpretation is radical. It was put forth by LeShan (1974), who argues that in an altered state it is possible to perceive an altered reality. In our everyday reality, objects and individuals are separate in space and can be separated by time; events are causally determined; we make value judgments of good and bad. But this is not the reality that psychics or mystics—or physicists—describe. To support his argument, LeShan gives a brilliant compilation of quotations about reality from physicists, mystics, and psychics. The descriptions from these three groups are almost indistinguishable. They tell of a universe in which all parts are interconnected, distinctions between past and future are not absolute, there are no value judgments (what is, is), and so on. He argues that, while our common sense view of reality is valid, another valid view is that of the physicists. Psychics and mystics can perceive both everyday reality and also the reality that physicists describe. Thus entering an altered state of consciousness may permit a different and valid way of perceiving.

And now a different kind of speculation, about applying rather than interpreting the results. Suppose that any one of these methods for changing mood or attitude or state of consciousness is psi-conducive. Can we induce that state in ourselves? The frequent successes of feedback techniques for self-training (e.g. in lowering blood pressure or preventing headaches) imply that some of us, though not all, can learn a change in mental set. Thus, if a state of consciousness permits use of psi, and if some can learn to enter that state, they will have learned better control of their psi ability. (The point is raised again on page 136.)

Overview

Occasionally, in trance, psychics give striking qualitative evidence of psi. There is statistical evidence for psi success in hypnosis, meditation, the Ganzfeld, and dreams. These five are altered states of consciousness, but comparable evidence of psi success comes from the remote viewing technique. Although it is not considered to produce an altered state of consciousness, it shares with those states a detachment from everyday reality and a readiness to accept incoming impressions which at other times might be rejected as illogical. Psychological interpretations are proposed.

Some of the findings are well replicated, and one method especially shows a high level of replicability. When the same subjects take ESP tests both while hypnotized and while in their normal condition, and the hypnotist knows whether or not they were hypnotized, scores are higher in the hypnotic than in the control condition. These results in psi research are parallel to the results with other tasks that were found in prior psychological research.

10. Perception

Perception is what gave ESP its name, but surprisingly little research has tried to find if there is the family resemblance that the name implies, or if psi in general functions as perception does. This chapter will begin with a rough outline of some questions about perception that psychology studies, and then turn to the psi research that comes closest to addressing the questions.

A basic concept behind psychologists' questions is that the brain acts as a filter. It acts in other ways too, of course, but one of its important functions is to screen out from consciousness most of the sensory input that bombards us. Examples come from every sense modality. A few follow.

Ordinarily we screen out stimuli from the surface of the body—though if we choose to attend to the tip of the nose or the soles of the feet, we can feel sensations there. When we are engrossed in what we are doing, we are likely to screen out internal sensations that tell us we are hungry or thirsty or need to empty the bladder, although we can become acutely aware of those sensations when the other action stops. The profile of the nose covers a sizable part of each eye's visual field, but even with one eye closed we seldom notice it. We become habituated to the ticking of a clock, unless there is some reason to listen for it.

This gives rise to one of the earliest questions of research on perception: What passes through the filter? Typical lists of these "determinants of attention" include four major categories. They begin with sensory variables like the loudness of a sound or the brightness of a light. Next come stimulus patterns, like symmetry, closure, textural differences, abruptness of change, and contrast or assimilation in figure-ground relationships. The lists then move along to stimulus variables dependent on prior learning, like familiarity or novelty, and finally to motivational variables. These include both short-term mental sets, such as a search for particular items, and also long-term emotional readiness, like alertness to the sound of one's own name. The lists are obviously highly relevant to psi. We ask if similar factors determine which psi targets will elicit a response.

Another set of questions asks what becomes of the perceptual input which did not reach consciousness. Was it truly filtered out, and erased as if it had never come in? Or can it become available to consciousness if we later try to observe it? Do we respond to it even without awareness, because it is part of the perceptual flow? Is it transferred to long-term memory, so that it affects later behavior? If the input which did not reach consciousness affects us, is it processed differently from input which reached awareness? The answer to each of these questions seems to be: "Yes, to some extent, under certain conditions." Here also we need to learn if similar conditions influence psi responses.

The units below are a survey of all the psi research I could find that seems to bear directly on these questions—with one exception. Motivational readiness is omitted here because it crops up so often in other chapters.

Sensory Variables

It was the orderly relation between sensory variables and our responses to them, i.e., psychophysics, that established psychology as a laboratory science. Psi research, so far as I can see, yields nothing comparable. When we look for orderly effects of sensory variables on psi we find a series of null or ambiguous reports.

The classic research here was done by Pratt & Woodruff (1939), whose subjects called three sets of ESP symbols: large, small, and the usual size. Order of presentation was counterbalanced. Generally an attempt was made to present each size as a special challenge. The results showed no effect of size, but instead reflected the challenge. While the challenge was fresh, scores were high; the first calls for each new size had significantly higher scores than the later calls. Data apparently related to motivational change but not to the sensory property of the targets.

There are several other examples of such null results, and I cite three. Carr (1983) found no significant ESP difference between responses to targets which were visually clear only to a color blind person and targets which were visually clear only to a person with normal vision. Woodruff (1960) wrote 60 percent of his targets in black and 40 percent in red. He found nonsignificant psi missing on black targets; nonsignificant psi-hitting on red; and a nonsignificant difference between them. Mitchell & Drewes (1982) examined differences in modality by having all their subjects take one ESP test with kinesthetic or motor emphasis (walking to six openings arranged in a circle and putting the ESP response into one) and another with a visual or verbal emphasis (while resting, imaging and naming one of six colors). Half the subjects used motor skills professionally (dancers, painters, etc.) and half used verbal skills (writers, teachers, etc.). Subjects took standard tests of ability and of interest. The ESP scores showed no difference between the tasks nor any interaction with profession or aptitude, but they related to interest.

These null effects of sensory variables have several apparent exceptions. At first glance some results may seem to show that more readily perceived targets give higher ESP scores, but a closer examination suggests the data are best interpreted in terms of preference or motivation. I cite a single example. Chauvin (1961) tested himself and four children on two sizes of ESP targets: one 12 mm. high, the other on microfilm, so that it could be read only with magnification. The children (but not Chauvin) scored higher on the larger targets. Is this opposed to the Pratt & Woodruff finding? Does it show that ESP depends on the target's perceptibility? No. When we look at the data, we find that those higher scores on the legible targets were close to the chance level. It was the low scores on the microfilmed targets that were significant: they were significantly lower than expected by chance. This implies that it was the illegible targets which the children identified by ESP—identified and then avoided.

As the Mitchell & Drewes work implies, even gross differences among sensory modalities have not shown any consistent psi effect. A good many studies used nonvisual targets such as sounds or right versus left position, but no results are distinctive except as they apply to particular subjects' preferences.

Studies from gifted subjects point to the same null conclusion, but with the same exception. For a particular individual, some idiosyncratic sensory condition may be a requisite for psi. In general, however, a psychic may at one time report visual imagery, give some correct responses, and—more interestingly—make errors that look as if they were visual, like mistaking an F for an E. At another time the same person may report hearing a voice, give some accurate responses, and make errors that sound as if one word were wrongly heard as another. Sometimes psychics report kinesthetic impressions, or a pain that corresponds to a pain which a distant person is feeling. There are individual differences in what is psi-conducive for one person or another, but no general relation, among gifted subjects, between sensory variables and psi.

The irrelevance of simple stimulus variables has been accepted for some time by many who do psi research, and in retrospect I recognize how I have taken it for granted in my own work. Only now, while writing this, did it occur to me with a shock that in a sense I lied to my subjects by describing their targets as colored ESP cards when in fact the (physical) targets were only an assistant's notation, for instance the letters YS for a yellow star. In the most extreme case (Schmeidler, 1964a) the subject was shown as the target pool a 5 by 5 array of ESP cards with each symbol painted in five colors, but the targets were selected by a computer and never printed out. Physically, they were only imperceptible changes within the computer. My presumption was that the meaning of the target was important but its physical structure or sensory quality was not, and significant data seemed to bear out the presumption.

For sensory variables, then, there seems no relation between psi and psychological findings. It is a topic where the theory that this book examines is disconfirmed.

Perceptual Patterns; Figure and Ground

Sensory input largely depends on the sensitivity of the sense receptors. The input is preliminary to perceptual processing, and the first step in this processing is organization into figure and ground. What we attend to or notice is figural and all the rest is background (though of course if we attend to something else within the perceptual array, that becomes figure and the previous figure is now part of the background). This leads to several questions. I turn first to those that ask what determines the figure and then, under the subhead of Contrast and Assimilation, to those that ask about the effect of the background.

Figural Properties

What makes a "good" figure, one that is readily perceived? There is rich psychological material here, but no consensus in parapsychology, except perhaps that targets should be interesting but should not encourage response biases. Neither of these is relevant to figural properties. It seems to me that the lack of consensus is itself a datum, because so many of us have devised novel targets, but found our pilot studies not promising enough for a follow-up. Some of the null results have been published; Nash (1985), for example, found no significant difference in ESP responses to words that resembled the target in meaning or in shape (e.g., bed-cot or bed-bad).

It may be that I am generalizing about this null relation too soon, because there are occasional reports of affirmative findings. Here are two. The most systematic study was by Camstra et al. (1972), who examined the size, complexity, contrast and symmetry of the targets in relation to the sex of the subjects. The only significant result was that ESP scores were higher for asymmetrical targets than for symmetrical ones. Since there seem to have been no replications, we do not know if the finding is stable.

Recent research that may be relevant to simplicity versus complexity is reported by Vassy (1985). Each of his RNG targets was a unit, but the unit was constituted from a sequence of binary choices. Sequences were of five different lengths. His first series tested naive subjects. Overall data were not significant, but comparison of different lengths of sequence showed significantly higher scores for the shortest, simplest sequence than for the next. A replication with experienced subjects found similar, fairly high scores for both these sequences. This could be taken to mean that for psi as for other repsonses, practice produces perceptual learning and thereby changes the optimal level of complexity, but the finding was not predicted and has not been replicated.

Here, too, a long list could be added of reports where a first look implies that some shape or pattern gives distinctive psi scores, but a second look implies that what was distinctive was not the percept, but only its meaning. An example comes from Fisk & West (1955a, 1955b). A subject responding to ESP cards had a significantly high score when the target was a circle, but scored at chance on other symbols. Inquiry found that for this young man, the circle connoted female. In a second ESP series he again scored high on the circle (and also on the plus, now interpreted as a male symbol) but not on the other targets. Clearly it was not the figural property per se that related to the score.

For figural properties, then, there is no clear evidence that psi and perception are similar.

Ambiguous Figures

Two studies that I hesitate about including examined telepathy with ambiguous figures (drawings which can represent either of two pictures, and where attention to one relegates the other to the background). Agent and percipient reported which part was figural. Neither study found a significant correspondence between agents' and percipients' reports. Because the drawing stayed the same throughout, and the target was the agent's conscious experience, it may not be proper to class these studies under the topic of perception.

Contrast and Assimilation

In psychology it is usual to speak in the same breath of two opposite processes: contrast and assimilation. Both relate to figure-ground patterning. Assimilation describes the pull of the background upon the figure, and is well established; it often occurs. Contrast describes the accentuation of some figural characteristic because of its difference from the background, and is also well established and frequent. A good deal of psychological research has begun to clarify the conditions under which one rather than the other will appear.

Are these processes also found in psi? The relevant research has never been collated, and I attempt here to put it together. The overview goes back forty years (but omits post hoc analyses unless a later series tried to check them out). My first search found nine procedures that seemed relevant. I describe them and the interpretation they suggested, then add four studies turned up in a later search, which give only partial support to the interpretation.

The list begins with Carington (1944, 1945), who describes years of work with an unusual technique. His targets were drawable words. His subjects agreed to make an ESP call of a drawable word on ten successive days, then mail the records to him. He selected each target on the day it would be used, either by opening a dictionary at random and using the first drawable word on the page, or by selecting at random from a pool already prepared. He displayed each day's target in a closed room, with windows covered. Scoring followed a formula devised for him by R.A. Fisher. It evaluated hits by taking as the baseline for each word the frequency with which that word was reported when it was not the target. The 741 subjects of his seven series showed highly significant success in hitting the targets, as did the hundreds of subjects of 28 other experimenters who used his method.

What is relevant here is an internal pattern that Carington first observed post hoc, then checked and confirmed in later tests. Not only was there, on average, a significant correspondence between the target for a day and the responses of that day, but also a strong correspondence between one day's target and responses on adjacent days, tailing off to smaller but still more than chance correspondence on days that were more remote.

Carington's two methods of target selection deserve separate consideration. His first was to open the dictionary each day to select a fresh target. Responses had not yet been mailed to him, and therefore could not have normally influenced his target choice, and yet he found that responses made on preceding days (as well as on subsequent days) corresponded to the target. This implies that subjects were responding precognitively to the targets he would later select, and it implies an odd sort of mistaken psi: making the right response at the wrong time. (Similar results have been found so often since Carington's work that the term "displacement" is now used to describe them.)

His other method was to select targets randomly from one of the pools he had previously prepared. This method found the same correspondences as his previous one, and it uncovered another oddity. As before, the average score was high for that day's target and was lower, but still significantly high, for the nine other targets of that series. He also found another significant effect: a score that was lower than the others, but still significantly high, for the unused words in that target pool, compared to other target pools.

The first two of these displacement effects were replicated by the other investigators who used Carington's method. For the words in their series, scores were separately significant for the correct day, for preceding days, and for following days. The only appropriate way to interpret this, it seems to me, is to conceptualize temporal differences as if they were spatial ones. This leads us to think of the ten targets as if they formed a group in which each day's target was the figure and the other targets were the background. The immediate surround of the target was the other nine words in its batch. Those words apparently exerted a strong pull. The more remote background, the unused words in the target pool, exerted a measureable but weaker pull. There was a tendency for the figure to be reported, but also a tendency toward assimilation, so that the background was reported too.

That was temporal background. What of spatial background? Convincing evidence for its effect on psi comes from another long series. Pratt (1973) summarizes ten years of research by himself and others with a gifted subject, Pavel Stepanek. Stepanek preferred to work with a binary ESP choice: whether the green or the white side of a card was uppermost. Cards were enclosed in opaque envelopes and were freshly randomized after each run. Stepanek initially had an extraordinarily high hit rate. As tests continued it was observed that responses to some envelopes were consistently hits but responses to other envelopes were consistently misses. This now became the new focus of research.

The first question, of course, was whether responses to an envelope had been consistent because the envelope had distinctive markings. To control for the possibility, each envelope was now enclosed in a larger opaque envelope; otherwise the procedure was unchanged. Stepanek called green or white. He continued to score high on the target but also to make consistent hits on certain envelopes and consistent misses on others, although now no sensory cues were available. Again the results were highly significant.

The research was conducted with meticulous care and had many other interesting findings, but this partial statement shows the general pattern. Although Stepanek was trying to respond to the card, his response was partially determined by the surround of the card. It is perhaps like a person trying to judge a picture but being influenced by the frame. If we take spatial relations as equivalent to temporal ones, these results are like Carington's in showing that the target's background can influence response to the target.

For both Carington and Pratt, an apparent background effect was first observed post hoc, then stated as a hypothesis and confirmed in later tests. Child & Kelly (1973), however, designed their research to study the effect of background. They used conventional ESP cards with 25 in a deck, but arranged the cards so that one of the symbols would appear only once, and the others three, five, seven, and nine times. Frequency of symbols was counterbalanced; cards were arranged randomly within the deck. They worked with a single gifted subject, L.H., who was told that decks would not hold five of each symbol, but was not told the details of the arrangement. Overall hits were significantly high.

Child & Kelly examined the data to find if the more frequent symbols would be called more often than the less frequent, i.e., if L.H. was in part responding to the deck as a whole. Their painstaking analysis made all necessary corrections for call and target frequency. The data gave a highly significant affirmative answer: there were many more calls for symbols that appeared seven or nine times than for those that appeared only one time or three. This was true separately for hits and for misses.

The preponderance of misses which showed the frequent symbols is especially interesting. It replicates the Carington and Pratt findings of a psi response that is appropriate to the background but not to the target.

Child & Kelly report one important further finding that at first seems an anomaly. The difference between targets that appeared one and nine times was less than the difference between targets that appeared three and seven times. Their further analysis showed that this reflected a high number of calls for the target that appeared only once, i.e., they found a contrast effect. The unique target stood out from its background. Their data seem to demonstrate both assimilation and contrast.

Two indirect partial replications came years later, using unselected subjects. In mine (Schmeidler, 1985), subjects took a standard psychological test (the Matching Familiar Figures Test) to show their tendency toward being impulsive (fast responses and many errors) or reflective (slow responses and few errors). Subjects also made three ESP runs: the first at their own pace; the next quickly, in half the time they had taken for the first; and the third slowly, taking at least twice as long as at first. The target pool was the 12 hour positions on a clock face. Each run had 12 targets, all on a single page.

To examine background effect, the twelve targets were selected so that four would be the same (constituting the background) and each of the other eight would be different. Backgrounds were rotated among the twelve possibilities; placement on the page was random. For 30 subjects, the only interesting finding was that fast subjects on their fast run seemed influenced by the background: they made a significant surplus of calls on the repeated target. A direct replication with 30 new subjects was undertaken to find if this unpredicted result would reappear. The replication gave an almost identical significant pattern. These unselected subjects, unlike L.H., had no overall significant psi-hitting; but like L.H., the fast subjects who were responding quickly, on their misses, made responses corresponding to the background of the target.

Crandall (1985) had previously (see Chapter 5) been examining a narrower effect of background: the immediate surround of the psi target. He used their hits on the target to divide his subjects into psi-missers and psi-hitters, and he found repeatedly that the calls of psi-missers showed a displacement effect: an extrachance correspondence to the items on the target list that immediately preceded and immediately followed the target. It seems a specific type of assimilation, confusing with the target the two items that, as it were, framed the target.

Crandall (1986) followed up the Child & Kelly research and mine by using still another way to examine background. Targets were the digits 1–5, written in black ink on each subject's target sheet. On each sheet a single one of the same five digits was also written both at the left and at the right of each target. The background symbols were rotated among target sheets; they were written in black ink on some sheets, in red on the others. Crandall's analysis of the data followed his usual pattern: dividing subjects into psi-missers and psi-hitters, and predicting that psi-missers would show displacement. He stated three other predictions, and all four were significantly supported.

Two of the others are relevant here. One was that psi-missers (but not psi-hitters) would show a significant surplus of calls on the symbol that formed the target background; and they did. The other was that either the red or the black would show more background effect (a nondirectional hypothesis). Here Crandall found contrast. There was significantly more background effect with the red. This resembles what Woodruff (page 113) had seen, though Woodruff's data showed only an insignificant tendency toward higher scores on the (unexpected) red symbols.

Meanwhile a clever PK experiment by Stanford (1983) had also supported the general argument that nontargets in the background would influence psi responses. In Stanford's careful double blind procedure, subjects used an RNG and had a picture as the target. After PK success the RNG exposed the target; after a PK miss the RNG exposed a nontarget. The nontargets had been pretested and were (a) highly similar to the target, (b) partly similar, and (c) dissimilar. There were 180 subjects, randomly assigned to the three nontarget conditions. As Stanford had predicted, PK success was significantly higher (by a one-tailed *p*) for dissimilar nontargets than for the pooled scores of similar and partly similar nontargets. Subjects were more likely to psi-miss if the background resembled the target.

The next reports describe psi responses to the temporal rather than the spatial arrays in which the target is embedded; they variously find contrast and assimilation. Tart (1978) used selected subjects and immediate feedback. He examined the hits to see how they related to other items in the target series, and found the hits' correspondence to the immedately following item was less than expected by chance. Calls that were hits on the target showed significant psi-missing for the next item in the target series.

Tart then made an interesting analogy between this and the physiological process called lateral inhibition. Lateral inhibition is well demonstrated in the retina. Input from the immediate surround of a stimulus is inhibited. This accentuates the edges of the stimulus and therefore makes the stimulus more distinct; it produces greater contrast. Tart hypothesized that psi uses lateral inhibition both transspatially and transtemporally. His initial finding was supported (but shown to need minor modification) in a follow-up study with Swann, a gifted subject. Here a hit on the target was also a hit on the next item but in addition was a psi-miss on the item after that, two ahead of the target.

Radin & Bosworth (1985) describe extensive RNG research with two gifted subjects. The purpose of their work was to test the response distributions against four models of psi. They report that the data supported three of these models, but gave strongest support to the transtemporal inhibiton model, i.e., the model where a hit was simultaneously a psi-miss for the items immediately preceding and following the target.

It is provocative to compare these results from gifted subjects to Crandall's mirror-image results. Apparently gifted subjects psi-missed on items adjacent to the target; Crandall had found that psi-missers hit on adjacent items. Crandall & Covey (1986) point out how neatly the findings dovetail, and suggest that a small change in Tart's hypothesis could combine them. They also suggest that all are compatible with Helson's sophisticated theory of perception (1964), where response to a stimulus shows contrast to some parts of the stimulus background and assimilation with other parts.

A psi effect, a type of transtemporal assimilation, was reported with some surprise by Klintman (1983). He had been doing psychological research on reaction time, using sequences of similar and dissimilar stimuli, and had also been administering the spiral afterimage, one of Eysenck's tests of extraversion. He found an interesting interaction. Extraverts had faster reaction times if stimuli were dissimilar; introverts had faster times if stimuli were similar. This is just what Eysenck's theory predicts (see Chapter 7).

Then Klintman noted an unanticipated pattern that looked like precognition. His procedure had been to present a color, find the subject's reaction time to it, and after a short interval present either the same or a different color. An RNG determined whether the second color would be the same or different; the research was double blind. Reaction time to the first stimulus was the baseline. The second reaction time would be measured against it—but Klintman found that the first reaction time varied according to what the unknown second stimulus would be. Where the second stimulus was the type that would be facilitative, the reaction to the first stimulus was faster.

In four subsequent series Klintman (1984) examined and supported hypotheses about this "perceptual feedback loop," that is to say, the precognition. He varied the length of the interstimulus interval, changed the stimuli from colors to digits, etc., and continued to find significant evidence that responses were influenced by a future stimulus, although that future stimulus was randomly determined and known to no one. The method has not been used by others, but it was well replicated by Klintman. As it stands it constitutes a strong body of systematic replications which show transtemporal assimilation.

These, then, are the nine procedures turned up by my first search (see page 117 above) for evidence on how a psi call related to its target's background. Do all study this relation? Only if we stretch the definition of background to include items adjacent to the target, more distant items in the target array, the object around the target, the temporal sequence of which the target is a part, and the nontarget to be shown if the target is missed. Each seems a legitimate example of a background, but are all of them, as a group? I am not sure.

If most or all of these are accepted as examples of the psi target's background, the methods of examining them, with their replications, provide a long list of significant findings that converge on the same conclusion. The conclusion is that in psi research as in psychology, the background of a figure affects, either by contrast or by assimilation, the response to that figure.

If that conclusion is valid, it needs to be refined. The next step must be distinguishing the conditions that lead to assimilation from the conditions that lead to contrast. I try to take this step in the next three paragraphs, but my speculations rest on an uncomfortably small data base.

They start with the fact that assimilation was found rather often: by Pratt and by Child & Kelly with gifted subjects; by Crandall with psi-missers; by Carington, Stanford, Klintman, and myself, with unselected subjects. With one exception (discussed later) contrast was found only with pretested, gifted subjects: by Child & Kelly, Tart, and Radin & Bosworth. The difference implies that assimilation is rather common in psi responses but that contrast will occur only when psi ability is stronger (and perhaps better trained).

If this is true, it makes sense psychologically. Assimilation of the background to the figure shows an incomplete discrimination of figure from ground. It is an inaccurate, primitive response. Contrast represents the first step in accurate discrimination; and we see it, for psi, in the more gifted subjects.

What then do we make of Crandall's having found a color contrast effect in psi-missers? If this unpredicted effect replicates, it might be explained psychologically by the difference between color and form discrimination. Color discrimination seems the more primitive process. (This is indicated by many findings. Color constancy is an example. It is less complete than form constancy and it reaches its maximum at an earlier age.) Perhaps in making color discriminations, even those whose psi is weak can advance from assimilation to contrast, whereas in making the more difficult discrimination of form, only those whose psi is stronger are likely to make this advance.

Now turn to the studies that I found only after writing those rather bold interpretations. As before, I excluded post hoc or exploratory work, and also the free response data where there was no baseline for chance correspondence. Four studies remained. All examined calls on ESP or similar cards, and described backward or forward displacement to items one (or two) away from the target.

Bindrim (1947) claims he supported a prestated hypothesis by reanalyzing 1494 ESP runs with null on-target scores. His new method compared displacements in the two halves of a run. The 345 runs with 0–3 hits (but not others) were consistent in showing more of either forward or backward displacement in both halves. There has been no follow-up.

Abbot (1949), an astrophysicist, used himself as subject in a replication attempt. Eleven years before, he had found that he psi-hit when he felt well, but when he was tired or ill he did not. Instead his calls corresponded to the items preceding or following the target. This fits my speculations neatly—but on replication his scores were null when he was tired. When he was rested, calls on-target were suggestively high. They showed significant psi-missing for the item preceding the target (contrast) but significant psi-hitting for the item following the target (assimilation).

Mangan (1955) retested a subject interested in precognition. On prior clairvoyance tests she had tended to psi-miss on the item preceding the target, but she had significantly psi-hit on the item following the target. The new series tested precognition, and both patterns reappeared. Psi-missing on items preceding the target was again suggestive and psi-hitting on items that followed the target was highly significant. The pattern seems idiosyncratic but perhaps it is not: it resembles Abbot's scores on the second (but not the first) of his self-tests.

Thomson (1973) gave group tests at fast speeds (2.5 seconds per trial) or slower ones (3.5 to 4 seconds per trial). On the basis of prior work he hypothesized that for the slower runs he would find what I call a contrast effect: psi-hitting on the target and psi-missing on preceding and following items. For the fast runs he hypothesized a mirror image of these scores. His hypothesis for the slow runs was significantly supported. For the fast runs the data showed no clear evidence of ESP.

How do my speculations fare? The Bindrim analyses and the null data from Thomson's fast runs are perhaps irrelevant. Abbot's initial work and Thomson's data from the slower runs are consistent with my interpretations. Abbot's later work and Mangan's data, each obtained in retests of one gifted subject, imply the need for some revision that will specify the particular combination of contrast and assimilation that those two subjects showed.

The Development of a Perception

Since the 1920s, a truism in psychology has been that experience comes as a meaningful whole—but obviously the raw sensory input needs perceptual processing before that whole appears. The earliest perceptual stages can be studied when unfamiliar material is presented to the subject. They seem typically to involve three steps. First comes a vague general impression; then discrimination of one detail after another after another; then a chunking or integration of the parts into a higher order of structure, the meaningful whole.

I know of no laboratory studies of psi that show even a hint of all three stages in this orderly developmental sequence. What we find, it seems to me, is one or the other of the first two stages. An example of the first stage came in the preceding unit: assimilation of the background to the target, which is a global, undifferentiated confusion of figure with ground. Spontaneous cases also seem often to remain at this stage of perception. Many report a strong impression of disaster or impending harm, or sometimes of happy relief, either without specifics or with some sparse, inadequate detail, like harm to Jonathan or danger in the northwest direction. They are worth attention when the feeling drives a person to some unusual and illogical action which is appropriate to an unexpected crisis or when the timing coincides with an event that matches the impression (Stevenson, 1970).

What of the second stage of a developing perception, discrimination of detail? Studies in the preceding unit which found contrast seem to exemplify it. In addition, observations from many and varied sources strongly suggest that it occurs in psi. Some came in comments from Targ & Puthoff (Chapter 9), who found their best results in remote viewing when subjects reported separate, fragmentary, meaningless impressions. Research from Ganzfeld and dream studies also found that judges made good matches by noting unusual but fragmentary details in the responses that corresponded to details of the targets.

Further informal supporting evidence comes from inspection of drawings made as ESP responses. Several investigators (e.g., Musso & Granero, 1973; Sinclair, 1930; Warcollier, 1948) have reproduced dozens of these records. Frequently a distinctive part of the target configuration appears in the response but appears out of context and without apparent meaning. Thus, repeatedly, qualitative analysis of ESP responses corresponds to the second stage of perceptual development. As suggested in the preceding unit, this second stage seems to be shown most clearly in studies of gifted subjects, or else when conditions are strongly psi-conducive.

I have found no psi data that correspond to the third stage. Three lines of psi research might at first seem to be evidence for it: complex targets which elicit significant psi scores; repeated administration of the same target set which leads to identifying the target accurately; and qualitative data from gifted psychics. I will discuss them briefly to argue that none of the evidence is satisfactory.

A sizable body of psi research uses targets so complex that they could ordinarily be perceived only in the final, integrative stage of perception. An example is a photograph with many irrelevant details where the target is only a conclusion to be drawn from the picture, or an equation for x, where x is the target. But psi success here need not mean that subjects went through the steps that would give them the answer. The responses may be precognitive. They might bypass the intermediate steps and home in on whatever the experimenter will later identify as a hit.

Repeated responses to the same target set have yielded, when pooled, extremely accurate psi-hitting (see, e.g., Ryzl, 1962). But the later responses are not consistently more accurate than the earlier ones. This indicates that continued exposure to a psi target does not make the target more perceptible. Only the experimenter's statistical analysis retrieves the information and yields the accuracy.

Occasionally, with a gifted psychic like Mrs. Leonard, repeated proxy sessions (sittings with a blind note taker, who can give no clues) have culminated in an accurate and detailed account, although early sessions gave only fragmentary bits (see, e.g., Thomas, 1935). Even with gifted psychics, however, such sequences are rare. Further, the later success can be attributed to the psychic's intelligent inferences from memories of the fragments reported earlier.

In summary, there is evidence that psi sometimes shows the first, global stage of developing perception, and also that psi sometimes shows the second stage where clear details emerge, but there is no satisfactory evidence that psi shows the third, integrative stage that is part of the sequence of perceptual development.

Familiarity and Novelty

In perception, either a familiar figure on an unfamiliar background or its opposite, a novel figure on a familiar background, will attract attention. Although I know of no psi research which juxtaposes the familiar and novel in this way, we are indebted to K.R. Rao and his coworkers for a series of psi studies which use an interesting method to study familiarity versus novelty. In a typical procedure, five words are used instead of the classic five ESP cards; the subject tries to respond with the word that matches the target. In one condition, the targets are in the subjects' own language; in another, the target words are translated into a language the subjects do not know.

Rao (1979) summarized the findings of eleven studies. There was a significant difference in ESP scores between unknown and familiar words in seven of the studies (and for two of the others, a significant difference in one of their two series). The high ratio of significant findings seems to demonstrate that in psi, as in perception, subjects respond to the difference between familiarity and novelty.

What do we see when we look more closely at the findings? Scores were sometimes higher and sometimes lower for familiar words. This occurs in perception too, so it should not be unexpected, but of course it makes us wonder about the reason for the shift.

One clue comes from another finding. Frequently the significant result was only an interaction between familiarity and sex, with males scoring higher on the foreign language and females on their own. I propose, tentatively, a post hoc interpretation. It is based in part on Rao's statement that as experimenter, he presented the foreign words as a challenge, and in part on the place and time of the research: the South, beginning in the early 1960s.

At that time, psychological tests were finding rather pronounced differences in the South between the approved social roles for males (active, seeking adventure, etc.) and for females (gentle, with domestic interests, etc.). This seems to me to clarify the typical pattern of the psi data. For subjects who conformed to the stereotype for their own sex, it would obviously be the males who welcomed the challenge of foreign words and females who preferred the security of the language with which they were at home.

A check on the interpretation could come from research where predictions were based not on sex alone, but on the subjects' scores on tests of masculinity-feminity and of sensation-seeking. If in addition the subjects took a test of empathy, an experiment would present the foreign language to half the subjects as a challenge, and to the other half as a study of empathy with other humans who are basically similar to themselves. The prediction here is that sensation-seeking, masculinity-femininity, and empathy would interact with the two test conditions.

In summary, findings on familiarity versus novelty are not inconsistent with data from perception, but can be interpreted as bearing more directly on motivation or personality than on perception.

SUBLIMINAL PERCEPTION

Psychologists use diverse approaches to studying the effect of input that was not consciously perceived. A good many psi studies have used one of those approaches: subliminal perception. Stimuli are defined as subliminal when they are too weak to reach the limen or threshold of consciousness; the threshold is usually defined as the level at which a stimulus will be reported correctly 50 percent of the time. Thus stimuli can be called subliminal not only when they are so weak that they are never consciously perceived but also when they approach the threshold and can be correctly reported, say, 40 percent of the time.

The history of subliminal perception begins like that of parapsychology. Claims that stimuli too weak to reach consciousness could affect behavior were greeted with attempts to explain away the findings as due only to errors such as inaccurate scoring or insufficient care in using a low enough level of presentation, or to response bias, etc. Well controlled, ingenious research answered these criticisms and later ones. By now it is well established that, whether or not the earliest experiments were faulty, their general conclusions are valid. Sensory input of which we are not aware can be processed in the brain and transferred to long term memory (Dixon, 1981).

How does subliminal perception relate to psi? I will give two examples of differences between them, then two of possible similarities, then summarize the two cases where predictions about a relationship were supported.

Differences

A pretty technique in subliminal research is called masking. It demands careful timing. If, for example, a row of three digits is exposed very briefly, a subject's image of them will last longer than the exposure, and the subject can recall them. But if, soon after that exposure, a circle slightly larger than a digit is shown around the space where one digit had been, the subject's image will show two digits and a slightly larger empty circle. It is as if the circle erased the digit. And now comes the next step. When those two exposures are followed by a third, with a still larger circle where the first circle had been, the subject's image shows all three digits, but with a large circle around one of them.

This forces us to conclude that the first circle had only masked, not erased, what it surrounded. The first circle inhibited the digit, but the second circle inhibited the first circle and thus disinhibited the digit. In psi there is no comparable tidy way of disinhibiting whatever prevents awareness of a target.

Another curious and well replicated effect comes with repeated presentations of a very weak stimulus. If a word is exposed very briefly on a tachistoscope, the subject will see only a flash of light. Now (with intervals long enough to let all retinal effects disappear) the same presentation is repeated many times. The subject will for the first several trials continue to see only blank light, but later will see lines or blurs in it, than a letter or two, and then eventually a word. Any of the presentations in isolation would give nothing, but presumably some residual effect in brain processing makes the series of nothings add to something. Psi scores do not show this cumulative effect of accurate report after repeated presentation of a target.

Possible Similarities

Two patterns within subliminal perception look to me as if they might hold true for psi, but so little psi research bears on them that this is only a speculation. One is a comparison of free responses with forced choices (one of the three predictions to which I referred in Chapter 4). Partly because of my reading of the subliminal research, and partly because of an (unpublished) M.A. thesis done under my supervision, I suspect that more evidence of subliminal effects will appear with free responses than with forced choices. I suspect this is also true for psi. Back in the 1960s I put together the two expectations, and predicted that the relation between ESP and subliminal responses will be stronger when both are measured by free responses than when they are measured by forced choices.

A review of research (Schmeidler, 1986) did not support the hypothesis but also, I think, did not disconfirm it. Only two studies had used free response for both variables. One found a nonsignificant trend in the predicted direction. The other yielded very high scores in the predicted direction but had only six subjects, so that the correlation between psi and subliminal scores was not clearly significant. In contrast, forced choice methods (see below) have often shown significant correlations. What we really need for a clean test of the hypothesis is a research design with four test conditions: subliminal perception with forced choices and with free responses, and ESP with forced choices and with free responses; but this research has not been done.

The other approach where a similarity seems likely examines sensitivity to specific messages. Here the findings in subliminal research are strong and well replicated. Subjects are pretested and divided into criterion groups. The groups are known to be (or known not to be) sensitive to some message: perhaps of closeness to one's mother, or violence, or cigarette smoking. Responses to subliminal input are clearly different when messages are relevant or irrelevant to the subjects' concerns. I would expect psi research to give parallel results. Many hints of this come from post hoc analyses, for example of Ganzfeld responses, but there has never yet been formal research designed to test the hypothesis, using psi targets that are appropriate or inappropriate for criterion groups.

Similarities

The two ways in which subliminal perception seems to relate closely to psi were stated briefly in Chapter 4; they are the two predictions I made which were supported by later research.

One was based primarily on the findings of Eagle (1962). He listed seven major personality variables that correlated with subliminal sensitivity. As I read his list I recognized each of them as a variable that some other research worker or I had found was related to psi sensitivity. Eagle's wording (sometimes shortened) appears in quotation marks below, along with citations to the psi studies that match it.

Three of Eagle's variables are astonishingly like what I had seen in Rorschach analyses (pages 70ff)—and of course what others had also found—"openness rather than constriction"; "intuitive, introspective and insightful, and capable of fantasy and vivid imagery"; "responsive to people." Two are like the description in Chapter 6 of psi findings on dominance or of the anecdote about B in Chapter 8: "non-submissive"; "more concerned with his own aggressive impulses than with being aggressed against from without." And the last two closely resemble some research that I had been puzzling over, in the 1960s, which described gifted psychics as disintegrative personalities (Tenhaeff, 1962) or as showing ego unsteadiness (Sannwald, 1963). Eagle's two descriptions were like a paraphrase of these: "tends to use non-cognitive defenses" and "shows a diffuse, non-crystallized identity." The close overlap in personality decriptions naturally led me to expect a positive correlation between subliminal and ESP scores, but I soon modified the expectation, and predicted a positive correlation only when (as in Eagle's work) the subliminal stimuli were far below the threshold.

The reason for this modification was primarily a finding on subliminal perception which looked as if it related to psi-missing. Significant psi-missing poses a vexing problem. We can think of it as failure, because the subjects did not call the targets correctly. But from another point of view it is success, because the subjects identified and avoided the targets. I associate it with resistance (defensiveness). The well controlled short experiment below seems to demonstrate just such resistance when subliminal stimuli are strong enough to be near the threshold. I take this experiment as presenting an analogue of the shift between psi-hitting and psi-missing.

Mattson & Natsoulas (1962) used as their subliminal stimuli a set of four pictures, arranged in a diamond shape. The 24 diamonds included all possible placements. For each, the subject was to say which of the four positions looked clearest. One picture was considered emotional because preliminary instructions had made the young male subjects associate it with masturbation. The other pictures were considered neutral. The diamonds were exposed both at a weak level, far below the threshold, and at a higher level, only a little below the threshold.

Was the emotional picture the clearest? Or least clear? Both. Data showed, as predicted, a significant interaction with level of exposure. The emotional picture was chosen as clear when it was far below the threshold, but avoided when it was near the threshold. This is, as it were, emotion-hitting with weak subliminal stimuli; emotion-missing with stronger ones.

The data seem like those for psi-hitting and missing because psi, too, is so often emotionally loaded (see Chapter 6 and elsewhere). It therefore modified my first expectation. Now I predicted that when subliminal stimuli were very weak, there would be a positive relation between psi and subliminal success, but that when the subliminal stimuli were so strong as to be near the threshold, there would be a negative relation between subliminal sensitivity and psi. In other words, there would be the opposite relation.

The pair of hypotheses, taken jointly, made what I thought was an exciting, nonobvious prediction: that psi scores would reverse, in respect to subliminal scores, when the subliminal stimuli were strong and when they were weak. These are the other two hypotheses mentioned in Chapter 4. If either was supported, that would be good; but if both were supported, that would be very much better.

My search to find whether or not any of my predictions were supported covered publications from late 1971 to early 1984 (Schmeidler, 1986). It found 16 reports (including 24 separate series) to test the two predictions about strong and weak subliminal stimuli. There were 22 series with weak subliminal stimuli, and 17 of them showed the predicted positive relation between subliminal scores and ESP scores. Nine of the 17 were significant with a one-tailed p; five of those nine were significant with a two-tailed p. The five that did not conform with the hypothesis were all nonsignificant. Only two series used stronger subliminal stimuli and thus could test the hypothesis of a negative relation between subliminal and ESP scores. Both gave significant results in the predicted direction. The first hypothesis seemed very well and the second moderately well supported, and thus there was rather strong support for the nonobvious prediction that was made by the two, considered jointly.

Sidelights

Three sidelights may be of interest. One is a correction. In Chapter 4 I told you that Eisenbud (1965) had reported no relation between psi and (weak) subliminal sensitivity. It was overhasty of me to accept this statement of his. Stanford (1974) reexamined the data and found that they showed a significant positive correlation between subliminal perception and ESP.

Another sidelight is more important: a general question that often recurs. Here it applies especially to research with the Defense Mechanism Test, a sensitive and well validated measure of response to threat. (Pictures of something threatening are shown subliminally, each first at a very low level, then at increasingly higher ones. Scores depend on how soon the subject reports the threat.) According to Johnson & Haraldsson (1984) 12 studies with 15 series related scores on the Defense Mechanism Test to ESP scores, and 14 of these 15 series showed a positive relation between ESP and nondefensiveness (i.e., openness). Nine of the 14 were significant with a one-tailed *p*; five of the nine with a two-tailed *p*. Readiness to respond to subliminal input clearly related, as predicted, to ESP success.

My question about these strong data is whether they would be even stronger if attitude were built into the design. The significant correlations were only moderately high. Would they have been higher with a control for attitude? Questionnaires to a similar sample of subjects have found a few subjects who accept ESP comfortably. For them it is not a threat. Just as goats should be segregated if research looks for psi-conducive conditions, should not subjects wholly accepting of psi be segregated if research looks for a correlate of defensive resistance to psi?

A third point that I found of special interest comes from intensive research on two gifted subjects. Kelly, Kanthamani, Child, & Young (1975) tested them for ESP and also presented the ESP targets subliminally, then examined for types of error. One subject, B.D., showed an extraordinarily high correspondence between his subliminal errors and his ESP errors. One example out of many, with playing cards as targets, is that if the target was a picture card and he missed it, he would (far beyond chance expectation) call another picture card rather than a number card, both for ESP and for subliminal presentation. This implies similar visual perceptual processing of ESP and of subliminal input. But a parallel procedure with L.H., the other gifted subject, showed no relation between his errors in the two procedures. Is psi input sometimes processed visually, but sometimes not? the first subject's data are too strong to ignore; the second subject's data show we dare not generalize from the first.

In summary, subliminal perception differs from ESP, but two predictions about the relation between these different processes have both been significantly confirmed.

Overview

For many perceptual areas, psi data show no general relation to the findings in perception. Psi scores are null or ambiguous or unreplicated for changes in sensory modality, sensory variables within a modality, the figural properties of psi targets, or perceptual learning. For some individuals, psi scores change with one or another of these, but the change apparently reflects the motivation or interest of the individual rather than a generally valid pattern for psi.

A comparison of novel and familiar targets shows that they produce significantly different psi scores. This is similar to what is found in perception, but it also may be a motivational rather than a perceptual effect.

In two other topics there is strong evidence that psi functions as perception does. One is the relation of the target's background to the responses. Psi responses, like perceptual ones, sometimes show an assimilation of target with background, and sometimes a contrast effect. The other topic is subliminal perception, where there are significant correlations between psi success and subliminal sensitivity, and where it has been possible to predict whether the sign of the correlation will be positive or negative.

11. Cognition

Cognition used to include only learning, memory, and thinking, but by now it covers a wide range of topics, from perception and language to the making of decisions. The thread that holds cognitive topics together is learning, which influences almost everything we do. Some psychologists argue for many kinds of learning, others for only one or two, but all (I think) agree that one method of learning is conditioning, especially when positive reinforcement (reward) immediately follows a response. Three stages have been suggested for the learning-memory process: encoding material, storing it, and retrieving it. Two types of thinking are often treated separately: convergent thinking, which homes in on a single correct answer, e.g. for some problem in arithmetic, and divergent or creative thinking, which finds one of many possible good answers.

Some topics in cognition have already been reviewed, for example attitudes (Chapter 6) and perception (Chapter 10). This chapter reviews psi research on five other topics within cognition. Often, however, because the psi data seem so inconclusive, only a few samples of the reports will be cited and the comments will be brief.

Learning to Improve Psi Success

There are at least three reasons for expecting research on the learning of psi to give positive results. One is the vague expectation that psi ability will improve with practice because most abilities do, but obviously this reason is not compelling. A second is that some internal patterns appear to be similar in learning and psi. This can be taken to imply that psi functions as learning does. An early example (J.B. Rhine, 1941) points out that on average, ESP scores are better at the beginning and end of a deck of 25 ESP cards than in the middle, and learning a long list is similarly better at its beginning and its end. This also is not compelling, because the changes could reflect interest: higher at first than later, with a small final upsurge. Third, and more impressive, gifted psychics tell us that over the years, with self-discipline, self-training, and sometimes training from others, they have learned how to make increasingly effective use of psi.

Many experimenters, naturally, have set up experimental conditions that they hoped would lead to learning ESP or PK. Although several initially claimed success, no method has as yet stood up to replication.

A fairly recent example comes from Tart (1976). His persuasive theory starts with the well established finding that reward or informative feedback immediately after a desirable response leads to learning. He then examines psi procedures. With binary targets or ESP cards, a hit (the desirable response) is often due only to chance. If so, feedback showing psi success after every hit gives false information; it will teach nonpsi responding. Thus for psi learning, it is important that the probability of chance success be low; that hits due only to chance should be rare. But if rewards are rare, subjects will probably grow discouraged. It is therefore also important that subjects with good likelihood of psi success be tested. This means that subjects should be pretested, and only those with high pretest scores be put through the learning procedure. Further, informational feedback helps learning. It is therefore desirable that feedback for incorrect responses should show where the error lies.

Tart's theory thus accounts for the null data about psi learning that have often been reported by experimenters who use targets with a high probability of chance success, but who give feedback for success with hits on those targets.

Tart tested his theory with an experimental arrangement that met all his conditions. He pretested subjects and used only those whose high scores indicated they might show an adequate level of psi success in the early learning trials. He used apparatus with high odds against chance success. After each trial he gave immediate informative feedback (e.g., with a circular arrangement of targets, the feedback showed both magnitude and direction of any error). These and other details of his research, which maintained interest by introducing minor novelties and encouraged a reasonably but not excessively high level of motivation, seem to me to provide an exemplary test of his theory.

Tests of a large number of subjects showed, on average, the progressive increase in psi scores that had been predicted. Then, properly, a replication was conducted; and although there were many other interesting results, the progressive improvement did not appear (Tart, Palmer, & Redington, 1979). This led to further detailed examination of the first experiment's scores, which found that the evidence for learning was due almost entirely to subjects tested by a single one of Tart's subexperimenters. Post hoc, the best interpretation of the original indication of learning is perhaps that this experimenter was enthusiastically convinced of Tart's theory and also was able to impart his enthusiasm to his subjects. As a result, his subjects scored well at first, but then later scored even better; they scored in accord with the experimenter's expectation.

There is a discouragingly long list of other novel methods that have failed on replication to show the progressive improvement which would indicate learning of psi. Often, though, initial work with one or another method looked as if there had been psi learning. I have been wondering why they had initial success, and propose two possible explanations.

One explanation is that the apparent learning can be due to an experimenter or a "good subject" effect. In research that hopes to find learning, the experimenter is likely to convey the expectation that later on, scores will be high. This implicitly conveys the expectation that at the beginning, scores will be low. The negative expectation can apparently result in psi-missing on the first runs (Jackson, Franzoi, & Schmeidler, 1977). Comparison of initial low scores with later scores that are at chance or slightly above will show an upward slope, but this is not learning, although a graph of the scores looks like a learning graph.

The other explanation follows Tart's line of thought. When a method was first used successfully with a naive and exceptionally gifted subject, but the subjects in replications were anyone who came along, the replications were systematic rather than direct. The replications show the procedures were not generally applicable but leave open the question of whether a direct replication, one that tests a naive but gifted subject, will show the learning of psi.

One such method is of special interest. Ryzl (1962) trained Pavel Stepanek (and reports training others) by a series of hypnotic sessions. First came hypnotic suggestions for sensory hallucinations. After the subject reported hallucinations, Ryzl told the subject to keep his eyes closed. He then put an ESP target in front of the subject, and suggsted that the subject would be able to say what the target was. Here, obviously, one quick opening of the eyes would let the subject give the correct answer and apparently have an ESP success. Only after successes here, did Ryzl give suggestions for ESP success with properly concealed targets. The interest of this method lies in its similarity to the procedure of Brugmans, Heymans, & Weinberg (1924). Their well controlled and spectacularly successful ESP tests of a gifted subject were preceded, in each session, by a muscle-reading test where success could have been due to sensory cues. Perhaps, with a gifted subject, establishing an expectation of continuing successes is psi-conducive.

One recent report seems to show learning of psi, but as far as I know there has been no attempt to replicate it. Since it has not been disconfirmed, it will be discussed at some length. W.G. Braud (1983) tested seven subjects on an RNG which showed a red light after a hit; scores were nonsignificantly higher than chance expectation. The subjects then had six weekly sessions in which Braud gave them imagery training in visualizing colors, and also assigned practice exercises for them to do daily at home. A posttest on the RNG showed a level of PK success that was highly significant and significantly greater than the pretest scores. Each subject scored higher on the posttest than the pretest, and there was a significant positive correlation between reported amount of home practice and PK scores. Braud suggests that prolonged training in imagery may facilitate psi, even if short training does not.

What do these strong results imply? Until others replicate what Braud himself called only a pilot study, it would be unwise to draw firm inferences, but here are some possibilities. Braud imposed a lot of labor upon his seven subjects, both in the sessions with him and the practice at home. The subjects had an investment in success. Braud also put a lot of labor into the project and had an investment in it, and he is considered a psi-conducive experimenter. Thus heightened motivation of subjects and experimenter might account for the single set of highly significant posttest trials. We do not know if the high level of psi scoring would be maintained.

But suppose high scores could be maintained. We note that what Braud trained was visual imaging, and that feedback was visual. This raises the question of whether prolonged visualizing is conducive to psi success in any procedure (although the mix of negative and supportive evidence on imagery collated by George, 1982, seems to me to suggest otherwise) or whether a nonvisual type of training would have been needed with nonvisual feedback. And a further, related question is whether prolonged practice in visualization or in other subjective processes will produce a moderately relaxed and confident mood, perhaps somewhat similar to an altered state of consciousness, and whether it is this state rather than the specifics of the practice that is psi-conducive. If the results are confirmed, a whole series of systematic replications would be needed to tease apart the possibilities.

Overall, then, it would be a Type I error to claim that psi success can be learned. But if desire to avoid a Type II error keeps us from concluding that psi cannot be learned, at least two hints seem worth following up. One, consistent with Tart's theory, derives from the statements of psychics and from reports like Ryzl's. It is that gifted subjects can learn effective use of psi, whether or not other subjects do so.

The second hint is derived from much of the material in preceding chapters, and from the just cited work by Braud. It is that subjects can learn to put themselves into a mental state which is psi-conducive and therefore can learn how to increase their psi scores. But if further research shows this can be done, it will raise another issue—one that sounds like hair-splitting, but that I think is important. Would this have been only a learning of increased control over one's mood or state of consciousness? If so, it would have been learning the conditions for releasing psi, for permitting one's psi to function, but would not have been learning within the psi process itself.

In summary, learning to improve psi ability is another area where the data do not support the theory that this book examines. No replicated evidence shows that psi can be learned.

Learning and Memory Scores and Psi

A good many experiments have asked for both learning responses and psi responses, then examined the relation between them. Ingenious methods permitted many types of comparison. For one example, subjects may try to learn a list of paired associates, then write their responses in one location or another. Choice of location is the ESP response. So many of the experiments report a significant relationship that the results are worth attention, but particular relationships seldom replicate.

I have been unable to find a meaningful pattern in the data. There are sometimes positive and sometimes negative correlations between learning and psi scores, and in some cases but not others the effect varied with the strength of the associations in the learning task. (See Palmer, 1978, 1982.) Post hoc interpretations can of course, as ever, appeal to differences in motivation. If subjects are eager to do well for the experimenter, scores on the psi and learning tasks should correlate positively. If the learning is difficult, subjects who know their learning scores are poor may be eager to compensate by succeeding at the separate ESP response. In this case, scores on the two tasks should correlate negatively. But since there is no independent evidence about how the subjects felt, such interpretations are unsatisfying.

Several interesting methods arrange that the learning response is also the ESP response. Stanford (1970), for example, had 30 male subjects hear a recording of what they were told was a girl's dream, then respond to multiple choice questions about the dream. The answers were scored for correctness. In addition, within each set of answers, one was randomly selected as an ESP target.

Where the answers were correct, ESP scores were at chance. Two types of answers were scored as incorrect. One was an answer that contradicted the recording. The other was the case where the recording had given no information about the question; here all answers were incorrect. For these two sets of answers, ESP scores were significantly high.

The results seem to imply that the subjects used ESP if their memory failed to supply the answer they looked for. However a replication by Sheargold (1972) found insignificantly low ESP scores for all categories of responses.

A half dozen reports study classroom tests and ESP. Unreplicated research by Cashen & Ramseyer (1970) asked students to guess which topics would be included on a forthcoming quiz. Correct choice of topic correlated significantly with scores on a standard ESP test, but did not relate to grades on the quiz or to overall course grades.

A different and deceptive technique incorporated an ESP test into a class examination. Johnson (1973) attached extra pages beneath his examination papers, and told students that the purpose of the extra sheets was to facilitate scoring. In fact, he had concealed on those extra pages some correct answers to the examination questions and some incorrect answers. Johnson found significantly higher grades for questions with concealed correct answers than for questions without correct answers, and significantly lower grades for questions with concealed incorrect answers than for questions with no answers.

Four attempts at replication have been reported. Two of the attempts failed to show the effect: Tedder (1977) in a test of prisoners, and Willis, Duncan, & Udolfia (1974). Two series of attempts significantly replicated Johnson's finding. W.G. Braud (1975) found significant results in the predicted direction in each of two series, and he adds a datum that relates the finding to learning. Half of his examination questions had no concealed answers; their scores show how well the class material was learned. There was a significant negative correlation between ESP scores and the grades on this part. This implies, as did Stanford's 1970 research, that ESP is more likely to be used when memory fails.

Schechter (1977) describes three series of experiments, with significant support for Johnson's findings in two of them, and an insignificant trend in the same direction for the third. But an inference from Braud's data was not supported: a correlation between grades on other examinations and ESP scores was near zero.

(I feel obliged to interject a personal comment here. With three out of five researches significantly supporting a hypothesis, the data are strong; but they seem to me not to make sense. ESP can be effective over long distances. But in this body of research, answers attached to one's own paper affect responses; answers attached to a neighbor's paper do not. I would have expected the ESP target to be the textbook, or the instructor's notes, rather than the page attached to one's questions. Schechter, also troubled by this anomaly, suggests several possible explanations. Perhaps the most plausible, though to me still an unsatisfactory one, is that students were focussing their attention on their own sheets of questions.)

A nondeceptive method was used by Kreiman (1978) to test a theory he proposed: that attempts to recall well learned material will be accompanied by psi-missing, but that attempts to recall poorly learned material will show psi-hitting. His subjects were 16 eagerly interested parapsychology students. Their learning material was a list of 50 words but they had only five minutes to read and reread the list. They then had a 15 minute period to try to recall it. Each subject had an ESP target list consisting of 20 of the learning words;

thus the probability of hitting a target by chance was 20/50 or 2/5. Kreiman made the natural assumption that in the recall period, subjects would write first the words they had learned best; words written later were words that were harder to recall. He therefore predicted psi-missing (scores lower than 2/5) on the words first recalled, and psi-hitting (scores higher than 2/5) on words recalled later. His data significantly confirmed the two predictions.

Both Weiner & Haight (1980) and I (Schmeidler, 1980) tried to replicate this but found only insignificant trends in the predicted direction. I continued with indirect replications and eventually used as subjects only sheep who were in a happily confident mood, as Kreiman's subjects had been. The data showed that the happy sheep had significantly higher psi scores for poorly learned words than for well learned ones, and this clearly supported Kreiman's basic prediction.

But did it support his theory? Not necessarily. When I thought about it, I saw two other possible explanations for my significant finding. One was that psi had guided which words the subjects learned from their lists, rather than which they recalled. I therefore ran another series to check this out. It was different in just one way. The previous instruction had told subjects that when they had trouble recalling words, their ESP might help them (i.e., ESP might help recall). The new instruction omitted that. Instead it told subjects that when they were trying to learn the words, their ESP might help them select the right words from the learning list (i.e., ESP might help learning). This series gave null results. It thus implied that the retrieval, not the initial learning, had been guided by ESP.

The other possible explanation was that the data were due, somehow, without my knowing it, to an experimenter effect. I therefore arranged to have a direct replication of my earlier procedure but without me. Graduate students administered the tests. This replication also found that the happy sheep had significantly higher ESP scores for poorly learned words than for well learned ones. The three series of tests (Schmeidler, 1983a) therefore seem to add up to rather strong support for a slightly modified version of Kreiman's theory: ESP success is more likely to accompany attempts to recall poorly learned material than attempts to recall material that was well learned. The theory is also consistent with some of the results reported above, especially those of Stanford (1970) and W.G. Braud (1975).

What, then, has been found about psi in relation to learning or memory? Let us divide the learning-memory process, as psychologists often do, into the three stages of encoding material, storing it, and retrieving it. We find little evidence for a relation between psi and encoding or storage. There are, however, a good many research reports which suggest that ESP helps the retrieval of material that was not well learned.

INTELLIGENCE AND COGNITIVE DEVELOPMENT

Research with either gifted or unselected subjects suggests that there is no direct relation between intelligence and psi success. So far as my own thinking is concerned, this broad negative conclusion was established in the 1940s, because by then Bond (1937) had found significant psi-hitting in a class of retarded children, while Humphrey (1945) found significant positive correlations betwen IQ and ESP scores. Later research (see Palmer, 1978) has given the mixed results that might be expected when attitude is not controlled: often a positive relation between intelligence test scores and ESP scores (though seldom a significant one); sometimes a negative relation.

The mixed results, like the mixed results on values (Chapter 6), seem to me best interpreted in terms of attitude—but I must add that no research has checked out my interpretation. When a bright instructor or experimenter presents ESP as an ability to be prized by the brightest, I would expect the correlation between ESP and intelligence test scores to be positive. When ESP is presented as a superstition of the ignorant, I would expect the correlation to be negative. If ESP is presented as a special skill, I would expect correlations to be near chance.

Few studies examine cognitive development. Drucker, Drewes, & Rubin (1977) administered one of Piaget's tests of cognitive development (conservation of liquids) and found chance ESP scores for children in the early, prelogical stage and for children in the logical stage, but high ESP scores for children intermediate between those two stages. There has been no confirmation of this unanticipated pattern. Winkelman (1981) gave informal tests to Mexican children and reports a negative relation between psi success and schooling; careful research in the Philippines failed to confirm the relation (Murray, 1983). There have been other direct comparisons of different age groups but I think most of them give little information because the research conditions seem more suitable for one age than another.

Here is another topic where the book's theory has not been supported.

CREATIVITY

Several studies of creativity and psi have administered more or less adequate creativity tests or have compared criterion groups of creative and noncreative persons. Of the 14 projects I have found, 9 report a positive relation between creativity and ESP; 3 are essentially null; 2 (both by me) found a negative relation. A large exploratory project yielded little more than anecdotes and suggestions (Murphy, 1966). I will summarize two of the positive research reports, then try to explain away my two embarrassingly negative ones.

Moss (1969) compared 30 agent-percipient teams of artists with 43 teams of nonartists. The GESP targets were slide sequences with accompanying sound, and had strong emotional impact. Nonartists scored negligibly above chance; artists scored significantly higher than nonartists.

L.W. Braud & Loewenstern (1982) administered a standard test of creativity (alternate uses) to their 20 subjects, followed by a 45 minute period during which a tape expected to be psi-conducive was played, and then by a five minute period during which subjects tried to respond to a target picture. Overall psi scores were null, but subjects who psi-hit had significantly higher creativity scores than subjects who psi-missed.

Now for my two reports. One (Schmeidler, 1963) describes tests administered by a colleague who was unsympathetic to parapsychology. After a creativity test, subjects tried to call ESP symbols. Subjects who scored higher in creativity scored lower on ESP. This might mean that if students had run out of creative ideas while their neighbors were still writing away, they tried to compensate by doing well on the ESP test that followed. It might be an example of the experimenter effect and reflect creative subjects' sensitivity to the instructor's feelings. It might show that more creative subjects felt constrained by the forced choice targets. The last interpretation could also apply to my other negative finding, also with ESP cards, in the project where targets were selected and responses were scored by a computer (Schmeidler, 1964b).

Is that interpretation contraindicated by a report from Honorton (1967) which also used ESP symbols as targets and found significantly higher scores for the more creative subjects? Perhaps, but in defense of the interpretation we note that (a) the ESP scores of Honorton's high creatives were only slightly better than chance, and the significant difference depended on the very low scores of the less creative; and (b) Honorton's instructions may have been so much more appropriate than my own that they persuaded subjects to think that calling ESP symbols partook of a creative achievement.

On the whole, research suggests a positive relation between creativity and psi success.

Cognitive Controls and Response Biases

Cognitive Controls

Individual differences in the way we organize information are called cognitive controls. Psychologists study many, with an especially large amount of research on field dependence/independence. Two techniques are usual. One displays a luminous rod inside a luminous frame, in a room which is otherwise dark. The subject tries to identify when the rod is vertical. Some subjects do so accurately even when the frame surrounding the rod is tilted; others make judgments influenced by the frame. The other method asks subjects to identify a particular pattern embedded in a more complex one. Some do this well; others find it difficult to separate out the pattern from its field.

Of the nine psi reports I have found that examine field dependence, only three used orthodox measures. Buzby (1967) used the Embedded Figures Test to divide subjects into field dependent and field independent. He found that the ESP scores of the field dependent subjects had a higher variance than the ESP scores of field independent subjects. C.S. Nash & C.B. Nash (1968) report the same finding for precognition scores but do not describe the clairvoyance scores which they also obtained. Roll (1982) reports that four mediums were tested with the rod and frame, and all were field dependent. The other research projects, taken as a whole, also tend to find more evidence for psi from field dependent subjects.

Locus of control scores describe whether a person feels considerable control over events, or feels that events are largely determined externally. Stanford (1972) found no main effect for internal-external locus of control in a precognition study, nor did my coworkers and I when we studied PK (Schmeidler, Gambale, & Mitchell, 1976). Wollman (1982), however, reports an interesting series of significant relations between psi scores and both locus of control and another cognitive control, augmenting-reducing (i.e., noting or minimizing differences).

Response Bias

In forced choice tests with ESP cards, when each deck holds five of each symbol, one type of response bias is making only five (or about five) choices for any symbol. Stanford (1966a, 1966b) found and replicated the finding that such attempts to equalize were associated with low variance of ESP scores, and his data point to an explanation. He found that, at the free beginning of a run, there was a tendency toward psi-hitting. In the latter part of the run, when subjects turned their attention to counting and equalizing, there was a tendency toward psi-missing. For the run as a whole, since the two tendencies cancel each other, scores were near chance and thus variance was low.

Another common type of response bias is the more frequent calling of some responses than of others. Kreitler & Kreitler (1972, 1973) repeatedly found higher ESP in responses less likely to be given, i.e., responses opposed to the subject's bias. Lübke & Rohr (1975) replicated one of their methods, with a similar result. Child (1977) criticized the statistical treatment; Kreitler & Kreitler (1977) responded. Stanford (1973), using a different method, also concluded that ESP was more likely to be found in responses that were seldom given, but Stanford & Schroeter (1978) failed to replicate the results.

Schouten (1972) made an interesting use of the same concept, with mice as subjects. He discarded the trials which showed only stereotyped behavior, where the mice followed their usual patterns, i.e., their response bias. In trials which departed from the response bias, psi scores were significantly high. The method was successfully replicated by Parker (1974) with gerbils and by Terry & Harris (1975) with rats, but a systematic replication with humans gave null results (Schouten, 1975).

Nash (1978) argues that response bias shows the opposite relation to psi success. In six experimental series which he analyzed, there was a higher hit rate for preferred responses than for nonpreferred. Post hoc examinations occasionally find one or the other of these tendencies, but most reports fail to mention either. (The silence is, or course, consistent with the fact that most experimenters try to make all target choices equally attractive.) I have seen no general review of the topic, and suspect that this is because most data, like mine, hint weakly at results that go in both directions.

In summary, there is some evidence for a positive relation between field dependence and psi. Research on response biases indicates that in rodents, departure from stereotyped responses is associated with psi success. Research with humans suggests that deliberate attempts to adjust responses to a predetermined pattern is associated with lowered ESP scores or variances. No firm conclusion about preferred versus nonpreferred targets is justified, but this may be because for most subjects, under most conditions, target preferences are not strong.

Speculation

It is tempting to take the strongest subsets among these scanty or inconsistent findings and tie them in to other findings. One example would be the association between psi and creativity. Creative thinking goes far afield to remote associations and integrates them with familiar ones to form a new constellation. Thus if psi helps to retrieve poorly learned information, it is helping the creative process. Creative processing and, typically, creative individuals, are open rather than constricted; this fits well with evidence (Chapter 7) that openness is psi-conducive. It also fits with the research in this chapter showing that free rather than stereotyped responses will show psi. But unfortunately for such theorizing, on this last point the good evidence comes from rodents and not humans, a reminder that the base for the line of thought is shaky.

Another temptation is to begin with field dependence. On the cognitive side it ties into evidence for other field effects like assimilation or displacements, and on the personality side it ties into the evidence that extraversion and sociability (both typical of the field dependent) are psi-conducive.

If the findings were firm, theoretical relations could readily be developed among topics that I have been discussing under separate headings.

Overview

No replicated research has shown that subjects are able to learn to increase their psi scores, nor does there seem to be a direct relation between intelligence and psi scores. Psi research on learning and memory has in general not given clear results, except for the fairly strong suggestion that attempts to recall inadequately learned material are associated with ESP success. Among other cognitive processes, there is fairly strong evidence that field dependence and (in rodents) departure from stereotyped responses are psi-conducive, and that there is a relation between creativity and psi.

12. Brain and Other Body Changes

Recent years have seen great advances in physiological psychology and neuropsychology, largely due to new instruments and techniques, to neurochemistry, and to use of new, careful controls. Parapsychologists also study these topics: over a hundred studies examine brain or body change in relation to psi.

The major impact of the new methods on psi research comes from the electroencephalograph (EEG). Studies that used it to help identify dreaming were summarized in Chapter 9; those with waking subjects will be summarized here. Most examine what are called brain waves (because the EEG records make wavelike tracings), and the types most often described when subjects are awake are alpha (rather slow, regular waves of high amplitude), beta (irregular, faster tracings of lower amplitude), and theta (waves that are slower and of lower amplitude than alpha). Alpha is usually associated with drowsiness or with a relaxed awareness of whatever comes to consciousness; beta with normal waking activity; theta with an extremely relaxed, perhaps altered state. The general expectation among parapsychologists has been that relaxed waiting for impressions is psi-conducive and therefore that psi-hitting will be indicated by alpha or perhaps theta.

With more than fifty psi studies on the brain and almost as many on other physiological topics, it would be impractical to describe them one by one, and it is hard to organize them. The units that follow will group them according to the purpose or method of the research, even though this means that EEG or autonomic nervous system studies are scattered under different subheads.

The methods fall into four categories which overlap only a little. One measures body changes that are concurrent with psi responses; it looks for a relation. Another examines psi responses in some unusual or changed body state, which the experimenter either produced (e.g., by drugs) or found (e.g., after concussion). A third attempts to use psi to produce a body change, as in psychic healing, and measures body changes. The last category is subtly different. It examines a body change to find if that change (rather than a button push or a verbal response) gives evidence of ESP.

Predictions from the theory this book examines are only that a relation to psi will be found by all four methods.

CONCURRENT MEASURES OF BODY CHANGE AND OF PSI

Brain Changes

Although over thirty reports describe the slow waves of alpha or theta in relation to psi, their methods vary too much to permit a simple summary. Electrodes are placed above different brain areas; this may mean that they measure different processes. Both the instruments and methods of measurement vary in sensitivity and accuracy (e.g., scoring is automated in some, in others it is by visual inspection). Criteria for identifying alpha differ, so that the alpha of one study overlaps with, but is not the same as the alpha of another. Checking for artifacts is sometimes careful and sometimes apparently omitted. Instructions to subjects are sometimes to keep eyes closed (which ordinarily makes alpha more frequent), sometimes to keep eyes open, sometimes not stated. And the psi tests differ. In short, even with so many studies there are few direct replications. Three examples follow.

Honorton (1969) pretested teenagers for psi, then studied ten whose scores had been above the mean chance level. Targets were ESP cards. He found a highly significant positive relation between ESP scores and the percentage of time that alpha was present during their ESP runs (made with eyes closed). I know of no other study with pretested teenagers, but most investigators used a similar EEG measure: percentage of time of alpha, or "alpha abundance."

Stanford and his coworkers used a measure that is considered more reliable: the frequency (cycles per second) of the waves within the alpha band. They compared frequency in the test period to frequency in a baseline period. When frequency increased from baseline to test, psi scores were significantly higher than when it did not, both in two projects with ESP cards as targets and a third where Stanford was the only subject and the target pool was 100 simple drawings (Stanford & Stevenson, 1972). A fourth project using free responses to picture targets did not show this; it showed a tendency toward higher scores with more alpha abundance (Stanford & Palmer, 1975). The initial result and its successful replications with forced choice, then failure to replicate with free response, seem well worth following up, and we are left to wonder why no others measured alpha frequency. Was it because scanning their earlier records did not show Stanford's pattern? Or only because their equipment made this scoring too difficult? I do not know.

For another procedure that no one has tried to replicate, take Lewis & Schmeidler (1971). We recruited subjects for four sessions in which they would try to learn to produce alpha and ESP. The first two sessions were for alpha learning. Subjects pushed a button when they thought they were producing alpha; visual feedback showed when they were correct. The subjects did not know this, but each button push also activated an RNG and was scored as an ESP trial. There was a significant positive relation between alpha abundance and psi-hitting. The next two sessions were for ESP learning. Subjects pushed a button to make their ESP response, and the same visual feedback showed an ESP hit. They did not know that their alpha was also being recorded. These two sessions showed a significant negative relation between alpha and psi hits: significant hitting when alpha was diminished or absent and chance scores when it was abundant. What accounts for this mirror-image change in results when the task changed? Nothing that I have read in others' reports seems to explain it. (I add, for completeness, that we saw no learning.)

Even though differences in method make it improper to group all the EEG studies (see Palmer, 1978, for a careful early review), I was curious to see if they tended to find the generally expected association between psi success and slow brain wave activity. I made a quick division using the authors' reports of significant findings. Disregarding a few where I could not make sense of the results, the tabulation of alpha (or theta) in relation to psi scores showed 14 reports of a null relation, 14 reports of some significant positive relation, and 5 where there was a significant negative relation. Even with allowance for the file drawer effect and for multiple analyses, the 19 significant findings seem to justify inferring there is some relation between slow wave brain activity and psi, though the relation is not necessarily that alpha accompanies psi-hitting.

In an important recent article, Healy (1986) collated findings from an extraordinarily wide range of methods, and argues that they converge to show that the theta rhythm is associated with psi success. One of the many implications of her review is that it might be useful to reanalyze the better controlled studies of alpha and find if psi scores were higher in the slower part of the alpha wave band.

A handful of EEG studies examined psi in relation to evoked potential (the pattern of EEG change within a single brain response). These patterns are highly variable both between and within individuals, and the method requires that large numbers of traces be summed to find the average wave form. Provocative results are sometimes reported, but replications, even by the same investigator, have not been successful (see, e.g., Hearne, 1981). I am indebted to R. Reinsel for suggesting one reason why replications have failed. She points out that recent research shows it is important to correct evoked potential recordings for varying levels of activation in the area that is being recorded. This correction has not as yet been made in psi studies.

Other Body Responses

Other physiological research on psi was described in Chapter 8: W.G. Braud (1981) cited a dozen studies where physiological measures permitted a conclusion about relaxation. He found that nine showed significantly better ESP scores with more relaxation. The few that can now be added to his list strengthen the finding. Almost all used a measure of skin conductance. The pattern is clearly consistent with the overall tendency to find better psi scores when there is more alpha.

A few other questions have occasionally been studied, but I have found only two problems that were examined more than a single time: eye movements and the menstrual cycle. Both Ludwick (1980) and Kreiman (1981) measured eye movements and ESP; both report higher ESP scores with eye movements to the nondominant side. Schmitt & Stanford (1978) found a relation betwen menstrual cycle and psi success, but the relation was not replicated by Keane & Wells (1979).

Summary of Concurrent Measures of Body and Psi

Many studies are inadequately replicated or null or contradictory, but two patterns are worth attention. A high proportion of reports find some significant relation between psi success and the slow brain waves of alpha or theta, and a very high proportion find that a moderately relaxed body state is conducive to ESP success. The two patterns are clearly consistent.

RESEARCH ON CHANGED BODY STATE

Surgery

Smythies & Beloff (1965) gave ESP tests before and after surgery to patients suffering from Parkinsonism. The ESP scores were null at both times. There seems to have been no similar research.

Drugs

Several of the older studies (often nonblind) describe psi tests after the administration of drugs. When subjects had taken alcohol or stimulants, ESP scores were sometimes high, sometimes low. When subjects took sedatives, ESP scores were often null but sometimes showed significant psi-missing. The most elaborate experiment, and also one of the more recent (Huby &

Wilson, 1961) selected subjects whose pretest scores were at least slightly above or slightly below the mean chance level. On different days during a week, each subject took a placebo, a stimulant, and a sleeping drug. All drugs were made up into pills with identical appearance; thus all subjects had the same dosage. Subjects made two ESP runs after taking the drug. In the first series, ESP scores were significantly high in the placebo condition, and tended to be high in the control (no pill) but low in the sedative and stimulant conditions. None of these effects appeared in a second series, using many of the same subjects and a largely similar method.

Published research on psychedelic drugs shows chance scores on the experimenter's targets but it often adds anecdotes of unanticipated impressions that sound like spontaneous ESP. There has also been considerable unpublished research on marijuana, reported only by the grapevine. Usually both subjects and experimenters felt strongly favorable toward both marijuana and ESP, and often but not always the reports tell of high ESP scores.

The inconsistent data about drug effects might have been expected from what has been found in psychological research with humans. After a low level of drug dosage, results show an interaction with motivation. Performance often is good on a task important to the subject but poor on a task important only to the experimenter. Post hoc, for example, psi-missing after a sedative could be interpreted to mean that drowsy subjects were exasperated at being kept awake; null scores to mean that they tolerated the ESP task but did not care about it. No psi research has formally tested for this interaction.

Brain Hemispheres

The left brain hemisphere has more direct input from the right side of the body than from the left and more direct control of motor activity on the right than on the left. The opposite is true of the right hemisphere. In the 1960s, some research led to a facile overgeneralization about the hemispheres: that the left functions verbally and logically but the right does not; and the right functions globally and intuitively while the left does not. This led some to expect that right hemisphere functioning would be psi-conducive, left hemisphere functioning would not.

Broughton (1976) initiated experimentation on whether the brain hemispheres differ in ESP ability. His ingenious method tried in half the ESP trials to keep the left hemisphere occupied, by simple arithmetic or by reading law reports, so that it would not interfere with ESP. Subjects were blindfolded in the other trials. The ESP task was to choose one object from a set of five small objects with different shapes. In half the trials of each condition, subjects made the selection with the right hand; in the other half, with the left.

Each of three series tested 20 right-handed subjects, but the series differed in minor ways and gave somewhat different results. Broughton considers that the overall data suggest both that the right hemisphere is more successful than the left with at least some forms of ESP, and that the left hemisphere is inhibitory, so that a nonpsi task which occupies the left hemisphere is conducive to psi.

Later modifications tried to make the procedure symmetrical (see Maher, Peratsakis, & Schmeidler, 1979). Half the trials tried to occupy the right hemisphere with a pictorial task; the other half tried to occupy the left hemisphere with a verbal task. For each task, half the trials were for verbal ESP targets and the other half for nonverbal targets. In each of the four subsets, half the responses were made by the right hand and half by the left. The first of two experiments showed highest ESP scores in the condition that was a mirror-image of Broughton's: choice of verbal targets with the right hand during the pictorial task. The second series gave essentially null results, but a selective pooling of the data from both series implies that when both the type of target and the hand that responds are appropriate for one hemisphere, keeping the inappropriate hemisphere occupied with a nonpsi task can be psi-conducive.

Other methods have studied hemispheric function in relation to psi, and though they are summarized elsewhere in this chapter, I add them here for cross-reference. Two were already mentioned: Ludwick (1980) and Kreiman (1981). Maher (1984) is reported at the end of the chapter. A few of the concurrent studies with the EEG (above) also examined the hemispheres separately, and some but not all found hints of a hemispheric difference. One of the strongest follows.

Kobayashi, Terry, & Thompson (1979) gave pretests for psi to 50 subjects, then classed 15 as a psi group and 13 as a nonpsi group. Both groups then performed a psi task while their EEGs were measured. Three hypotheses were tested. Two were not confirmed: that during the psi task the psi and nonpsi groups would differ in alpha level (a) for the right hemisphere or (b) in total alpha. The third was significantly supported (if we do not correct for selection): right hemisphere alpha increased from the relaxation period to the psi period for the psi group but decreased for the nonpsi group. The work has not been replicated.

Other Observations about Brain Function

Several interesting observations about brain function and psi have not been investigated further. Here are three examples.

Ehrenwald (1978) points out a marked similarity between the drawings made as ESP responses, which so often give an accurate but meaningless reproduction of some part of the target (described in Chapter 10), and the attempts at reproducing drawings made by patients with lesions in the left parieto-occipital brain area, which also show distinctive but only partial resemblances to what they are trying to copy.

In a series of articles, a parapsychologist and a neurologist (see Roll & Montagno, 1983) argue that brain injury which will cause psychomotor epilepsy may be the model for poltergeist effects. They examined some individuals who seemed to be the cause of poltergeist disturbances, and suggest that when the brain injury is in the temporal lobe, poltergeists will be "smart" with responsive sounds or the slow falling of objects, but if the locus of brain injury is the limbic system, poltergeists will be "crude," with explosive sounds and indiscriminate breakage.

An unanticipated finding came from my single attempt to examine brain injury and psi (Schmeidler, 1952a). Only concussion patients were available. The ESP card tests showed, rather to my dismay, that their ESP scores were significantly high. A control group, hospitalized for accidents without brain injury, tended to score low. Rorschach responses suggested that the concussion cases, but not the others, showed a vague, uncritical acceptance of any incoming impressions; a relaxed, acceptant state. No one has tried to replicate the finding with concussion cases, but a systematic replication (Gerber & Schmeidler, 1957) tested subjects in the most relaxed, acceptant state we could think of: new mothers still in the hospital, who had recovered from anesthesia and whose babies were well. They, too, had significantly high ESP scores.

Summary of Psi Research on a Changed Body State

Psi research on the effects of drugs is inconclusive. There is no well replicated research on the effect of brain function on psi, but several reports suggest psi differences related to functioning of the right and left hemispheres.

Attempts to Use Psi to Produce a Body Change

Good research is disappointingly meager for the question of whether psi produces body change. The natural place to look is in reports of psychic healing, but critical analysis will dismiss many or all of the reports that involve healing humans. Reasons for dismissal include a possible placebo effect in studies that were not double-blind, the absence of objective evidence for both the initial impairment and its betterment, and (in the occasional accounts of sudden recovery from a dread disease) the absence of adequate baseline comparison for spontaneous recovery without psychic healing. And there are other reasons too; one example is fraud.

But it would be a Type II error to take this as a dismissal of psychic healing. Viewed by the standards of naturalistic research, evidence for it is strong. Further, two extrapolations from well controlled research seem strongly to support the possibility that it occurs. One is the excellent evidence that PK can change the growth of plants or microorganisms (for summaries, see Schmeidler, 1978, 1987). The other inference comes from the repeated finding that some who are considered psychic healers can, under tightly controlled conditions, produce changes in unicellular organisms or chemicals or physical objects (see, e.g., Dean, 1983; Edge, 1980; Rauscher & Rubik, 1980; Smith, 1972). Lack of good evidence on human healing may be due only to lack of good research.

An example of good research on nonhuman mammals comes from Watkins & Watkins (1971). They report that when psychics ("healers") tried to use psi to help mice recover from anesthesia, those mice recovered faster than a control group. Certain patterns in the data suggested another remarkable possibility: that the effect of a psychic's efforts might persist in the place at which the psychic was concentrating. Watkins, Watkins, & Wells (1973) made a careful test for this "linger effect" and confirmed that it occurred. After the healer left, mice placed in the spot where the healer hoped for recovery had a faster recovery time than mice placed elsewhere. Wells & Watkins (1975) add further evidence for a linger effect. The method of attempting to speed resuscitation after anesthesia has not been replicated by others.

A series of experiments from W.G. Braud's laboratory began with striking findings. The PK agents were a gifted subject, Matthew Manning, or Braud himself, or unselected subjects. The agent was always in a separate room, sound-shielded from the target. Targets included the galvanic skin response of human subjects, the spatial orientation of swimming fish, a gerbil's running on an activity wheel, or the rate of hemolysis of human whole blood. There were significant changes in all these types of targets, and with all types of agents (Braud, Davis, & Wood 1979).

W.G. Braud & Schlitz (1983) integrated a psychologically interesting variable into their research design: the strength of the need for healing. All their subjects wanted help for anxiety or a psychosomatic problem implying overtension, but pretests of skin resistance indicated that some needed help more than others. Subjects were divided into the 16 with higher tension levels and the 16 with lower. In the key part of the procedure, the agent, who was in a separate room from the subject, tried in randomly ordered periods of 30 seconds each either to calm the subject or to think of something else. The subjects' skin conductance levels showed significantly less tension in the calming than in the control periods for the 16 whose tension had been higher; there was no difference between periods for the others. The authors suggest that healing is more effective when the need for it is greater. Further research from the same laboratory, though interesting, has not yet identified other key variables.

A few studies found evidence that psi could influence gross body activity. Randall (1971), for example, reports that 3 of 12 schoolboys significantly influenced the direction in which wood lice would crawl. C.B. Nash & C.S. Nash (1981) tested chicks and mice on a "visual cliff" (a sturdy glass slab, partly over a gap). With PK, both species stepped more often on the part that was over the gap.

Summary of Using Psi to Produce a Body Change

Well controlled research shows that PK can change the growth of plants and simple organisms, and some well controlled research also found that PK can change gross body activity or an internal body process in insects, humans, and other mammals. Extrapolation from these results implies support for the possibility of psychic healing.

Body Change as an ESP Response

Tantalizing data come from the plethysmograph. The instrument measures fluid volume, usually in the finger. It thus indirectly measures vasodilation or vasoconstriction, an indicator of autonomic arousal. After earlier studies had shown mixed ESP results with plethysmograph changes, Dean (1962) developed a neat technique for studying the relation between them. The subject lies quietly in one room. In another room, an agent looks in random order at three types of ESP targets: names important to the subject, important to the agent, or important to neither. Blind scoring of the plethysmograph records permits comparison of levels of autonomic arousal with different targets.

Dean repeatedly, but not invariably, found significantly more arousal when the agent looked at names that were meaningful to the subject. Both his and other findings are mixed. A summary by Beloff (1974) shows that the strongest results come when there is a long series of tests on a single individual, and that results often show an interaction with other variables, e.g. familiarity with the procedure. Statistical evaluation of all studies combined looks as if the results are promising but are not strong.

The only study I have found that was later than Beloff's summary also gave mixed results. Schouten (1976) measured both plethysmograph changes and skin conductance. There were two types of targets: names, as in Dean's work, and loud sounds which the agent heard through earphones. Plethysmograph responses showed a significant change when the agent looked at names meaningful to the subject but showed no change with the loud sounds that the agent heard. In contrast, changes in skin conductance were significant for the sounds but not the names. If the findings replicate, this is a line of research that can lead to important inferences about the way psi input is processed.

One general consideration that applies to much of the other research is pertinent here. It comes from the well replicated psychological finding that individuals differ in their autonomic responsiveness. For one person the heart rate is a sensitive measure of arousal but skin conductance is not; for the next person the opposite can be true. Research projects that use the same measure to test everyone will look tidy, but can give weak results because their measure is inappropriate for some subjects. It is noteworthy that the clearest data with the plethysmograph come from repeated tests with the same individual, presumably a person for whom this measure is a sensitive one.

It should also be mentioned that Dean, who has done the most research with this technique, describes data that lend themselves to clinical rather than statistical evaluation. For one example, he reports on a subject who in repeated sessions showed least arousal for the set of names important to him. Dean describes the young man as having little self-esteem. Late in the series of tests there was one day when the responses showed most arousal, consistently, for names important to the subject. Dean inferred that the day was special, asked if it was, and the young man told him yes, today was his birthday and a party would be given for him. On that day but not the others, he was an important person. A series of such anecdotes tells of changes in response that were unpredicted but seem meaningful. Because the anecdotes are reported by a cautious and conscientious investigator, they seem to me to carry considerable weight. They argue that test conditions which appeared similar to the experimenter were in fact different for the subject.

In the foregoing studies, the subject knows the general plan of the research, but is expected to rest quietly, thinking whatever happens to come to mind, without conscious attempts to respond to the agent. Tart (1963) did not impose this restriction. He used himself as agent and used as targets occasional electric shocks to find if his subjects would respond to what he felt. He recorded their EEGs, plethysmograph changes, and skin conductance changes, but he also asked them to give ESP responses: to signal by a key press when they had an ESP impression of the shock. The key tap responses gave null results, but each of the other measures changed when he was shocked. Thus, in this unreplicated research, conscious response gave no evidence for psi, but unconscious bodily responses gave such evidence.

Two studies with physiological indicators of ESP used twins as subjects.

Duane & Behrendt (1965) report that of the 15 pairs of twins they tested with an EEG, the 13 pairs to whom the EEG was unfamiliar all gave null results. For two pairs familiar with lab methods, however, the authors state that when one twin was stimulated and his EEG showed the expected response, the other unstimulated twin also showed that response. Barron & Mordkoff (1968) tested pairs of identical twins, all girls, and measured their skin resistance, heart rate, and respiration. For four pairs, one twin watched a traumatic film while the other, in another room, was to try to imagine what the first was seeing. There was negligible overall correspondence in their autonomic records.

Extraordinary results come from a pair of EEG studies on a gifted subject. Targ & Puthoff had presented light flashes to an agent, distant from the subject. The subject's EEG showed a psi correspondence to those flashes: the alpha blocking that would be expected if he himself had seen the light. A replication (May, Targ, & Puthoff, 1979) also showed a significant correspondence between the distant flashes and the subject's EEG, but the results reversed: now there was stronger alpha, not alpha blocking. This effect was more pronounced in trials without an agent than with one. As in Tart's work, the subject's conscious attempts to respond to the flashes gave null results. Post hoc examination of both experiments analyzed cycles per second during alpha, and found that peak alpha frequency was different in the two experiments. The authors suggest that the change in alpha frequency might have caused the reversal in psi responses.

A recent experiment also found evidence that brain changes can in themselves be ESP responses. Maher (1984) used two videotapes, markedly different from each other, as ESP targets. One was expected to produce more activity in the right hemisphere than the other. There were 20 right-handed subjects. Four sets of EEGs were taken: the first two when the two tapes were played as ESP targets; the next two while the subjects were observing the two tapes. After the ESP period the subjects tried to respond to the tapes by describing their impressions, and after they had observed the tapes, they tried to designate which had been played first when it was an ESP target. Two blind judges also tried to match the tapes to the subjects' impressions.

Data from these judgments varied according to who made the judgments (as is often found in scoring free responses, e.g., in dream research). Subjects' attempts to identify the target and the scores of one of the blind judges were only slightly better than chance. The scores of the other blind judge, a clinical psychologist, were significantly correct.

The EEG data gave an important result. Hemispheric dominance during the ESP period significantly correlated with hemispheric dominance during the actual observation of the tapes. Brain processing was similar for ESP and for sensory input.

Summary of Body Change as an ESP Response

Even when subjects are not consciously aware of an ESP target, their brains and bodies can respond to it.

OVERVIEW

EEG studies tend to show some relation between alpha (or slow brain wave activity) and psi success. Results are mixed and thus do not confirm the expectation that alpha is conducive to psi success, but they tend more toward supporting than toward disconfirming it. No method for psi study of brain activity has been adequately replicated, but several reports indicate a relation between psi scores and hemispheric function.

Psi research on the effect of drugs is inconclusive.

Research on autonomic nervous system activity shows strong evidence for higher ESP scores when arousal is moderately low than when there is higher arousal.

There is strong evidence that a person can, by psi, cause body change in another living being, but well controlled research on body changes in humans is sparse.

There is strong evidence that body (including brain) changes can show a direct response to ESP targets even when subjects give no conscious response to the targets, or fail in conscious attempts to identify the targets.

13. Evaluation of Replicability and of the Theory

Chapters 5–12 tried to make a full survey of the psi research that directly relates to psychological topics. The purpose of so detailed a review was to provide a base for evaluating a prediction: the prediction that psi findings would make a fit with psychological findings. The chapters included evaluations for some but not all of the topics. Now it is time to put together the pluses and minuses; to judge whether as a whole they tend to support or disconfirm the theory that psi is a psychological process.

Evaluating Replicability

The first step in judging whether or not psi findings match a theory must be to determine what the psi findings are. We ask: What research outcomes are so well replicated that we can feel confidence in them, and use them to see if a theory's predictions are or are not supported? What other outcomes are fairly well replicated, so that they may be put to similar use? What outcomes are so inconsistent that they are a clear mismatch to any affirmative prediction?

Evaluating the strength of replications demands multiple criteria, and mine can be boiled down to three sets of questions. One set centers around quantity; it asks if there was enough research to justify any generalization. (Was it research from different laboratories? Research with many subjects?) A second set centers around quality. (Were the studies well designed? Well controlled? Carefully conducted? Were the data analyzed appropriately?) The third set asks if the findings were consistent. (What proportion of the results showed the same trend? What was the significance level for supportive results? For nonsupportive?)

The outcome of using this variety of criteria was a rough ranking of the forty-odd topics in chapters 5–12. The two highest rankings came for the experimenter effect (Chapter 5) and the effect of hypnotic induction when subjects acted as their own controls and the hypnotist was not blind (Chapter 9).

Next came many topics where the level of replication seemed satisfactorily high (and where the difficulty of weighting multiple criteria made it tempting to give them tied ranks). Some examples are the comparisons (Chapter 7) of extraversion versus introversion and of openness versus withdrawal, with its strong subset on defensiveness; the level of autonomic arousal (chapters 8 and 12); the weak but fairly consistent sheep-goat effect (Chapter 6); and subliminal perception (also partly dependent on its defensiveness subset).

Lower ranks went to several topics like creativity and the retrieval of poorly learned material (Chapter 11) and to brain changes in relation to psi (Chapter 12). The bottom of the list, where replicability was clearly inadequate, included learning to improve psi scores (Chapter 11) and research on values (Chapter 6), on positive and negative affect (Chapter 8), and on sensory or figural variables (Chapter 10).

EVALUATING THE THEORY

The Stronger Results

Let us look first at the two best replicated findings. Psychological data on the experimenter effect show better scores with a warm rather than a cold experimental climate, and with positive rather than negative expectations from the experimenter. Psi data showed the same effects and also gave convergent evidence, e.g. for certain experimenters being self-consistent in the scores they elicited.

In psychology, when the same subjects act in both hypnotic and control conditions and the hypnotist is not blind, hypnotic induction usually facilitates scores on whatever task the hypnotist assigns. In psi research also, especially when both those conditions were present, psi scores were higher with hypnotic induction than without it.

These two lines of research strongly support the theory that psi results will relate to psychological ones. Does this mean the theory is supported by two separate topics? Not necessarily. Many psychologists class them as a single topic that is studied by two methods. They consider nonblind hypnotic induction as a special case of the experimenter effect, because hypnotists ordinarily create a warm climate and expect higher scores in the hypnotic condition than in the control. (Other psychologists consider the difference in method important enough to justify separate categories.) But whether these are two topics or one, the psi tests that replicate best give data that are consistent with what is found in psychology.

Also high up on the list of topics with satisfactory replicability is a batch of five findings on attitude and personality. Lack of defensiveness (chapters 7 and 10) is psi-conducive; here the data are remarkably consistent. Sheep-goat inquiries (Chapter 6) tend to show fairly consistently that psi scores are higher for those who accept some possibility of success in the test they are taking than for those who reject the possibility. Chapter 7 gives three additional sets of results that should be considered at least moderately strong. Several methods in addition to tests of defensiveness compare the more open, expansive subjects with the more withdrawn or constrained; all find or tend to find that psi scores are higher for the more open. Extraverts tend to have more psi success than those with higher scores. Subjects with lower scores for anxiety (or for indications of neurosis) tend to have more psi success than those with higher scores.

Here are five well replicated or moderately well replicated patterns, but the list raises again the question that was asked about the experimenter effect and hypnotic induction. Are these separate results? Or are they only separate methods that converge on a single finding?

Often, with alternatives like these, the best answer lies somewhere between them. The answer to the question is, I think, that the various findings are not identical but they interrelate. It is even possible to argue that each relates to the process shown by the experimenter effect.

Here is a rough sketch of the argument. Both a warm emotional climate and expectation of success will tend to make subjects less defensive. The sheep-goat difference refers to the subject's expectation of success. Although this is separable from an experimenter's expectation, the two tie in with each other. Openness and low anxiety are likely to be associated with a warm experimental climate; constraint and higher anxiety with a cold one. Extraverts, with their ability to inhibit prior restraints, are more likely to accept the suggestion implied by the experimenter's expectation, and research has shown that on average, they tend to have low scores for neuroticism.

At a minimum, these differently named traits or attitudes have some overlap. For each the relation to psi scores is what would be expected to follow from the findings on the experimenter effect. The results cluster; they hold together psychologically. This makes them consistent with the theory's prediction.

Three other topics that were high or fairly high in my rankings fit into the cluster too. One is physiological measures of arousal, with their evidence that a moderately low level of arousal is more ESP-conducive than a high level (chapters 8 and 12). This is in accord with the findings that low anxiety and a warm research climate are psi-conducive. A second, but a weaker one, is the usual positive relation between psi and creativity scores (Chapter 11). Higher scores on creativity are expected with openness than with constraint. A third is the relation of psi scores to scores on subliminal perception (Chapter 10), where there are two complementary interpretations. One applies to subliminal stimuli far below the threshold. Here positive correlations with ESP were predicted and found, and the common factor underlying the two sets of scores is taken to be openness versus defensiveness. The other interpretation applies to stimuli near the threshold. Here negative relations were predicted and found, and the key difference between the two is taken to be that a near-threshold subliminal task mobilizes reality-orientation, which is associated with a healthy but psi-inhibitory defensiveness.

Three methods of conducting research seem psi-conducive (Chapter 9) and also seem to belong in the same cluster. Dreams are usually considered more open and less defensive than waking responses. And in both remote viewing and the Ganzfeld, the introduction ordinarily encourages expectation of success, the climate is warm, and the setting is planned to induce both moderate relaxation and an openness to incoming impressions which would otherwise be dismissed as illogical.

For four other topics the findings are less well replicated, but the trend that they show makes a fit with the cluster. Meditation is one (Chapter 9). Field dependence is another (Chapter 11). Another is group relations (Chapter 6), where results seem to converge toward showing higher psi scores for those who are more secure in a group and more comfortable with it. Studies with EEGs (Chapter 12) tend often to show some relation between psi and slow wave brain activity, a relation that is consistent with openness and relaxation.

Only a few other topics had rankings that were even fairly high. One is the indication that ESP facilitates retrieval of poorly learned information (Chapter 11). It perhaps relates to creativity, since in poorly learned information the associative structure is weak, and creative persons tend to respond on an association test with items that are low in their hierarchy of associations. Another is the effect of a psi target's background upon response to the target (Chapter 9). It, like the retrieval of poorly learned information, perhaps implies openness to peripheral material, an openness that is opposite to the barriers that a defensive subject might erect. (A more elaborate possible interpretation is suggested below.) Goal orientation, on the face of it, seems more relaxed and open than its opposite: emphasis on the process by which one reaches the goal. The indications that physiological responses show psi even when conscious responses do not is consistent with the general line of argument; it implies defensiveness in conscious response.

This survey of psi findings, from the well replicated down to those which only hint at a consistent trend, indicates that they are interrelated. The relation is often close, like the similar expectations in the experimenter effect and the sheep-goat effect, but sometimes more remote, as for the assimilation of target and background. All or almost all cluster in a way that is consistent with psychological expectations. They thus tend to be supportive of this book's theory. But it is noteworthy that almost all come from a limited number of psychological areas: personality traits and attitudes, experimenter-subject or other interpersonal relations, and the data from physiological psychology that seem to relate to these.

The Nonreplicating Results

Although psi research in the social-personality area often gave results that supported this book's theory, there were two topics within this area where it did not. Neither for values nor for positive versus negative affect did psi research yield consistent findings. For both these topics, however, it seems possible that the lack of replications is due to defects in the research methods. Each topic, I think, demands either a multivariate design or a research project tailored to the particular individual who is acting as a psi subject. Some examples follow, to illustrate this need.

Begin with affect, and its extremes of elation and misery. How will a high spirited, elated mood affect the way subjects approach an assigned task, like a psi test? Their happy mood may make some go at their psi calls with enthusiasm, but it may make others feel too carefree to take the testing seriously, and instead enjoy themselves by giving flip, irrelevant responses. Or suppose subjects take a psi test while feeling miserable, perhaps because of a recent failure or rejection. Unhappiness might make some inattentive because the test is irrelevant to what concerns them. For others misery might spread into a feeling of worthlessness, so that they do not hope to succeed because they do not deserve success. Still others might try to compensate for whatever single event went wrong, and latch eagerly onto the psi test because it provides a new chance at showing how good they really are. Moods produce different reactions, predictable only with knowledge of the different persons.

For values, we must expect an interaction between the value and the specific task or situation. High religious values have made some feel sympathetic toward psi but have made others reject psi as the work of the devil. For someone with high social values, a GESP psi test may call forth an eager response, but a clairvoyant psi test may be rejected as ego-alien. If one's values differ from those of the person who administers the psi test, that lack of basic sympathy might in itself be a determinant of attitude toward the task.

Psi research on affect and values has not addressed the issues raised by these examples. It may therefore be legitimate to set aside the null data on affect and values rather than conclude they disconfirm the book's theory.

On many topics, psi research was too sparse to warrant any conclusion. On many others, especially physiological studies, data showed little replication from one study to the next, but procedural differences or lack of adequate control for key variables might have been the reason for the lack of replication. Here also, in my opinion, no conclusion should yet be stated.

Strong disconfirmation of the theory, or at least strong partial disconfirmation, comes from the major psychological area of cognition (Chapter 11), which includes perception (Chapter 10). Cognition is basic and important within psychology, yet psi research that studies cognitive problems has failed to find orderly data—except for the few subtopics already mentioned: subliminal perception, creativity, figure-ground relations, and the retrieval of poorly learned material. But these four topics are not major exceptions. Each is marginal rather than central to the large body of psychological research on discrimination in sensory processing, or on learning and closely related cognitive processes.

On the one hand, then, psi research on cognitive processes has shown so many ambiguous or null results as perhaps to lead to the general statement that psi does not function as cognition does. On the other hand are four sets of affirmative (or possibly affirmative) findings. I suggest that those data justify some modification of the blanket negative conclusion about psi and cognition.

The suggestion starts with the figure-ground relation. This relation is probably the first, primitive step of perceptual discrimination. If we collate the scattered psi data that bear on it, they indicate that unselected subjects or psi-missers and perhaps fast, hurried subjects tend to assimilate the psi target to its background. They thus fail to discriminate figure from ground. Gifted subjects, although they may assimilate, also seem able to discriminate: they show a contrast effect between the target and its surround. Perhaps then we have a right to infer that when psi ability is weak and untrained, the processing of psi input resembles the "blooming, buzzing confusion" that William James saw in the neonate, whereas when psi ability is stronger or more practiced, the processing of psi input resembles the first stage of figure-ground separation. The implication is that psi processing is similar to the earliest stages of sensory processing but not similar to later, finer discrimination.

An extension of this line of reasoning might also account for the resemblance between psi and subliminal responses. Subliminal input is, by definition, processed and stored without awareness. Presumably it, too, represents an early stage of perceptual processing.

The two other exceptions, creativity and the retrieval of poorly learned information, can be considered jointly. Success in either of them demands, at least initially, a readiness to let come what may; to make responses that might be right but might be absurdly wrong. Both seem to involve a temporary suspension of critical judgment or of checking for precision and certainty. This readiness seems to relate closely to personality variables; it seems to show a (temporary) lack of defensiveness.

I therefore suggest an inference from the combined null and affirmative data on cognition. In cognition, psi findings relate to psychological findings only for the most primitive perceptual processing and for that part of cognitive processing which is modulated by personality.

Overview

For psi research on the more than forty psychological topics summarized in the preceding chapters, the level of replication of the results was assessed according to three sets of criteria: the quality of the research, its quantity, and how consistent its outcomes were. On some topics the level of replication was high, on others it was moderately high, on others there was some trend that was strong enough to deserve attention, and on others it was inadequate.

Where the psi data were well replicated, the findings were consistent with psychological ones. These consistent psi patterns clustered in the social-personality area. Most were studies of attitudes and personality variables, of some interpersonal relations such as the experimenter effect, and of autonomic arousal, which is related to these.

In contrast, psi research on perception, learning, and other cognitive processes typically, with few exceptions, gave null or ambiguous results. These results imply that psi does not function like sensory discrimination except for the most primitive responses, nor like cognitive processes except when those processes are modulated by personality. Thus the theory that there is a relation between psi and psychological processes has been well supported in some areas of psychological research but has not been supported in others.

III. Speculation

14. Physicists' Theories of Psi

Back when I began to learn about ESP, it seemed to me to contradict the laws of physics. When the distance of the target varied, scores did not show the changes that are expected from the inverse square law. Information came from well shielded targets, or even worse, from targets that had not yet been selected. Something was wrong. What I first thought wrong were the claims of ESP, but by now I see the error lay in my simplistic notions of space and time. The "Laws of Physics" I had been taught were the classic, Newtonian ones, but the findings that support relativity theory and quantum theory show that classical physics was not the last word.

Are ESP and PK compatible with modern physical theory? Physicists' opinions differ. Some find no place for psi in the universe (see Wheeler, 1981, for a forceful statement of this position, but later in the same book, see Jahn's corrections of a part of the statement). Other physicists like Wigener (1981) are noncommittal; they hold open the possibility that psi may eventually be integrated with physical concepts. Others go further and present theories that include psi.

A few of these theories are briefly described below, but all my descriptions are incomplete. They omit interesting parts of every theory, and they omit the mathematical formulations that give the theories meaning and permit prediction. The relevant research is barely mentioned. Nevertheless, I hope the survey can show the general lines of thought that some modern physicists follow.

Thermodynamics

In thermodynamics it is conventional to solve quadratic equations involving time only for the case where time moves forward and entropy increases toward the future. It is as if we solved the square root of four for $+2$ and disregarded -2 as a possible answer. That is not what we were taught to do in elementary algebra, but the solutions usually give appropriate answers (though there are occasional anomalies or violations).

Donald & Martin (1976) examined the implications of solving thermodynamic equations in both the ways that are mathematically correct: the conventional solutions and also solutions for the case where time moves backwards. The conventional solutions take the past as fixed and not to be changed, so that its order is given; entropy or disorder increases toward the future. Donald & Martin tentatively assume that this is the usual but not the complete description of our universe now; they assume that there are lcoal exceptions where the opposite, symmetrical description applies. They built their assumptions into a series of formulas which extend thermodynamics in a time-symmetric way.

The formulas make predictions about psi, and especially about precognition. Donald & Martin write that after having developed the formulas, they read parapsychological reports and found support for those of their predictions that had been tested. Some predictions are yet untested, for example that psi will be more effective with random than with pseudo-random targets. What makes their approach especially interesting is that it is consistent with quantum mechanics (Walker, 1984) and with some astronomical concepts, notably black holes and the theory of an oscillating universe.

HOLOGRAPHY AND THE IMPLICATE ORDER

Bohm (1980, 1986) presents a theoretical framework intended to reconcile relativity and quantum theory, bring together mental and physical realities, and suggest a theory for parapsychology.

His theory can perhaps best be understood as an extension of holography. In a holographic image, say of an automobile, what we see looks like an image of the whole automobile. But if instead of seeing the whole we see only the part that had been a wheel, that part now shows the whole car. Each part enfolds and "implicates" the whole, just as the whole that we saw enfolded and implicated each part.

In Bohm's theory the explicate order, for example each of the separate things we can identify, has implicit within it the relation of the parts to each other—and to everything else. An example from physics, on a small scale, is that the trajectory of an electron depends on its field of surrounding electrons. An example from mental reality is that our perception of the meaning of a new stimulus depends on the world in which that stimulus is a part. The whole is implicit within each specific. This resonance of meanings and field relations encompasses and accounts for psi.

(I must add a note here. The esteem which other physicists have for Bohm implies that many research predictions are implicit in his theory. But he has not spelled them out, and my own ignorance of holographic principles makes it impossible for me to explicate them.)

Positive and Negative Time Frames

Tiller (1977) has developed a radically different theory of the universe. He begins with the commonly accepted four dimensions (including time) where substance is electromagnetic, mass is positive, and the highest velocity is that of electromagnetic light. He then posits that this is only one of the conjugate parts in a higher dimensional time-frame. Its conjugate part also has four dimensions, but its substance is magnetoelectric, its mass is negative, and velocities are greater than the speed of electromagnetic light.

With these postulates, Tiller's theory readily includes not only PK and ESP but also such striking and bizarre paranormal claims as levitation or the passage of matter through matter. Tiller presents preliminary data that support several of his theory's postulates. One example is that magnetic shielding will inhibit successful dowsing. Another is that different images are produced when electromagnetic and magnetoelectric light pass through quartz or glass. Electromagnetic light slows down and magnetoelectric light speeds up. So far as I know, others have not tested his theory. I find this astonishing because the theory is so broad and provocative, because Tiller is a prestigious physicist with a respected academic position, and especially because his preliminary findings accord with his predictions.

Quantum Mechanics: the Observational Theories

Walker (e.g., 1975) has elaborated in great detail a quantum theory of consciousness and psi. Psi, he writes, accords well with quantum mechanics. Quantum events are nonlocal and time-invariant, and psi also seems not to be restricted by distance or time. Further, predictions of quantum events are probabilistic, and although individual psi events seem unpredictable, statistical or probabilistic data on psi are sometimes strong.

The key to his theory, and the base from which his formulas for psi are developed, comes from his interpretation of a statement generally accepted in quantum mechanics: that quantum events are indeterminate until they are observed. Before observation they can be described only as a set of probabilities: one outcome is more probable, another is less probable, and so on. Observation determines the outcome. For most physicists, "observation" can be an instrumental recording, but Walker interprets "observation" as requiring an observer. He argues that only a (conscious) observation changes the set of probabilities into a single event.

He uses neurological data to derive a value for the speed of conscious processing and to derive another, lower value for the speed of acts of will. He then works out a series of formulas to predict or retrodict specific effects of consciousness and of psi under different conditions. Walker (1984) lists 39 research tests of his theory, some relating to consciousness and some to psi; he reports that all support his formulations. Most of his predictions are admirably specific, e.g. for change in PK score with different rates of presentation. His theory has received a great deal of respectful attention from parapsychologists, some of whom have designed and performed research to test some of its predictions.

Schmidt (1975) published a mathematical model for psi that he hoped would serve the clarifying function that Maxwell's equations served for electromagnetism. Schmidt's formulas involve an individual, called the psi source, who can use PK if there is feedback but cannot use PK if there is no feedback. (The same requirement of feedback applies to ESP. Schmidt takes ESP to be a special case of PK in which the events to be influenced are one's own responses.) Because psi is postulated to be dependent on feedback (i.e., observation) but to be independent of space, time, and task complexity, the model leads to daring predictons, e.g. that with time independence, an unobserved past event can be influenced just as a future event can be.

Schmidt (1976) devised a clever method for examining such backward PK. An RNG creates target lists and records them on tape, but no living person observes them before the experimental session. The lists are randomly assigned to a high or to a low condition. In the experiment, subjects hear the tapes while trying to use PK to make their scores either high or low, depending on which they were assigned. The subjects are thus the first living beings to observe the tapes. Extrachance success is found in a good many but not all of the experiments with this method (see pages 53–54 in Chapter 6). Even the strongest results, however, are open to two interpretations. One is that PK acts to change the past. The other is that the random assignment of targets to the high or low condition was guided by psi, and thus extrachance success, when it occurs, is due to contemporary or precognitive psi in making the (random) target assignments.

More recently, Schmidt (1984) presented two models of psi, one teleological and one based on quantum collapse. They have different testable consequences for some procedures, e.g. when two subjects make successive attempts to influence the same events. The quantum collapse model predicts that a subject will be more successful as the first psi source than as the second, but this prediction is not a part of the teleological model.

An especially interesting approach to psi utilizing quantum mechanics is being developed by Jahn & Dunne (1984), who consider that consciousness, like mass, should be conceptualized in terms of quanta. Jahn & Dunne use known physical variables like momentum and density as the base for metaphors of consciousness. When these metaphors are applied to psi they show promise of important new predictive value.

Overview

Some brilliant and respected physicists have used modern physical concepts to develop theories of psi. We who are not physicists can therefore feel reassured that ESP and PK are not necessarily contrary to other parts of the body of scientific knowledge.

15. Psi: PK and the Subclasses of ESP

Is it proper to use psi as a general term for ESP and PK? If it is — if they are enough alike to be classed together — is there any need for the separate terms? And similarly, is the single term ESP appropriately used for clairvoyance, precognition, etc., as if differences among them were negligible? If so, should we discard the batch of polysyllabic words which imply that the processes are separate?

Logically it might seem that if we accept the broad terms we do not need the specific ones. This chapter argues that we should follow the common practice in other taxonomies and keep them all. The first section adduces three reasons, rather different from each other, for using specific terms; the following section gives reasons for thinking of psi as unitary. The next section discusses some problems raised by a unitary theory of psi.

Reasons for Distinguishing Subclasses of Psi

Operational Reasons

"Operationalism" is a set of rules introduced by Bridgeman, a physicist, and eagerly adopted by many psychologists. It has one outstanding merit: it avoids the mess that comes from fuzzy use of language.

Take the example of length. Given a standard meter or yardstick, we measure the length of an object by laying the standard along it. Well and good. But in the old days, introductory physics texts or popular articles that tried to give a notion of the size of a hydrogen atom might write that some huge number of them, laid next to each other, could fit into an inch. This is absurd and misleading; it implies that hydrogen atoms can be arranged neatly side by side and then counted. Physicists must use a different operation to measure atoms. Operationalism corrects this kind of error. Its major principle is that information derived by one operation must be distinguished from information derived by a different operation.

Or take another example: the value of a baby's body. What is it worth? If measured by the resale price of its chemicals its worth is small. When it is the body of your own sick child, and is measured by how much you will gladly pay to restore it to health, the amount is very much greater. The two statements of value do not contradict each other; they have used the same word to refer to different operations.

The virtues of operationalism, therefore, are that it demands a clear description of what we mean when we use a word and that it keeps us from being confused when a single word is used with different meanings. It resolves apparent difficulties which are not real ones. It prevents our expecting anxiety measured by a paper and pencil questionnaire to be the same as anxiety measured by physiological recordings. It keeps us from expecting that intelligence measured by an IQ test will tell us how intelligently a person handles an emotional crisis.

(Although it is somewhat out of place in this section, I must add that when operationalism is pushed to its extreme, it has the defect of its virtues. It distinguishes among different methods, and there it stops. It is a useful tool, but should not be our only one. Almost everyone agrees that once we have used it to separate and differentiate, we need to go further. We must reintegrate, judiciously, if we are to have either meaningful concepts or a practical use. Among the methods that let us put ideas together again, after operationalism has taken them apart, are indirect replication and convergent validation.)

Now turn to psi. When we employ the useful tool of operationalism, we can find a clear difference between ESP and PK. Extrasensory perception is tested by recording a subject's response, which is then compared to some target. Psychokinesis is tested by recording a physical change that is beyond the subject's bodily control. The operations are different; we therefore need both terms.

For three classes of ESP, operational distinctions are equally clear. Clairvoyance is examined when a target exists but is known to no one. General ESP is examined when a target exists and is known to someone. Precognition is examined when a target does not exist at the time a subject responds, but will exist in the future.

An operational definition of telepathy needs more consideration. Ideally, it would be examined when a target is known to someone but has no physical existence at present (which makes it different from clairvoyance and GESP) and will not have a physical existence in the future (which makes it different from precognition). But there is controversy about whether this ideal operation can ever be performed. Here is the classic example.

McMahan (1946) tried to examine telepathy. She used a private code, never written or spoken, to translate digits into ESP symbols. (She might, for example, have translated 5 as a circle because the previous evening she and four friends sat around a circular table.) She then selected targets by following the order of digits in a table of random numbers. She mentally translated each digit into a symbol and tried to send messages about the symbols to her ESP subjects. Subjects did not know she was making the mental translations; they responded with ESP symbols. Both she and others who used similar methods found extrachance scores. Because the objective, physical record showed only digits, not symbols, extrachance scores on the symbols seemed to demonstrate telepathy.

But did they? Although J.B. Rhine had suggested the method, he argued later it did not exclude the possibility of clairvoyance. When McMahan thought of a symbol there was presumably a physical change in her brain. The subjects might have responded clairvoyantly to her brain changes. Thus her subjects' extrachance scores do not show that the subjects responded telepathically to her thoughts. It was not an adequate procedure for telepathy.

Rhine's argument is unanswerable at the metaphysical level, but it is uncomfortably reminiscent of arguments about how many angels can dance on the head of a pin. Operationalism lets us bypass it. Operationally, we can define telepathy as what is examined by McMahan's method, then continue to use the term. And we have even more freedom. We can define telepathy operationally in any way we choose, for instance as what is examined in GESP. We need only specify the operations we mean when we use the word.

This is obviously convenient. It not only lets us be clear, it also lets us follow Humpty Dumpty's excellent precedent: when we use a word, it means just what we choose it to mean. But it demands two precautions. We must be careful to state our own definition precisely (and forcefully) enough that others know what we mean. And in addition we must be careful, when others use the same word, to check out if they define it as we do. In short, when telepathy is defined operationally, it is a legitimate term.

Retrocognition has been suggested as another classification within ESP, and here the problems are even stickier. One early claim of demonstrating retrocognition can act as an example. During an archeological dig, a man dreamed of a medieval monk who told him many things, among them that digging at a particular unlikely site would show certain artifacts. A dig was conducted at that site and it found artifacts like those the dream had described. There was no check on the other parts of the dream.

Suppose we accept this account as true. Should we infer that the information was retrocognitive, that it came from the past? Most of us would say no to this question. Our reason is that the only verified part of the dream fits the operation for clairvoyance. Targets (the artifacts) existed and were known to no one. All the other interesting impressions may have been only dreamwork or fantasizing; embroidery around a clairvoyant core. They are unconfirmed.

The case is typical of most claims for retrocognition. Either information to check it exists and the operation is the same as for clairvoyance, or else it is unchecked. Because of these considerations, the term retrocognition has almost disappeared from parapsychology.

But the concept is important theoretically (as well as fascinating to those of us who enjoy science fiction). I suggest an experimental arrangement which might legitimize it: the breaking of an apparently unsolvable code for which a solution was known in the past. Suppose, for example, there is no equivalent of a Rosetta stone for writing from a certain ancient civilization and experts agree it is too fragmentary to read. Suppose then that someone ignorant of the civilization sees a sealed, opaque box that holds the writing and translates all of it, including the missing parts. Experts now agree the translation matches the symbol pattern and also explains previously unexplained artifacts. All agree the translation is correct. This would give a situation which is not clairvoyance (because we postulate that no translation exists) and which is not precognition (because experts agreed that no translation could be made in the future) and which therefore is to be described as a different operation: retrocognition. So far as I know, the method has never been used. My suggestion is therefore only that retrocognition is a potentially useful term, which can properly be retained as a possible topic for study.

In summary, operational definitions of subclasses of psi show that they are distinguishable and therefore meaningful.

Psychological Reasons

Most subjects in psi experiments are more comfortable with one procedure than with some other. Usually GESP is preferred to clairvoyance, and either is preferred to precognition or PK. But there are marked individual differences in these subjective reactions. With GESP, subjects are ordinarily comfortable when the agent is someone they trust and like or love, but are likely to feel strong reserve or desire for avoidance with an agent they distrust or dislike.

Precognition can arouse eager interest in those like the dynamic executives described by Dean et al. (Chapter 6) who hope to find they have a precognitive ability that will help their work; but a precognitive procedure can arouse abhorrence in someone like Meseguer (1959), a Jesuit, who believes that telepathy is a natural ability which is interesting to explore but that foretelling the future is prophecy and is forbidden to all except the prophets to whom God gave this gift.

Some subjects who eagerly accept telepathy think that clairvoyance is impossible; others find a clairvoyant task attractive but recoil from telepathic influence; PK fascinates some but frightens others and seems absurd to many. In short, subjects react differently to the different methods, and their attitudes can lie anywhere on the continuum from strong, emotionally toned eagerness, through mild interest and mild dislike, to strong, emotionally toned dislike. And as we have seen in Chapter 6 and elsewhere, there is a good deal of evidence that such attitudes can influence psi responses.

The same considerations often apply to other participants in the research. We experimenters may also have different feelings about different methods. I well remember one of the times that this was true of me. I was testing for precognitive clairvoyance, which seemed to me to have exciting implications. For a third of the calls, a computer would select the targets and score the responses; the targets would never be known to anyone. When I knew subjects were going to make those calls I felt—and may have conveyed—more eagerness than when they called the other precognitive targets that they or I would later see. Scores for precognitive clairvoyance were high. In a later series I was blind to which responses were which; the zest was gone; and the overall scores were low (Schmeidler, 1964a). I have wondered ever since whether the change in me might have influenced the scores.

Other experimenters, surely, sometimes feel more enthusiasm with one or another procedure, and the data from Chapter 5 indicate strongly that changes in experimenter attitude can relate to changes in subjects' scores.

From the psychological point of view, therefore, the particular operation used to study psi can be an important determinant of the attitudes of the participants. The operation therefore needs to be specified. It would of course also be highly desirable to build into the procedure a direct measure of those attitudes, so as to give firmer ground for inference about what was going on.

Empirical Reasons

Do the data show different outcomes for different subclasses of psi? Some early suggestions of such differences have not been supported, but other suggestions deserve attention. I list four, two for differences between precognition and contemporary ESP, and two for differences between ESP and PK.

One difference comes to us from collections of spontaneous cases. They repeatedly show that precognitive impressions occur more often in dreams than while awake, but that the opposite is true for psi impressions of contemporary events. (See West, 1948, for cases that were carefully investigated, and L.E. Rhine, 1981, for an analysis of thousands of unvalidated cases.)

Does this mean that precognition differs from contemporary psi, and that some process in sleeping or dreaming is conducive to precognition? It may, but it can also be explained away in two common sense ways. One is that most contemporary events occur during the usual waking hours; this explains why contemporary impressions are more frequent while awake than asleep. The other is that our learned, rational distrust of precognition can prevent our being aware of precognitive impressions while awake. Dreams are irrational and permit such impressions more readily.

Tart (1983) reports another difference. Because he wanted to learn what ESP method gave maximal success as measured by bits per trial, he reviewed prior reports. He confined his review to those fairly recent articles in three parapsychological journals which reported significant results as a main effect. Of these reports, 53 tested GESP or clairvoyance and 32 tested precognition. Mean success was significantly greater for the clairvoyance or GESP reports than for the precognitive ones.

He suggests three interpretations: that our cultural preconceptions make precognition seem harder and thus result in a less favorable attitude toward it; that the process or mechanism of present-time ESP is different from that of precognition; and "that external reality itself is strongly different for the present moment and for any future moments." The first of these has considerable support, but a priori, the others are also possible.

One possible difference between ESP and PK was mentioned in Chapter 8. W.G. Braud (1985) found strong evidence both in his own and in others' research that relaxation and moderately low autonomic arousal were ESP-conducive. When he examined reports of gifted PK subjects, however, he collated many descriptions of high autonomic arousal when their PK was effective. He holds open the possibility that this may show a difference in processing between PK and ESP.

Another possible difference between PK and ESP is the "linger effect," sometimes called a "release of effort effect." Chapter 12 described it after PK attempts to help mice recover from anesthesia. Mattuck (1977), a physicist, gives another example. He was testing a subject reputed to be gifted, and asked her to increase the temperature registered by a thermometer. At the end of her effort he carefully recorded the new reading, which did indeed show an increase, then set the thermometer aside (far from a source of heat or any possibility of tampering) while they continued with other tests. After these he looked again at the thermometer and found its temperature had risen further during the interval.

Other experimenters using other procedures have also reported such linger effects. For one example, Palmer & Kramer (1984) used an RNG. They recorded its output both during the test period while subjects tried to use PK to influence it and during the next period, after the subjects had stopped trying. Scores were significantly high in the prescribed direction for the posttest period, and this seems especially interesting because test scores were null.

The many indirect replications provide strong evidence for a linger effect in PK, but it has not been reported for ESP. Can this mean that the PK process, whatever it is, continues or even grows in strength once it has begun, but that the ESP process does not? As things stand now, the question cannot be answered because no one has looked for the linger effect in ESP. Like Braud's suggestion of a difference in optimal autonomic arousal, it is a candidate for a difference in processing between ESP and PK.

Summary of Reasons

The subclasses of psi are different operationally. They appear different to many participants in research and therefore induce different attitudes; thus their psychological effects can influence research outcomes. There is some evidence that they produce different results or are processed differently. For all these reasons, terms which identify the subclasses of psi should be retained.

REASONS FOR GROUPING THE CLASSES OF PSI

Grouping Subclasses of ESP

Should ESP be used as a blanket term for telepathy and clairvoyance, precognition and retrocognition? Should we consider all of them the same process, though they are tested by different operations?

J.B. Rhine (1934) began to think so when he changed from a GESP to a clairvoyance procedure and saw no change in his subjects' high scores. Since then, many other experimenters have shifted from one category of psi to another, either for their own convenience or to suit their subjects' preferences. In general (when allowance is made for difference in attitude) they have found that an indirect replication with a different subclass of psi gave results comparable to a direct replication with the same subclass. This suggests that it is appropriate to group the subclasses indiscriminately as if all were equivalent.

Do the two examples of differences between precognitive and present-time responses forbid the grouping? Not necessarily. Each can be explained by our (waking) tendency to think precognition is impossible or difficult or morally wrong. The parsimonious interpretation of what differences were found is that they are due to differences in attitude.

In short, both the overall results of laboratory work and the principle of parsimony argue that the various ESP subclasses represent the same process, even though we use different operations when we test for them. Therefore ESP is an appropriate general term.

Grouping ESP and PK

For psi, the questions are parallel to those for ESP. Is psi an appropriate blanket term for ESP and PK? Should we consider them the same process though they are tested by different operations?

Intuitively, they seem opposite rather than the same. In ESP we learn something; in PK we do something. Some years ago parapsychologists used to emphasize the contrast by writing that in ESP, information came to an individual; in PK, an individual imposed a new order (i.e., imposed new information) upon a random process. Historically, too, the distinction was made long before J.B. Rhine gave us the terms ESP and PK. When psychics were studied, they were classed as either mental mediums who seemed to describe facts not normally known to them, or else as physical mediums who seemed to produce effects like levitation. Hauntings were mental; poltergeists were physical.

But there have always been ambiguities and a blurring of the mental-physical boundary. The ghostly apparitions of a haunting are sometimes accompanied by poltergeist effects. And it is not uncommon in a spontaneous case to be told that, just when some member of a family was in a serious accident, someone else had a feeling of grief or danger and also an object fell or broke without apparent cause.

Another source of ambiguity comes from the fact that several psychics show both physical and mental abilities. Here are three examples. Matthew Manning, who when he was a child seemed to produce poltergeist effects, has as an adult repeatedly produced significant scores in both PK and ESP (see, e.g., Gregory, 1982). B.D. had in social situations shown remarkable spontaneous ESP, and in the laboratory under well controlled conditions made significant scores at PK as well as at ESP (Kelly & Kanthamani, 1972). Mrs. Garrett, an intelligent and critical observer as well as an extraordinarily gifted psychic, reports that as a child she found herself producing PK effects and that only training and self-discipline taught her to eliminate them (Healy, 1986).

These examples argue against making a distinction between mental and physical psi, but someone who wants to maintain the distinction could brush away all of them. Any spontaneous case of both ESP and PK could be dismissed as only coincidence. Reports of haunting with poltergeist effects could be dismissed as unverified, or else one set of reports could be attributed to self-suggestion. That some psychics show both mental and physical effects could be explained away as due to some general trait of personality that facilitated two diverse abilities, just as a creative person might be good at both painting and poetry.

But other findings are not easy to dismiss. I will add four examples that seem to show concurrent ESP and PK, then return to the theory that treats

ESP and PK as one, and then cite recent research which tends to support the theory.

Two of the examples come from Ingo Swann. The first occurred when I was testing him to find if he could change the temperature of a distant thermistor (Schmeidler, 1973). After he worked with an unshielded thermistor, I asked him to change the temperature of one that was carefully shielded in a thermos bottle. He asked where in the thermos it was, but I did not know. He said he would "probe for it," i.e., use ESP to locate it. I therefore delayed testing, and we sat quietly while he probed—until L. Lewis, who was monitoring the temperature recordings, burst into the room to find out what had been going on. The record of temperature in the thermos, instead of staying level, had suddenly shown a large decrease. Its striking change in output coincided with Swann's ESP attempt to find the thermistor's location.

A few months later, in another laboratory, Swann was asked to change the readings from a well shielded and carefully tested magnetometer which was producing a regular curve (Targ & Puthoff, 1977). He asked where the magnetometer was, and was told to use his ESP to find out. Just when he succeeded in locating it by ESP, the frequency of oscillations doubled. The change in recordings was unheard of, and did not recur after Swann left the laboratory.

The third example comes from Ted Serios, who used PK to change pictures taken by either ordinary or video cameras. He was asked to reproduce a hidden picture, i.e., an ESP target. The ensuing pictures, strikingly different from the pictures that the camera would normally have taken, showed a strong resemblance to the ESP target (Eisenbud, 1967).

A fourth example comes from Alex Tanous. Osis & McCormick (1980) used apparatus which displayed a target so that a person could see it correctly from a particular position but would see it incorrectly from any other. Tanous was asked to go "out of the body" to the distant target, position himself in the correct place, and report what he saw. Unknown to him, a photoelectric cell monitored changes at the place from which the target would be viewed correctly. The photoelectric records showed a significant change when there was ESP success, indicating a tendency for physical change near the target to accompany ESP.

The examples suggest that ESP and PK are intrinsically related, though four cases are obviously too few for a firm conclusion. Let us consider the possibility. Theoretical support comes from some physicists (Chapter 14) who take PK and ESP to be the same process. And if information from ESP is integrally related to a change by PK, this seems to have an analogy at the quantum level. Quantum theory says that gaining information from a system perturbs the system.

Also weigh three opposing arguments: (1) That last inference about psi from quantum theory is weak; it is only an analogy. (This is surely true.) (2)

Quantum events are a far cry from the massive PK that is sometimes found. (Yes, but Mattuck [1982] extended Walker's quantum theory to fairly large PK changes, so the gap has lessened.) (3) Even if ESP and PK both cause physical change, they may do it in different ways. (This is unparsimonious and therefore unattractive.)

On balance, the theory of an intrinsic ESP-PK relation still seems worth considering, and recent research has given results in line with it. Reports from China described gifted subjects with extraordinarily accurate and frequent ESP responses (Chinese Academy of Sciences, 1982). Next to the targets of those subjects were sensitive instruments, capable of registering small physical changes. Successes at ESP were accompanied by changes in the instruments; failures at ESP were not. The investigators reported a variety of these physical effects. X-ray or photographic film clouded, and there were changes in the recordings of photoelectric tubes, thermoluminescence dosimeters, and biological detectors.

Following these reports, Hubbard, May & Puthoff (1986) tested for the clearest of the effects: increase in large amplitude bursts registered by a photomultiplier close to the target. They performed an indirect replication with four psychics, and computed the correlation of ESP scores not only with increase in those high amplitude pulses but also with three other sets of data (decrease in high amplitude pulses and low amplitude increase and decrease). Correlations with the other three measures were null, but the correlation between ESP scores and increase in high amplitude pulses was significant. Thus their findings replicated a finding in the Chinese report.

Summary

Recent experiments indicate that ESP and PK are integrally associated, and thus imply that psi is a unitary process. Support comes from some earlier laboratory research, some spontaneous cases and field investigations, and the abilities of some psychics. The theory is not inconsistent with some extrapolations from quantum theory.

Problems to Be Faced If PK and ESP Are Unitary

If empirical findings, or quantum theory, or both have persuaded us to accept as a working hypothesis that PK and ESP represent a unitary process, we have problems to solve. I begin with a list of six of the problems raised by research reports and my attempt to find answers for them.

(1) Why do ESP and PK apparently occur separately in the laboratory? An answer is easy for ESP. The apparent problem may be due only to our

ignorance. We do not know if ESP is accompanied by physical changes at or near the target because, except for the few studies that were cited above, no one has looked for those PK changes.

The answer is harder for PK. If ESP and PK are associated, we might expect that when PK is effective there will be awareness of it, yet ordinarily statements of confidence show only erratic correspondence to PK success. Does a subject's mood or orientation or response set, in successful PK, prevent responding to ESP? I return to this possibility later.

(2) Why do relatively few spontaneous cases report both ESP and PK? Here (perhaps because we know even less) post hoc explanations seem reasonably plausible. In spontaneous cases of ESP, those at the target site do not know that ESP occurred and obviously have not set up instruments to measure small physical changes. For PK in poltergeist cases, the person who seems responsible usually has strong emotional investment in denying responsibility and thus might suppress or repress whatever ESP occurred.

(3) Why do some gifted subjects who have been carefully tested apparently show either ESP or PK but not both? Here, again because we are ignorant, it seems plausible to suggest that they find one ability gratifying and try to use it, but find the other alien and choose not to use it.

(4) What of Braud's persuasive proposal that autonomic arousal is PK-conducive while relaxation is ESP-conducive? There are counterexamples. One is that Swann gives every appearance of quietude during a successful PK trial. Other counterexamples come from the occasional reports of striking ESP success while a subject is strongly aroused, e.g. while being filmed for television. In any event, the proposal is so recent that no research has tested it, and thus we are not yet obliged to give it much weight.

Let us suppose that research supports Braud's statement as a general proposition which admits of some exceptions. If so, two psychological explanations may account for it, so that it need not imply a physical difference between PK and ESP. One was proposed by Braud: the arousal may be a ritual that induces the right frame of mind. The other supplements this one; it involves the limitations of our attention.

Ordinarily attention has only a single focus. If I try to proofread a text for typographical errors but find myself thinking about the ideas in the text, I miss many of the typos. If I look at the ocean and attend to the shimmering play of colors on its surface, I am only vaguely and peripherally aware of the ripple patterns; if I try to analyze the intersecting ripples I barely notice the colors. And consider how this limitation of attention might affect someone who thinks that PK involves actively doing something but that ESP is passive. The person tries to produce an excited, active body state for PK and then, because attention is on the PK pattern, does not become aware of ESP.

(5) Does the linger effect show a difference between the two processes? Until there has been research to find if a linger effect occurs in ESP, we cannot

say. We can even, if we stretch, find a scrap of information here and there which indicates that for ESP too, more accurate information is reported after the formal inquiry has ended. I will give one example.

It comes from Mrs. Piper, the oustanding mental medium who was intensively investigated after William James brought her to the attention of those in psychical research. She would go into trance, and in trance often gave remarkably accurate information, which she could not have normally known. After a time the flow of information would diminish and she would, fairly slowly, come out of trance. Sometimes while in this "waking stage," when the sitting was formally ended, she would unexpectedly make further comments. When she did, what she said in that post-trance, waking stage was likely to be spectacularly accurate, the best part of the sitting. It was as if her ESP had lingered.

(6) Another potential problem arises from details of PK-ESP research. Chinese data were not published in a form that permits careful study, but we can look at the data from Osis & McCormick (1980); and Hubbard, May, & Puthoff (1986) have also made their data available. Both sets show that although there is a statistically significant relation between ESP success and physical change, there is no one-to-one correspondence between them. This would seem an anomaly to an old-fashioned determinist.

Perhaps, however, it is no problem to quantum mechanics, which deals with probabilities. Parts of some quantum theories of psi also deny the need of one-to-one relationships. An example is their requirement of feedback, where both Schmidt and Walker consider that feedback about the particular target is unnecessary and that a vague or statistical statement about overall success can be sufficient feedback. The inexact, statistical relation between ESP success and physical change may therefore satisfy the requirements of quantum theory.

Should we therefore conclude that PK and ESP are intrinsically the same process? These six empirical difficulties in considering that psi is unitary do not seem insuperable. The hypothesis that it is unitary is parsimonious, and parsimony of hypotheses is always desirable. It seems to me that we should accept the unity of ESP and PK tentatively, as a working hypothesis, and hold it unless further research disconfirms it or (as seems likely) shows it must be modified.

But aside from the narrow, research-oriented questions that were just raised, the hypothesis gives rise to broader and more troublesome questions. Here are some of them.

Should time be considered a dimension that is equivalent to a spatial dimension? Are temporal direction and distance as irrelevant to psi as spatial direction and distance seem to be? If so, retrocognition is equivalent to precognition, and PK can change past events as it changes present or future ones. Those would be radical conclusions.

Or alternatively, were Donald & Martin (Chapter 14) on the right track when they suggested that in our universe, now, time usually moves forward? If so, when and why do the exceptions occur?

Will quantum theory ever be able to account for the well validated instances of massive PK? Until it does, it is not a fully adequate guide for understanding psi.

Does the sender in telepathy exert a force (or help to create a field) that, by PK, directly affects the percipient's body and responses? Such a force or field seems implied by the theory that PK and ESP are unitary and is suggested by Murphy (pages 55–56) and by some data. If so, what are the implications for psychic healing and psychic hurting? Further, if there is such a force or field, how should we evaluate the frequent claims (usually but not exclusively made by psychotics) that someone else is forcing them, by telepathy, to think and act in particular ways? Ordinarily, all such claims are dismissed as delusions. Must we now consider the possibility that some are valid?

And if there is such a force, is there also some shielding against it?

Summary

Parsimony of hypotheses argues for subsuming ESP and PK under the rubric of psi. Quantum theories describe ESP and PK as the same process. Some data support this contention. No data unequivocally contradict it. We should therefore consider PK and ESP to be a single process until new data demonstrate a difference between them.

OVERVIEW

Some recent research and some earlier findings indicate that PK and ESP are associated or even integrally related. A general review of PK and the subclasses of ESP suggests two directives. For theoretical purposes our working hypothesis should be the parsimonious one that psi is unitary and there are no intrinsic differences among the subclasses of ESP or between ESP and PK. For practical purposes, while conducting research, we must treat the subclasses of psi as separate.

16. Psi and the Self

In ESP, incoming information somehow bypasses shielding or distance. In PK, what we do somehow bypasses the muscles and other effectors. When we use psi we apparently transcend the limitations of the body. With psi we make contact with events that are distant in time and space, and we thus apparently transcend physical limitations. What are we, who have these abilities?

This chapter discusses only one of the theories that address the question. The theory is that each of us has a spirit or soul or inner self with different properties from the body's, and the theory is often extended to state that this inner self will continue to exist after the body's death or has existed before conception. The theory has been indirectly and partially examined by psychologists when they study the self, and its extensions have been examined by parapsychologists (who usually use the term spirit). Although soul, spirit, and self have different connotations, I will treat them as synonyms.

The theory that each of us is a self or has a spirit or a soul may sound simple and straightforward, but it gives rise to many problems. In this inappropriately short chapter I mention some of the problems and survey some of the attempts to find answers.

Some of the Problems

If each of us has a soul—one unitary soul—it should show itself in consistent ways during the life span. Is there evidence for such a consistent self? Psychologists have repeatedly looked for the evidence but there is no consensus that it was found.

A typical research method is to identify the psychological characteristics of a number of subjects at one age; to make a similar (blind) attempt when the subjects have reached some later age; then try to match the two sets. But again and again the matching is correct only for some of the subjects or for short time intervals. Often, especially with drastic changes in a person's life due to a disfiguring accident, a family break-up, etc., the person shows marked differences between infancy and childhood, between childhood and adolescence, between adolescence and maturity. This does not support the theory of a soul's continuity.

Does it disprove the theory? No; like any other theory, this one can be made so flexible that it is impossible to disprove. It needs, I think, only two further postulates. One is that the soul changes and grows; it is not static. The other is that the way the inner self shows itself is constrained by body and perhaps other processes, and of course by the environment. A critic can then argue that psychologists are misled by the growth changes and the constraints. The specifics which psychologists measured were only superficial, not the true, important, deeper ones, and this explains the failure to make correct matches. Thus with two extra assumptions we can continue to defend the thesis that each of us has a unitary self or soul.

Where does this leave the theory? What data we have permit us to hold it but give little support to it. If we stay with it we should try to think through what its mismatch with the data implies. Can we account for the anomalies? Can we specify when and under what conditions the earlier manifestations of a unitary self will differ from later manifestations? Which particular changes are predictable as part of the growth process? Can we identify which kinds of behavior are irrelevant to the theory so that they can legitimately be disregarded? They are not easy questions yet they need to be answered before the theory of a unitary self is on firmer ground.

Parapsychology raises further questions. If we take seriously the thesis that a self or soul shows by its use of psi that it transcends body functions, we must ask how psi ability originated. One possible answer is that it was produced by some stage of body development, but this leads to other hard questions. How and when and where did abilities that transcend bodily ones originate in the body?

If we reject this explanation of how the self began, the alternative is that it had some independent or prior source—but this raises a whole new set of questions. When and how did it enter the body? How does this self, which is capable of psi, interact with the body? Is it separable from the living body? What happens to it when the body dies? Does it too die, or does it continue? If it continues, does it change still further, and does it have a different set of constraints?

RESEARCH TOPICS AND ISSUES OF EVALUATION

Parapsychologists, and some research workers in other disciplines, have tried to collect data that bear on a few of the problems in the preceding unit. Three proposals they examined will be discussed briefly here: that the self can be at a place distant from the living body, that the self survives death, and that the self existed before conception.

For each proposal, it has been claimed that research demonstrates it is true. The same issues therefore arise as in any other type of research: whether there are possible sources of error, and whether the results of carefully conducted work can properly be dismissed as due only to chance.

But when evidence is well validated and seems extrachance, another issue arises: a new argument based on psi is used to refute the claims. The argument is called the super-ESP or super-psi hypothesis. It states that although evidence had been interpreted to mean a spirit or self was independent of the body, the evidence really shows only ESP and PK. It means nothing beyond those abilities.

The general problem, I think, boils down to three possibilities. One is that much of the apparent evidence is weak, and that the little that remains can be attributed to chance. (On some topics, in my opinion, this possibility must be discarded.) Another possibility is that the super-psi hypothesis can account for all the findings. The third is that the evidence is convincing: it goes so far beyond what ESP and PK have been shown to do that the super-psi hypothesis demands too many ad hoc assumptions and is implausible.

It is a paradoxical situation. The better the evidence for the effectiveness of PK and ESP, the weaker the argument for a spirit that separates from the body.

What follows is a quick rundown of some lines of research that bear on the topics. None is a full, adequate statement, but they give samples of the findings and of the arguments that make some thoughful persons accept the super-psi hypothesis but make others reject its adequacy.

Out of Body Experiences

The experience that one's consciousness, one's self, is located somewhere outside one's own body is fairly common in some cultures and among some groups (perhaps especially those that practice meditation) but is rare in others. This implies that the experience is partly dependent on one's readiness for it (Schmeidler, 1983b). Most psychiatrists consider the experience a symptom of psychosis. Parapsychologists test for evidence that the claims are valid, and while some conclude that the self can indeed temporarily separate from the body (see Mitchell, 1981) others explain the experience as a special combination of memory and imagination, i.e., as a type of fantasy (Blackmore, 1986).

What kind of evidence is there? Some comes from spontaneous cases. The most famous dates from the days before there was a transatlantic cable;

it was reported by a woman whose husband had gone overseas. She did not know when he would return home; she worried about his safety. One night she had a vivid experience: that she was in a ship's cabin and saw her sleeping husband in a lower bunk and a strange man in the upper one. In fact, her husband was asleep on a ship that night, and was in a lower bunk while a man the wife did not know was in the upper bunk. But now comes the striking part of the case. On what seems to have been the same night that the woman felt she was in the cabin, the man whose bunk was above her husband's was shocked to see a woman in her nightdress walk through the cabin, caress the man in the lower bunk, and then disappear (Myers, 1903).

There are other spontaneous cases of this type, some well attested, but any particular case can be attacked on various grounds. There has also been formal research on out of body experiences. Most of the research begins by finding some subject who claims to be able to go out of the body at will, then uses one of three methods, or a combination of them. The most common method is to ask the subject to go to some distant target's location and report on the target—but this is equivalent to the operation for clairvoyance or GESP. Another is to see if the person can produce an effect at some distant place—but this is the operation for PK, and PK can be effective at a distance. A third is to measure the EEG of a person who is succeeding at either of the first two methods.

Statistically significant success with the first two methods has been obtained but can readily be explained by the super-psi hypothesis. It may be only common, garden variety ESP or PK, accompanied by a fantasy. Most EEG reports indicate that the brain state in out of body experiences is similar to that of meditation. Thus the formal research leaves us essentially where we began.

But qualitative accounts are sometimes distinctive. What seems the most striking to me is the occasional statement that when the "out of body" person is obtaining an accurate impression of a distant site, that person is also seen at the site. This has been reported in a few spontaneous cases and once during formal research, but never, so far as I know, in other psi tests with distant targets.

Accounts of such sightings are rare, and because they have never been formally investigated, we cannot rule out the possibility that the reports are due to suggestion. But suppose that well controlled research shows that such sightings occur, more often than expected by chance, in association with out of body experiences. Could the super-psi hypothesis explain them away? Yes, by making some additional, ad hoc assumption. It could assert, for example, that some subjects while obtaining an ESP impression can also by PK project a visual image of themselves in the area of the target. It may seem strained, but it is relatively parsimonious.

Near Death and Deathbed Experiences

Near Death Experiences

Some persons in coma, and some who were medically diagnosed as clinically dead, have been restored to life. A large proportion of them report that they had vivid experiences while apparently unconscious. The experiences they describe often include one or more common elements, such as going through a tunnel, hearing a sound, coming to a light, or contact with a glowing, loving, powerful presence. Occasionally a report also describes accurately events which occurred while the person seemed unconscious and which the person could not have normally known even if awake. When such evidence of ESP occurs it is embedded in a description of out of body travel. A person may say, "I found myself looking down from such and such a place, and saw. . . ." A question raised about the reports is whether they represent a foretaste of life after death. Greyson & Flynn (1984) give a partial review of the findings and a fuller review of various physiological and psychological interpretations.

Deathbed Experiences

Osis & Haraldsson (1977) summarize earlier accounts of deathbed experiences which either are mystical or seem to show paranormal knowledge. Their own research is based on deathbed reports from hundreds of doctors and nurses in the United States and in India, and includes many interesting findings. Here is one set that they (and I) consider especially striking. Patients sometimes report that a deity, or the spirit of a loved person who has already died, has come to take them away. This, of course, is readily explained as a fantasy due to wish fulfillment or cultural expectation. But there have been occasions when the messenger is identified as a relative who is believed by the family at the bedside to be still alive. When there were follow-ups of these apparently absurd statements by the dying persons, it was found that in fact the relatives had already died. This makes the statements sound as if the dying persons knew paranormally of their relatives' deaths. The dying persons seem to give no other evidence of psi. Does this imply that the relative's spirit has come to help in the transition of dying? Or does it show only that one kind of ESP, though not other kinds, occurs at the deathbed?

Evaluation

For both deathbed and near death experiences, a psi or super-psi theory can encompass the cases of paranormal information. Physiological and psychological ad hoc explanations have been offered for the frequent similarities among near death experiences, such as the tunnel, the sounds, the light. The many ad hoc interpretations are intellectually satisfying to some. To others, the convergent reports imply that the experiences are valid.

SURVIVAL AFTER DEATH

Gauld (1982) gives a thorough, thoughtful, critical survey of the traditional lines of research on whether a self or spirit survives death. There are many of these lines; I will mention five that are cited by Gauld.

Sittings with Psychics

Some psychics, especially in trance, accurately report information that they did not know but that was known by a dead person. In what seems to me the most remarkable of those cases (Thomas, 1935), a "blind" note-taker asked a medium, Mrs. Leonard, about a little boy who had recently died. Notes from a series of sittings were mailed to the child's grandfather, who reported that many items were correct. The grandfather then asked the cause of the child's death. Mrs. Leonard said he had drunk polluted water from three springs on a nearby hill. The grandfather checked with the boy's friends and learned that the boy had played on a hill which matched Mrs. Leonard's detailed description. He searched for three springs on the hill, found them, and asked the local inspector to test the water. The tests showed the water was polluted.

It has also been sometimes asserted that the psychic's voice, gestures, phrasing, etc., are characteristic of the dead person rather than of the psychic. The only confirmation here is the subjective impression of the sitter, and thus the assertions can be attributed to suggestion.

Cross-Correspondences

A subject of special interest, called cross-correspondences, was found when workers at a central office compiled reports from a number of psychics (in England, India, the United States), e.g. when messages purporting to come from a dead scholar said he was preparing a test. Later messages, purportedly from the same person, were found to have odd fragmentary bits, a name here, an irrelevant comment there, meaningless in themselves, which intruded into coherent (and often nonevidential) passages. Intrusive items from different psychics were sometimes the same or similar (e.g. a word in

Greek, Latin, or English). When put together, the intrusions added up to a meaningful composite, consistent with the possibility of a spirit that was purposively giving each psychic an incomplete message.

Spontaneous Cases and Hauntings

A large number of cases tell of a ghost or apparition in a particular location that was described similarly at different times by independent witnesses, sometimes with statistically significant similarity between reports made under double blind conditions. Reports of nonrecurrent apparitions can also be impressive, especially when the apparition gives correct information that is apparently known to no living person, or else when a time coincidence is clear. An example of the latter comes from a pilot who reported that one afternoon, between 3:15 and 3:30 p.m., he saw and heard a friend, also a pilot, enter their quarters with his usual breezy greeting. He looked for his friend a little later, did not find him, and in the evening learned that the friend had died in an air crash that afternoon, and the friend's watch had stopped at 3:25 (Sidgwick, 1922).

Drop-in Communicators

A group will sometimes hold sittings in the hope that spirits of the dead will send them messages through table rappings or through a ouija board, planchette, or similar device. Occasionally the messages that are spelled out will include sufficient identification to permit checking. In several such instances the check has shown all or almost all of the information to be correct but not to have been known by any member of the group that received it. A case of this type is especially impressive when it takes considerable effort to track down sources which verified the information, and when the dead person had not been known by anyone in the group (Gauld, 1971).

Codes

Ingenious methods have been developed for preparing apparently unbreakable codes, which either translate a piece of writing or provide the key to a particular lock. A person prepares the code, tells it to no one, and promises that if he or she survives death, information about the code will be provided. None has yet been solved.

Evaluation

Case after case, from all these lines of investigation except codes, has been claimed to give such accurate information as to prove that a dead person's spirit has survived. Critical examination permits assigning many of the claims to mistaken memory, suggestion, and other normal causes. After all those cases are discarded, other cases remain. So many are well investigated and well verified that their number seems too large to attribute to a series of coincidences.

But for each of these cases, the super-psi hypothesis can be modified to explain it away. For the cross-correspondences, an interpretation could be that all the psychics were in unconscious telepathic communication with each other and arranged that there be both overlapping and nonoverlapping information. For drop-in communicators or the breaking of a code if one is broken, the argument could be that while the key person was alive, one or more psychics learned the relevant information by GESP, but reported it only after the person's death. As for the pilot's apparent apparition: an argument here could be that his friend learned by ESP of the pilot's death, repressed the knowledge, and demonstrated the Freudian defense of denial by hallucinating that the pilot was still alive.

Any single case, and some broad categories of cases, can be explained by making enough assumptions about psi ability. To explain all the well attested cases demands many such assumptions. There is no guide except one's judgment about whether the accumulated weight of all those assumptions about psi is more than the super-psi hypothesis can tolerate.

REINCARNATION

Head & Cranston (1977) survey writings on reincarnation from other cultures and our own. Stevenson (e.g., 1987) has investigated many cases where, typically, a child claims to be a person who has already died. His reports give scrupulous detail about the conditions of the investigation and itemize both the findings that support the claim of a past life and those that cast doubt on the claim.

Many of the cases are impressive, especially when Stevenson interviewed the child and those associated with the child before there was any attempt to verify the child's claims, then was himself present when the child was brought to a distant place where the dead person had lived. Often it was found that the child had stated correctly many of the names of those associated with the dead person, and was correct in describing not only relationships among them, but also unusual details of behavior, likes and dislikes, possessions, etc. Occasionally there was an especially striking incident, as when the child found, when requested, valuables which the dead person had secreted and for which the family had searched in vain. Many reports describe birthmarks on the child's body that correspond to scars or other malformations which the dead person was known to have. Stevenson puts special weight on the occasional examples of a living person's showing a skill that could not have normally been acquired but that the dead person possessed, such as understanding and speaking responsively in a language unknown to anyone in the claimant's family and circle of acquaintances.

But there are anomalies (or apparent anomalies) in the cases Stevenson reports. I give three examples, and take them to mean that anyone who defends the theory of reincarnation must either question the validity of these cases (and thus, by inference, the validity of other cases) or else must develop an elaborate rather than a simple theory of how reincarnation occurs. In one case that seems well supported, a child claimed to be a person whose death occurred after the child was alive. Another case describes a child's "remembering" many names and facts that fit exactly the life of a young man who had died fairly recently, but other names and facts that fit only the life of a cousin of the first man, who had died at about the same time. A third anomaly is the clear difference among cases from different cultures, for example that in some societies all cases are same-sex while in others many are cross-sex.

Critical examination can, of course, dismiss the cases that Stevenson considers weak. It can weight differently the ratio of matches to mismatches in some cases, then dismiss them too. It can appeal to statistics to dismiss some of the strongest cases as only what would be expected by chance when many claims are examined. Even then, other cases remain.

Can the super-psi hypothesis cope with them? Yes, of course. It can postulate freely; there are dozens of scenarios it can write. Take the birthmark cases, for example. The super-psi hypothesis might resort to some argument along these lines. If a child is troubled by a birthmark, the child may use retrocognition to learn about the life of someone with a similar body mark, then weave retrocognitive information into a fantasy of being that other person. Alternatively, explanations may posit PK as causing the birthmark, associated with some retrocognitive ESP. The explanations may seem implausible because they demand psi ability far stronger than what we know, but they are not atypical of the way the super-psi hypothesis is applied.

Overview

Many difficult questions arise from the theory that each of us is a unitary self during the life span, or that each of us has a unitary soul or spirit. The theory has little research support and is difficult but not impossible to defend.

There is controversy about whether a soul or spirit exists independently of a person's body. Many lines of research provide evidence that supports such independent existence. After the weak evidence is set aside, a substantial amount remains which is well validated and strong. Some interpret this evidence as conclusive, but others use ad hoc arguments to explain away each part of it. One group of these arguments, called collectively the super-psi hypothesis, dismisses each case as merely a demonstration of some exceptionally strong and perhaps hitherto unknown form of ESP or PK.

17. General Overview

How should we appraise parapsychology? This chapter makes an attempt to see it in historical perspective. The first unit comments on one issue that is typical of problems confronting new sciences; the next unit argues, briefly, that parapsychology meets the criteria for a science. The other two units discuss, first for the theory that this book examined and then for parapsychology as a whole, how far each falls short of what might eventually be achieved.

Historical Context

We know, of course, that philosophy used to encompass all the areas now classed as sciences. Over the years new methods of inquiry developed, using better instruments, more rigorous controls, finer quantitative statements of the findings. Although basic questions like the First Cause or the intrinsic nature of life were left unanswered, much was learned by applying the new methods. When, as occurred in one domain after another, what was learned became a large and coherent body of knowledge, the domain acquired a separate identity. It broke off from philosophy; it became a new science.

But often, even typically, the new science met opposition. Some who were recognized as authorities in an established discipline resisted accepting it. They derogated the new findings. They defended their territory by attacking the basic claim for a new field. A recent example comes from the mid-19th century, when respected philosophers argued that there could never be a science of psychology. It was impossible a priori. Why? For one obvious reason. Psychology claimed to be a science of the mind, yet it was inherently impossible for the mind to examine itself.

This may sound quaint to us now, but some contemporary criticisms of parapsychology are closely parallel. Many who are respected as authorities in their own fields, in physics or philosophy or neurology, use an a priori argument to oppose parapsychology's claim to be a new science. They tell us that ESP and PK are inherently impossible. Both ESP and PK violate known truths and therefore cannot occur. Precognition is often cited as a notorious example. The data show a correspondence between responses and future events, even if the future events are random and thus could not be inferred. The critics take this correspondence as a claim that the responses were caused by future events. They then deny that claim because it violates the Law that a cause must precede its effect.

There is, I think, only one suitable response to this type of argument against the legitimacy of a new science. The appropriate response is to ignore it. Patient parapsychologists must do what patient psychologists did: use carefully controlled methods of investigation, find what the facts are, and when the facts contradict old generalizations, let the facts speak for themselves.

Parapsychology as a Science

The facts—the well replicated, affirmative findings—sometimes speak loudly. One example of the things they say is that scientific research has whittled still another area out of philosophy: the classical problem of the relation of mind to matter. Up to now, inquiries about the mind-matter relation belonged in metaphysics, a part of philosophy. Philosophers proposed and defended many theories about it: that there is evidence for mind but not for matter; that there is evidence for matter but not for mind; that mind and matter interact; that mind and matter are parallel and independent, like two clocks that tell the same time; that mind is only an epiphenomenon of matter, and so on.

But now we have new methods of investigating the question. Although the basic issue of how mind relates to matter is left unanswered, we have some new facts. Consider one example. Random number generator research, from 1969 on, has examined records of random events to find if changes in those records corresponded to changes in an experimenter's instructions. The records are of physical events, e.g. changes in the rate of radioactive emissions. The instructions (at a minimum) represent mental changes in the experimenter, and they often produce mental changes in the subject. Research into RNGs thus brings mind-matter relations into the laboratory. Its method of testing is tight, because the random events that activate an RNG cannot be influenced by body activity and because all records are automatic. A good deal of research with this method accumulated over the next 15 years.

Radin, May, & Thomson (1986) used meta-analysis to evaluate one body of the RNG data. They examined RNG research with binary targets from 1969 to 1984, and found 73 reports, describing 332 experiments. They determined what allowance to make for a possible file drawer effect by a Monte Carlo simulation, which suggested there might have been 95 null experiments that had been left unpublished. Their meta-analysis added those 95 to the 332 published experiments, and tested the null hypothesis that all the results could be attributed to chance. Its outcome showed that the probability of having found such results by chance was less than one in ten raised to the 17th power, a probability that should lead any reasonable person to reject the null hypothesis and conclude that the results were extrachance. Other crosscuts of the findings (e.g., whether the affirmative findings came from only a few of the major investigators) showed no reason to question that the research had been carefully performed or that the results were due to any cause other then psi.

Here, then, is laboratory demonstration of a direct relation between the physical events of RNG recordings and the mental changes from the experimenter's instructions. What follows? Typical scientific questions. We ask, for example: Under what conditions are the effects stronger? Under what conditions are they weaker? What are the characteristics of the participants whose effects are stronger? are weaker? When the mind-matter relationship was part of metaphysics, it led to argument and more argument. Now that it has moved to the laboratory, we can hope that studying it will lead to more information.

(I add parenthetically that a related philosophical question, the relation of mind to brain, has no comparable findings from parapsychology. We can infer that if mental events relate to external physical changes they also relate to internal brain changes, but psi research gives no clear, well replicated data to support the inference.)

If parapsychology is to be a new science, it needs more than careful methods and well replicated results. One requirement is that it should have a coherent body of findings that lend themselves to theory. Some examples of its theories were given in chapters 6, 13, and 14. They show that parapsychology meets this requirement; theories of parapsychology abound.

Another frequently voiced demand for a new science is that its findings should relate to findings in established sciences. Many such relationships have been suggested. Some are broad, notably those from physicists like Walker, Schmidt, and Jahn (Chapter 14). Others are narrower: they suggest a relation to one or another specific in a different scientific field. An example (Chapter 10) is Ehrenwald's analysis of the similarity between drawings made as psi responses and drawings made by patients with brain lesions in the left parieto-occipital area. Another example comes from Persinger (1985) who examined tables of geomagnetic records in relation to psi, and collated evidence that psi is more effective when there is less disturbance in extremely low frequency electromagnetic waves. And still another example, of course, is evidence surveyed in this book which showed a close similarity, in some psychological areas, between psi data and prior findings in psychology.

By all these criteria, parapsychology is a new science. But it has reached only the first viewing point on the road toward what needs to be learned. The next unit discusses how much more is needed in the area I know best, the relation between psi and psychological findings, and the last unit briefly discusses the field as a whole.

The Theory That Psi Is a Psychological Process

Because the theory that psi is a psychological process has support from a number of psychological topics or subtopics, it seems to have made a beginning at putting the facts together. Because it has little or no support on other topics, and because there are still others that it entirely neglects, the theory obviously has a long way to go before it is adequate.

A revision of the theory was proposed in Chapter 13. For areas where the original broad version seemed supported (attitudes, personality, social relations, and their related physiological changes) and also for particular topics where it seemed to hold, such as figure-ground patterning and subliminal perception, the support needs further checking. If the affirmations hold up after those checks, they will then need to be extended and refined. If they do not hold up, the theory must be modified further. Apparent exceptions, especially relations to moods and values, should be reexamined to find if with better research design they too make a fit with the theory. If they do not fit even then, a further revision of the theory is demanded. For the topics within cognition where I reported no similarity between psi and psychological processing, the old data should be reexamined to look for patterns I failed to see, and of course new research should examine the topics further.

Suppose that this, or some later revision, makes a good match within the special area of relations to psychology. That would bring us only to one further stopping place on our road to knowledge, because psychology too has wide areas of ignorance. One that has especially troubled me is that we psychologists seldom can predict about individuals or about outstanding, exceptional events. An example is that though we know many of the correlates of creativity, we do not know when any artist will produce a masterpiece, nor do we know, from among thousands of potentially creative high school students, who will make remarkable creative achievements. The parallel in psi is that we know a fair amount about the subgroups of subjects who will make higher or lower psi scores in formal research, but this does not let us identify a gifted psychic, nor do we have even an inkling as to when there will be an instance of massive PK, or of the type of extraordinarily accurate ESP shown by the four subjects whom Rhine (1964) describes, with perfect scores on decks of 25 ESP cards.

It may be, of course, that such specificity is beyond our reach; that this will always be an area of ignorance. The goal of most psychological and parapsychological research is only the confirmation of some statistical prediction, and this is in tune with the times. Statistical predictions satisfy quantum physicists; their utility is shown by the earnings of insurance companies that use actuarial tables; they justify the use of standard psychological tests; and they show some lawfulness in parapsychological findings. But their own formulas tell us that a statistically based prediction will sometimes be in error, and they fail to pinpoint the cases that interest us most. Statistical confirmation tells us that our knowledge is moving forward. This is good; but dependence on statistical averages as opposed to specific predictions seems to me to imply that our contemporary scientific goals are not high enough.

Other Theories and Topics

My first general statement of a psychological theory, though it was too broad, was also far too narrow. It made no provision for a great deal of psi research, some of it well replicated, where psychological facts or theories seemed irrelevant. A few examples, the ones I could not resist mentioning in passing, are the linger effect (chapters 12 and 15), the low variance of psi scores in a depressed mood (Chapter 8), and the apparent double negative effect of two unfavorable conditions (chapters 5 and 11). If these or other patterns are distinctive to psi, they may become especially instructive in identifying the "para" of parapsychology. They need further research, of course, but also need some supplementary theory which should eventually become integrated with the psychological one.

We know too little, and need to know more, about many questions, for example about how psi relates to brain activity or to physical variables and physical theory. Further, because PK and ESP transcend known bodily limitations, they open questions that had seemed closed to scientific research (Chapter 16). Some are important questions, which ask about the possibility of conscious experience that is independent of the body. Research on these questions has as yet been primarily naturalistic rather than testing predictions from hypotheses, and it has not yielded answers with which all reasonable persons agree.

In summary, this book has examined critically one theory of psi. It found that a good many parts of the theory had strong research support. That partial support seems to demonstrate that parapsychologists have made a beginning at the work needed in a new science—but the inadequacies of the theory also demonstrate that there is much more work waiting to be done.

Glossary

ad hoc improvised for the occasion, e.g., an interpretation invented to explain some unexpected finding.

affect as a noun (af-fect), pleasantness or unpleasantness of mood.

analysis of variance a pretty statistical method for evaluating differences among means. It is especially useful when two or more types of conditions are examined. It can give a *p* for each type separately (the "main effect" of that condition) and also for the interactions between or among variables.

ANOVA analysis of variance.

arousal activity, especially emotional or autonomic activity.

attribution in psychology, assigning a meaning. Failure, for example, may be attributed to the difficulty of a task or to one's own habitual carelessness.

autonomic the part of the nervous system which controls the heart, digestive tract, sweat glands, etc., and ordinarily is not under conscious control. Autonomic activity is considered a measure of emotional level.

blind uninformed about the test condition.

call a single response for ESP or PK.

clairvoyance a psi procedure in which a target exists but no one knows it. Also used to designate the process which underlies psi information about contemporary objects or events.

cognitive control a way of organizing experience that has broad implications for many areas of behavior.

contamination the effect on response of some condition which the experimenter has not controlled or measured.

correction for selection allowance, in determining *p,* for multiple analyses of the data.

correlation a statistical measure of the orderly relation between variables. A positive correlation shows that when one increases, the other tends to increase. A negative correlation shows that when one goes up, the other tends to go down.

counterbalanced equalized by the experimental design, especially for the number of times that items are used, or for the order in which they appear.

criterion group a set of subjects who are known to share some characteristic.

debriefing at the end of a test, telling the subject about it and having the subject tell as much as possible about subjective reactions not previously expressed.

direct replication *see* **replication**

disconfirm disprove or tend to disprove, usually referring to data different from what a hypothesis predicted.

displacement a response to a target when the response was intended for some other target.

dissociation separation of some activities, memories, etc. from others. A major example is a case of multiple personality; a minor example is knitting while chatting.

double blind the term used when both subject and experimenter are uninformed about the condition being tested.

EEG the electroencephalograph, an instrument which records some brain changes.

ESP response to information which was not sensed or inferred. Extrasensory perception, or ESP, is one class of psi; the subclasses of ESP are clairvoyance, telepathy, precognition, and perhaps retrocognition. Sometimes "ESP" is used to designate the process which underlies an ESP response.

ESP card an object like a playing card, with one ESP symbol on it.

ESP symbols a circle, a plus, a square, a star, and a set of three parallel wavy lines.

extrasensory perception ESP.

falsify disconfirm.

field dependent having test scores that show the surround of a figure has a strong influence on one's perception of the figure. Its opposite is field independent. Field dependence/independence is considered a cognitive control.

file drawer effect apparent support for a hypothesis due to supportive findings' having been published while nonsupportive findings were unpublished (i.e., kept in the research worker's file drawer).

forced choice a procedure which restricts the subject's formal responses, e.g. to the five ESP symbols.

free response a procedure which asks for any impressions.

Ganzfeld in psi research, test conditions which include the subject's sitting alone, on a comfortable chair, wearing goggles which permit seeing only unpatterned light, and wearing earphones which feed in a meaningless sound.

GESP an ESP procedure in which a target exists and is known to someone. Also used to designate the process which underlies obtaining GESP information.

goat a subject who rejects all possibility of psi success under the research conditions (even if that possibility is accepted under other conditions). Sometimes defined more broadly, e.g. a subject who thinks psi is unlikely.

"good" subject a subject who guesses what the experimenter hopes, then tries to behave in conformity to that guess instead of trying to follow the instructions.

hit an ESP call which identifies the target, or a PK try accompanied by the target change which the experimenter requested.

hitting scoring above the level expected by chance.

indirect replication *see* **replication**

interaction the joint effect of two or more conditions.

kinesthesis sensory input from activity of the skeletal muscles.

labile changing readily, usually with frequent, smooth transitions. Labile is the opposite of stable.

linger effect a PK change after the PK subject has stopped attending to the target and trying to produce PK.

main effect *see* **analysis of variance**

mean the arithmetic average.

median split division of a group of scores so that half are below the middle and half above.

medium a psychic who purports to have contact with spirits.

meta-analysis a statistical method of evaluating support for a hypothesis on the basis of several replications.

miss failure to identify an ESP target or to produce an instructed PK change.

missing scoring below the level expected by chance.

multivariate examining more than one variable.

null hypothesis a statement of the chance results to be expected if the hypothesis is not valid.

one-tailed a *p* which evaluates the likelihood of only one direction of scoring (i.e., either high or low). It thus evaluates the data against only one "tail" of the distribution that is expected by chance. It is appropriately used when a hypothesis specifies the predicted direction of scoring and when scoring is, in fact, in that direction. A one-tailed $p = .05$ is the same as a two-tailed $p = .10$.

order effect change in response due to the sequence of test conditions or to the subject's prior responses.

p the likelihood that a given result would occur by chance. When *p* equals or is less than .05, it is called significant. Unless otherwise stated, *p* stands for a two-tailed *p*. See **one-tailed** and **two-tailed.**

paranormal due to ESP, PK, or some kindred process.

parapsychology the scientific study of psi and possible related processes. Sometimes called psychical research.

parsimonious making few new assumptions. "Parsimony of hypotheses" is theoretically desirable.

PK a physical change which could not have been produced by body change, has no other known physical cause, and is nevertheless inferred to be due to the action of some individual(s). The initials stand for psychokinesis. One of the classes of psi, PK sometimes is used to designate the process which underlies PK changes.

poltergeist massive PK effects, occurring spontaneously and apparently without conscious intent to produce them, usually associated repeatedly with a place or person.

pool a collection of items or individuals, from which a choice will be made.

postdiction a prediction that a previously unobserved pattern will be found in data that have already been examined, but not examined for that particular pattern.

post hoc after the facts are known. It refers to an interpretation made only after the data are examined.

precognition an ESP procedure in which the target is randomly selected after the subject's call. Also used to designate psi information about the future and the process which underlies obtaining precognitive information.

proxy sittings sessions with a psychic in which no one present has normal knowledge of the facts about which an inquiry is made.

psi-hitting *see* **hitting**

psi-missing *see* **missing**

psi ESP and PK.

psychic a person with unusually strong ESP and PK ability.

psychical research parapsychology.

psychokinesis PK.

repeatable similar outcomes for replications of research.

replication research which examines the same hypothesis as some previous research. A direct replication tries to use the same method as the prior research; a systematic or indirect replication uses a different method and thus tests the generality of the previous finding.

response bias tendency to make predictable choices. Examples, in calling ESP cards, are choosing a circle more often than a square, or avoiding repetitions.

retrocognition response to something known in the past, but not known or inferrable at present. It has been proposed as a subclass of ESP, but no procedure has as yet distinguished it from clairvoyance.

REG the initials stand for random event generator.

RNG in psi research, an instrument which provides random targets, and records number of responses and number of hits. The initials stand for random number generator.

run a unit consisting of a series of psi attempts. When ESP symbols are the target, a run consists of 25 calls.

selection *see* **correction for selection**

sheep a person who does not completely reject all possibility of psi success under the research conditions (even if psi success is considered very unlikely and the subject's own success is considered impossible). Sometimes defined in other ways, e.g. without reference to the experimental conditions, a person who thinks that psi occurs.

significant (statistically) p at or below a designated level. The usual practice in psychology is followed here; the level for significance is set at .05.

spontaneous case a report of an unanticipated event that is attributed to psi.

suggestive (statistically) not significant, but near the level of significance; usually a $p \lesssim .10$ but $> .05$. (Nonstatistically) a noncommittal term equivalent to provocative.

super-sheep a person confident of succeeding at a psi task.

systematic replication *see* **replication**

tachistoscope an instrument which exposes visual material briefly.

telepathy an ESP procedure which is interpreted as "mind to mind" communication. The target is someone's subjective experience. In the most rigorous definition, the target has no physical representation, and will have none in the future. By a less rigorous definition, the GESP procedure measures telepathy. Also designates the process which underlies mind to mind communication.

threshold the physical strength of stimuli at which they will be correctly perceived 50 percent of the time.

two-tailed the conservative p which evaluates data against both tails of the distribution that is expected by chance. See **one-tailed.**

Type I error accepting a false hypothesis.

Type II error rejecting a true hypothesis.

variance a statistical measure of the variability of scores.

veridical supported by independent evidence. Usually refers to statements from a psychic that correspond to facts.

References

Abbot, C.G. (1949). Further evidence of displacement in ESP tests. *Journal of Parapsychology,* **13**, 101–106.

Alvarado, C.S. (1980). On the "transference" of psychic abilities: A historical note. *European Journal of Parapsychology,* **3**, 209–211.

Anderson, M., & White, R.A. (1956). Teacher-pupil attitudes and clairvoyance test results. *Journal of Parapsychology,* **20**, 141–157.

Barber, T.X. (1969). *Hypnosis: A scientific approach.* New York: Van Nostrand Reinhold.

Barron, F., & Mordkoff, A.M. (1968). An attempt to relate creativity to possible extrasensory empathy as measured by physiological arousal in identical twins. *Journal of the American Society for Psychical Research,* **62**, 73–79.

Batcheldor, K.J. (1984). Contributions to the theory of PK induction from sitter-group work. *Journal of the American Society for Psychical Research,* **78**, 105–122.

Bellis, J., & Morris, R. (1980). Openness, closedness and psi. In W.G. Roll (Ed.). *Research in parapsychology 1979.* Metuchen, N.J.: Scarecrow Press, 98–99.

Beloff, J. (1974). ESP: The search for a physiological index. *Journal of the Society for Psychical Research,* **47**, 403–420.

Beloff, J., & Bate, D. (1970). Research report for the year 1968–1969. *Journal of the Society for Psychical Research,* **45**, 297–301.

Bhadra, B.H. (1965). Dissertation at Sri Venkateswara University, Tirupati, India.

Bickman, L.B. (1963). Report. *Journal of Parapsychology,* **27**, 269.

Bindrim, E. (1947). A new displacement effect in ESP. *Journal of Parapsychology,* **11**, 208–221.

Blackmore, S.J. (1986). Spontaneous and deliberate OBEs: A questionnaire survey. *Journal of the Society for Psychical Research,* **53**, 218–224.

Bohm, D.J. (1980). *Wholeness and the implicate order.* Boston: Routledge & Kegan Paul.

Bohm, D.J. (1986). A new theory of the relationship of mind and matter. *Journal of the American Society for Psychical Research,* **80**, 113–135.

Bond, E.M. (1937). General extrasensory perception with a group of fourth and fifth grade retarded children. *Journal of Parapsychology,* **1**, 114–122.

Braud, L.W. (1976). Openness versus closedness and its relationship to psi. In J.D. Morris, W.G. Roll, and R.L. Morris (Eds.). *Research in parapsychology 1975.* Metuchen, N.J.: Scarecrow Press, 155–159.

Braud, L.W. (1977). Openness versus closedness and its relationship to psi. In J.D. Morris, W.G. Roll, & R.L. Morris (Eds.). *Research in parapsychology 1976.* Metuchen, N.J.: Scarecrow Press, 162–165.

Braud, L.W., Ackles, L., & Kyles, W. (1984). Free-response GESP performance during Ganzfeld stimulation. In R.A. White & R.S. Broughton (Eds.). *Research in parapsycholgy 1983.* Metuchen, N.J.: Scarecrow Press, 78–80.

Braud, L.W., & Loewenstern, K. (1982). Creativity and psi. In W.G. Roll, R.L. Morris,

& R.A. White (Eds.). *Research in parapsychology, 1981.* Metuchen, N.J.: Scarecrow Press, 111–115.

Braud, W.G. (1975). Conscious versus unconscious clairvoyance in the context of an academic examination. *Journal of Parapsychology,* **39**, 277–288.

Braud, W.G. (1981). Psi performance and autonomic nervous system activity. *Journal of the American Society for Psychical Research,* **75**, 1–35.

Braud, W.G. (1983). Prolonged visualization practice and psychokinesis: A pilot study. In W.G. Roll, J. Beloff, & R.A. White (Eds.). *Research in parapsychology 1982.* Metuchen, N.J.: Scarecrow Press, 187–189.

Braud, W.G. (1985). ESP, PK, and sympathetic nervous system activity. *Parapsychology Review,* **16(2)**, 8–11.

Braud, W.G., & Braud, L.W. (1973). Preliminary explorations of psi-conducive states: Progressive muscular relaxation. *Journal of the American Society for Psychical Research,* **67**, 26–46.

Braud, W.G., Davis, G., & Wood, R. (1979). Experiments with Matthew Manning. *Journal of the Society for Psychical Research,* **50**, 199–223.

Braud, W.G., & Hartgrove, J. (1976). Clairvoyance and psychokinesis in transcendental meditators and matched control subjects: A preliminary study. *European Journal of Parapsychology,* **1(3)**, 6–16.

Braud, W.G., & Schlitz, M. (1983). Psychokinetic influence on electrodermal activity. *Journal of Parapsychology,* **47**, 95–119.

Braud, W.G., Shafer, D., & Mulgrew, J. (1983). Psi functioning and assessed cognitive lability. In W.G. Roll, J. Beloff, & R.A. White (Eds.). *Research in parapsychology 1982.* Metuchen, N.J.: Scarecrow Press, 182–185.

Broughton, R.S. (1976). Possible brain hemisphere laterality effects in ESP performance. *Journal of the Society for Psychical Research,* **48**, 384–399.

Broughton, R.S., Millar, B., Beloff, J., & Wilson, K. (1978). A PK investigation of the experimenter effect and its psi-based component. In W.G. Roll (Ed.). *Research in parapsychology 1977.* Metuchen, N.J.: Scarecrow Press, 41–48.

Broughton, R.S., & Perlstrom, J.R. (1985). A competitive computer game in PK research: Some preliminary findings. In R.A. White & J. Solfvin (Eds.). *Research in parapsychology 1984.* Metuchen, N.J.: Scarecrow Press, 74–77.

Broughton, R.S., & Perlstrom, J.R. (1986). Further studies using a competitive computer PK game. In D.H. Weiner & D.I. Radin (Eds.). *Research in parapsychology 1985.* Metuchen, N.J.: Scarecrow Press, 4–5.

Brugmans, H.J.F.W., Heymans, G., & Weinberg, A.A. (1924). Une communication sur des expériences télépathique au laboratoire de psychologie à Groningen. *Le Compte Rendu Officiel du Premier Congrès International des Recherches Psychiques,* Copenhagen, 396–408.

Brunswik, E. (1944). Distal focussing of perception: Size-constancy in a representative sample of situations. *Psychology Monographs,* **56**, No. 1, 1–49.

Buzby, D.E. (1963). Clairvoyance, precognition, and "religious" values. *Journal of Parapsychology,* **27**, 271–272.

Buzby, D.E. (1967). Precognition and a test of sensory perception. *Journal of Parapsychology,* **31**, 135–142.

Camstra, B., et al. (1972). The influence exerted by the characteristics of visual stimuli on ESP. *Journal of Parapsychology,* **36**, 89.

Carington, W. (1944). Experiments on the paranormal cognition of drawings: III. Steps in the development of a repeatable technique. *Proceedings of the American Society for Psychical Research,* **24**, 3–107.

Carington, W. (1945). *Telepathy: An outline of its facts, theory, and implications.* London: Methuen.

Carpenter, J.C. (1968). Two related studies on mood and precognition run-score variance. *Journal of Parapsychology,* **32**, 75–89.

Carpenter, J.C. (1969). Further study on a mood adjective check list and ESP run-score

variance. *Journal of Parapsychology,* **33,** 48–56.
Carpenter, J.C. (1983a). Prediction of forced-choice ESP performance: Part I. A mood-adjective scale for predicting the variance of ESP run scores. *Journal of Parapsychology,* **47,** 191–216.
Carpenter, J.C. (1983b). Prediction of forced-choice ESP performance: Part II. Application of a mood scale to a repeated-guessing technique. *Journal of Parapsychology,* **47,** 217–236.
Carr, B.J. (1983). An experiment to discriminate between telepathy and clairvoyance using Ishihara cards and colour-blind agents. *Journal of the Society for Psychical Research,* **52,** 31–44.
Cashen, V.M., Ramseyer, G.C. (1970). ESP and the prediction of test items in psychology examinations. *Journal of Parapsychology,* **34,** 117–123.
Chauvin, R. (1961). ESP and size of target symbols. *Journal of Parapsychology,* **25,** 185–189.
Child, I.L. (1977). Statistical regression artifact in parapsychology. *Journal of Parapsychology,* **41,** 10–22.
Child, I.L. (1981). Remarks on "psi-conducive and psi-inhibitory experimenters." *Journal of the American Society for Psychical Research,* **75,** 360–363.
Child, I.L. (1985). Psychology and anomalous observations. *American Psychologist,* **40,** 1219–1230.
Child, I.L., & Kelly, E.F. (1973). ESP with unbalanced decks: A study of the process in an exceptional subject. *Journal of Parapsychology,* **37,** 278–297.
Chinese Academy of Sciences (1982). Additional human body radiation. *Psi Research,* **1,** 16–25.
Collymore, J.L. (1978). Religious values and their effects on telepathic communications. *Journal of Parapsychology,* **42,** 153.
Condey, A. (1976). Non-verbal, non-proximic group and individual communication effects. Dissertation at the City University of New York.
Crandall, J.E. (1985). Effects of favorable and unfavorable conditions on the psi-missing displacement effect. *Journal of the American Society for Psychical Research,* **79,** 27–38.
Crandall, J.E. (1986). A model for receptivity to background stimuli in ESP research, with two further studies. In D.H. Weiner & D.I. Radin (Eds.). *Research in parapsychology 1985.* Metuchen, N.J.: Scarecrow Press, 40–43.
Crandall, J.E., & Covey, M.K. (1986). A model for receptivity to background stimuli in ESP research, with further data. *Journal of the American Society for Psychical Research,* **80,** 393–408.
Cronbach, L.J. (1957). The two disciplines of scientific psychology. *American Psychologist,* **12,** 671–684.
Crumbaugh, J.C. (1958). Are negative ESP results attributable to traits and attitudes of subjects and experimenters? *Journal of Parapsychology,* **22,** 294–295.
Dean, E.D. (1962). The plethysmograph as an indicator of ESP. *Journal of the Society for Psychical Research,* **41,** 351–353.
Dean, E.D. (1983). Infrared measurements of healer-treated water. In W.G. Roll, J. Beloff, & R.A. White (Eds.). *Research in parapsychology 1982.* Metuchen, N.J.: Scarecrow Press, 100–101.
Dean, E.D., Mihalasky, J., Ostrander, S., & Schroeder, L. (1974). *Executive ESP.* Englewood Cliffs, N.J.: Prentice-Hall.
Dixon, N.F. (1981). *Preconscious processing.* New York: Wiley.
Donald, J.A., & Martin, B. (1976). Time-symmetric thermodynamics and causality violation. *European Journal of Parapsychology,* **1(3),** 17–36.
Drucker, S.A., Drewes, A.A., & Rubin, L. (1977). ESP in relation to cognitive development and IQ in young children. *Journal of the American Society for Psychical Research,* **71,** 289–298.
Duane, T.D., & Behrendt, T. (1965). Extrasensory electroencephalographic induction between identical twins. *Science,* **150,** 367.

Dukhan, H., & Rao, K.R. (1973). Meditation and ESP scoring. In W.G. Roll, R.L. Morris, & J.D. Morris (Eds.). *Research in parapsychology 1972.* Metuchen, N.J.: Scarecrow Press, 148-151.

Dunne, J.W. (1927). *An experiment with time.* New York: Macmillan.

Eagle, M. (1962). Personality correlates of sensitivity to subliminal stimulation. *Journal of Nervous and Mental Diseases,* **134,** 1-17.

Edge, H. (1980). The effect of the laying on of hands on an enzyme: An attempted replication. In W.G. Roll (Ed.). *Research in parapsychology, 1979.* Metuchen, N.J.: Scarecrow Press, 137-139.

Edge, H., & Farkash, M. (1982). Further support for the psi-distributed hypothesis. In W.G. Roll, R.L. Morris, & R.A. White (Eds.). *Research in parapsychology 1981.* Metuchen, N.J.: Scarecrow Press, 171-172.

Ehrenwald, J. (1978). *The ESP experience: A psychiatric validation.* New York: Basic Books.

Eilbert, L., & Schmeidler, G.R. (1950). A study of certain psychological factors in relation to ESP performance. *Journal of Parapsychology,* **14,** 53-74.

Eisenbud, J. (1965). Perception of subliminal visual stimuli in relation to ESP. *International Journal of Parapsychology,* **7,** 161-181.

Eisenbud, J. (1967). *The world of Ted Serios.* New York: William Morrow.

Eysenck, H.J. (1957). *The dynamics of anxiety and hysteria.* London: Routledge & Kegan Paul.

Eysenck, H.J. (1967). Personality and extra-sensory perception. *Journal of the Society for Psychical Research,* **44,** 55-71.

Feather, S.R., & Rhine, L.E. (1969). PK experiments with same and different targets. *Journal of Parapsychology,* **33,** 213-227.

Feilding, E., Baggally, W.W., & Carrington, H. (1909). Report on a series of sittings with Eusapia Palladino. *Proceedings of the Society for Psychical Research,* **23,** 309-569.

Fischer, R. (1971). A cartography of the ecstatic and meditative states. *Science,* **174,** 897-904.

Fisk, G.W., & West, D.J. (1955a). ESP tests with erotic symbols. *Journal of the Society for Psychical Research,* **38,** 1-7.

Fisk, G.W., & West, D.J. (1955b). ESP tests with erotic symbols: Corrections. *Journal of the Society for Psychical Research,* **38,** 134-136.

Fisk, G.W., & West, D.J. (1956). ESP and mood: Report of a "mass" experiment. *Journal of the Society for Psychical Research,* **38,** 320-329.

Fisk, G.W., & West, D.J. (1958). Die-casting experiments with a single subject. *Journal of the Society for Psychical Research,* **39,** 277-287.

Friedman, R.M., Schmeidler, G.R., & Dean, E.D. (1976). Ranked-target scoring for mood and intragroup effects in precognitive ESP. *Journal of the American Society for Psychical Research,* **70,** 195-206.

Gauld, A. (1971). A series of "drop in" communicators. *Proceedings of the Society for Psychical Research,* **55,** 273-340.

Gauld, A. (1982). *Mediumship and survival: A century of investigation.* London: William Heinemann.

George, L. (1982). Enhancement of psi functioning through mental imagery training. *Journal of Parapsychology,* **46,** 111-125.

Gerber, R., & Schmeidler, G.R. (1957). An investigation of relaxation and of acceptance of the experimental situation as related to ESP scores in maternity patients. *Journal of Parapsychology,* **21,** 47-57.

Goldberg, J., Sondow, N., & Schmeidler, G. (1976). Psi and the experience of time. In J.D. Morris, W.G. Roll, & R.L. Morris (Eds.). *Research in Parapsychology 1975.* Metuchen, N.J.: Scarecrow Press, 152-155.

Gregory, A. (Ed.). (1982). London experiments with Matthew Manning. *Proceedings of the Society for Psychical Research,* **56,** 283-366.

Greyson, B., & Flynn, C.P. (Eds.). (1984). *The near-death experience: Problems, prospects, perspectives.* Springfield, Ill: Charles C. Thomas.

Haight, J., Kanthamani, H., & Kennedy, J.E. (1978). Interaction of certain personality variables and feedback in a computerized ESP test. *Journal of Parapsychology,* **42,** 51–52.

Hall, C.S., & Lindzey, G. (1957). *Theories of personality.* New York: Wiley.

Harris, M.J., & Rosenthal, R. (1985). Mediation of interpersonal expectancy effects: 31 meta-analyses. *Psychological Bulletin,* **97,** 363–386.

Head, J., & Cranston, S.L. (Eds.). (1977). *Reincarnation: The phoenix fire mystery.* New York: Crown Publishers.

Healy, J. (1986). Hippocampal kindling, theta resonance, and psi. *Journal of the Society for Psychical Research,* **53,** 486–500.

Hearne, K.M.T. (1981). Visually-evoked-responses and "ESP": Failure to replicate previous findings. *Journal of the Society for Psychical Research,* **51,** 145–147.

Helson, H. (1964). *Adaptation-level theory.* New York: Harper & Row.

Heyman, S., & Schmeidler, G.R. (1967). Attitudes toward time and the impatience effect. *Journal of Parapsychology,* **31,** 316.

Hodgson, R. (1892). A record of observations of certain phenomena of trance. *Proceedings of the Society for Psychical Research,* **8,** 1–167.

Honorton, C. (1967). Creativity and precognition scoring level. *Journal of Parapsychology,* **31,** 29–42.

Honorton, C. (1969). Relationship between EEG alpha activity and ESP in card-guessing performance. *Journal of the American Society for Psychical Research,* **63,** 365–374.

Honorton, C. (1983). Response to Hyman's critique of psi Ganzfeld studies. In W.G. Roll, J. Beloff, & R.A. White (Eds.). *Research in parapsychology 1982.* Metuchen, N.J.: Scarecrow Press, 23–26.

Honorton, C. (1985). Meta-analysis of psi ganzfeld research: A response to Hyman. *Journal of Parapsychology,* **49,** 51–91.

Honorton, C., & Harper, S. (1974). Psi-mediated imagery and ideation in an experimental procedure for regulating perceptual input. *Journal of the American Society for Psychical Research,* **68,** 156–168.

Honorton, C., Ramsey, M. & Cabibbo, C. (1975). Experimenter effects in extrasensory perception. *Journal of the American Society for Psychical Research,* **69,** 135–149.

Houtkooper, J.M., Andrews, R., Ganzevles, P.G.J., & van der Sijde, P.C. (1980). A hierarchical model for the observational theories: A study of subject identity and feedback in repeated retroactive psychokinesis. *European Journal of Parapsychology,* **3,** 221–246.

Hubbard, G.S., May, E.C., & Puthoff, H.E. (1986). Possible production of photons during a remote viewing task: Preliminary results. In D.H. Weiner & D.I. Radin (Eds.). *Research in parapsychology 1985.* Metuchen, N.J.: Scarecrow Press, 66–70.

Huby, P.M., & Wilson, C.W.M. (1961). The effects of centrally acting drugs on ESP ability in normal subjects. *Journal of the Society for Psychical Research,* **41,** 60–67.

Hudesman, J., & Schmeidler, G.R. (1976). Changes in ESP scores after therapy sessions. *Journal of the American Society for Psychical Research,* **70,** 371–380.

Humphrey, B.M. (1945). ESP and intelligence. *Journal of Parapsychology,* **9,** 7–16.

Humphrey, B.M. (1946a). Success in ESP as related to form of response drawings: I. Clairvoyance experiments. *Journal of Parapsychology,* **10,** 78–106.

Humphrey, B.M. (1946b). Success in ESP as related to form of response drawings: II. GESP experiments. *Journal of Parapsychology,* **10,** 181–196.

Humphrey, B.M. (1947). Help-hinder comparison in PK tests. *Journal of Parapsychology,* **11,** 4–13.

Hyman, R. (1985). The ganzfeld psi experiment: A critical appraisal. *Journal of Parapsychology,* **49,** 3–49.

Jackson, M., Franzoi, S., & Schmeidler, G.R. (1977). Effects of feedback on ESP: A curious partial replication. *Journal of the American Society for Psychical Research,* **71,** 147–155.

Jacobs, J.C., Michels, J.A.G., & Verbraak, A. (1978). An experimental study on the influence of experimenters' expectancies on life span age differences in PK-performance. *European Journal of Parapsychology,* **2,** 213–227.

Jahn, R.G., & Dunne, B.J. (1984). *On the quantum mechanics of consciousness, with application to anomalous phenomena.* (Technical Note PEAR 83005.1, 1st Rev., Princeton: Engineering Anomalies Research.) Princeton, N.J.: Princeton University School of Engineering/Applied Science.

Janet, P. (1886). Deuxième note sur le sommeil provoqué à distance et la suggestion mentale pendant l'ètat somnambulique. *Revue Philosophque de la France et de l'Etranger,* **21,** 212–223.

Johnson, M. (1973). A new technique of testing ESP in a real-life, high-motivational context. *Journal of Parapsychology,* **37,** 210–217.

Johnson, M., & Haraldsson, E. (1984). The Defense Mechanism Test as a predictor of ESP scores. *Journal of Parapsychology,* **48,** 185–200.

Johnson, M., & Kanthamani, B.K. (1967). The Defense Mechanism Test as a predictor of ESP scoring direction. *Journal of Parapsychology,* **31,** 99–110.

Kanthamani, B.K. (1966). ESP and social stimulus. *Journal of Parapsychology,* **30,** 31–38.

Kanthamani, B.K. (H.), & Rao, K.R. (1973). Personality characteristics of ESP subjects: V. graphic expansiveness and ESP. *Journal of Parapsychology,* **37,** 119–129.

Katz, R. (1982). *Boiling energy: Community healing among the Kalahari Kung.* Cambridge, Mass: Harvard University Press.

Keane, P., & Wells, R. (1979). An examination of the menstrual cycle as a hormone related physiological concomitant of psi performance. In W.G. Roll (Ed.). *Research in parapsychology 1978.* Metuchen, N.J.: Scarecrow Press, 72–74.

Kelly, E.F., & Kanthamani, B.K. (1972). A subject's efforts toward voluntary control. *Journal of Parapsychology,* **36,** 185–197.

Kelly, E.F., Kanthamani, H., Child, I.L., & Young, F.W. (1975). On the relation between visual and ESP confusion structures in an exceptional ESP subject. *Journal of the American Society for Psychical Research,* **69,** 1–31.

Kennedy, J.E., & Taddonio, J.L. (1976). Experimenter effects in parapsychological research. *Journal of Parapsychology,* **40,** 1–33.

Klintman, H. (1983). Is there a paranormal (precognitive) influence in certain types of perceptual sequences? Part I. *European Journal of Parapsychology,* **5,** 19–49.

Klintman, H. (1984). Is there a paranormal (precognitive) influence in certain types of perceptual sequences? Part II. *European Journal of Parapsychology,* **5,** 125–140.

Kobayashi, K., Terry, J.C., & Thompson, W.D. (1979). Left-right hemisphere differences between a psi and non-psi group. In W.G. Roll (Ed.). *Research in parapsychology 1978.* Metuchen, N.J.: Scarecrow Press, 41–43.

Kreiman, N. (1978). Memoria secundaria y ESP. *Cuadernos de Parapsicología,* **13,** 3–12.

Kreiman, N. (1981). ¿Lateralidad cerebral y ESP? *Cuadernos de Parapsicología,* **14,** 15–22.

Kreitler, H., & Kreitler, S. (1972). Does extrasensory perception affect psychological experiments? *Journal of Parapsychology,* **36,** 1–45.

Kreitler, H., & Kreitler, S. (1973). Subliminal perception and extrasensory perception. *Journal of Parapsychology,* **37,** 163–188.

Kreitler, H., & Kreitler, S. (1977). Response to "Statistical regression artifact in parapsychology." *Journal of Parapsychology,* **41,** 23–33.

Krippner, S., Ullman, M., & Honorton, C. (1971). A precognitive dream study with a single subject. *Journal of the American Society for Psychical Research,* **65,** 192–203.

Laubscher, B. (1938). *Sex customs and psychopathology: A study of South African pagan natives.* New York: McBride.

Layton, B.D., & Turnbull, B. (1975). Belief, evaluation, and performance on an ESP task. *Journal of Experimental Social Psychology,* **11,** 166–179.

LeShan, L. (1974). *The medium, the mystic, and the physicist.* New York: Viking Press.

Levi, A. (1979). The influence of imagery and feedback on PK effects. *Journal of Parapsychology,* **43,** 275–289.

Lewis, L., & Schmeidler, G.R. (1971). Alpha relations with non-intentional and purposeful ESP after feedback. *Journal of the American Society for Psychical Research,* **65,** 455–467.

Lovitts, B.E. (1981). The sheep-goat effect turned upside down. *Journal of Parapsychology,* **45,** 293–309.
Lübke, C., & Rohr, W. (1975). Psi and subliminal perception: A replication of the Kreitler and Kreitler study. In J.D. Morris, W.G. Roll, & R.L. Morris (Eds.). *Research in parapsychology 1974.* Metuchen, N.J.: Scarecrow Press, 161–164.
Ludwick, M. (1980). Lateral eye movements as they relate to ESP. *Journal of Parapsychology,* **44,** 80.
McCrae, R.R., Costa, P.T., Jr., & Busch, C.M. (1986). Evaluating comprehensiveness in personality systems: The California Q-Set and the five factor model. *Journal of Personality,* **54,** 430–446.
MacFarland, J.D. (1938). Discrimination shown between experimenters by subjects. *Journal of Parapsychology,* **2,** 160–170.
McMahan, E.A. (1946). An experiment in pure telepathy. *Journal of Parapsychology,* **10,** 224–242.
Maher, M. (1984). Correlated hemispheric asymmetry in the sensory and ESP processing of continuous multiplex stimuli. In R.A. White & R.S. Broughton (Eds.). *Research in parapsychology 1983.* Metuchen, N.J.: Scarecrow Press, 18–21.
Maher, M., Peratsakis, D., & Schmeidler, G.R. (1979). Cerebral lateralization effects in ESP processing: An attempted replication. *Journal of the American Society for Psychical Research,* **73,** 167–177.
Mangan, G.L. (1955). Evidence of displacement in a precognition test. *Journal of Parapsychology,* **19,** 35–44.
Markwick, B., & Beloff, J. (1983). Dream states and ESP: A distance experiment with a single subject. In W.G. Roll, J. Beloff, & R.A. White (Eds.). *Research in parapsychology 1982.* Metuchen, N.J.: Scarecrow Press, 228–230.
Mattson, J.M., & Natsoulas, T. (1962). Emotional arousal and stimulus duration as determinants of stimulus selection. *Journal of Abnormal and Social Psychology,* **65,** 142–144.
Mattuck, R.D. (1977). Probable psychokinetic effects produced in a clinical thermometer. *Psychoenergetic Systems,* **2,** 31–37.
Mattuck, R.D. (1982). Some possible thermal quantum fluctuational models for psychokinetic influence on light. *Journal of Psychophysical Systems,* **4,** 211–225.
May, E.C., Targ, R., & Puthoff, H.E. (1979). EEG correlates to remote light flashes under conditions of sensory shielding. In C.T. Tart, H.E. Puthoff, & R. Targ (Eds.). *Mind at large.* New York: Prager, 127–136.
Medhurst, R.G., & Goldney, K.M. (1964). William Crookes and the physical phenomena of mediumship. *Proceedings of the Society for Psychical Research,* **54,** 25–157.
Meseguer, P. (1959). *The secret of dreams.* New York: Tudor.
Millar, B. (1979). The distribution of psi. *European Journal of Parapsychology,* **3,** 78–110.
Miller, G.A. (1956). The magical number seven, plus or minus two: Some limits on our capacity for processing information. *Psychological Review,* **63,** 81–97.
Milton, J. (1985). The effect of agent strategies on the percipient's experience in the Ganzfeld. In R.A. White & J. Solfvin (Eds.). *Research in parapsychology 1984.* Metuchen, N.J.: Scarecrow Press, 1–4.
Mischo, J., & Weis, R. (1973). A pilot study on the relations between PK scores and personality variables. In W.G. Roll, R.L. Morris, & J.D. Morris (Eds.). *Research in parapsychology 1972.* Metuchen, N.J.: Scarecrow Press, 21–23.
Mitchell, J.L. (1981). *Out-of-body experiences: A handbook.* Jefferson, N.C.: McFarland.
Mitchell, J.L., & Drewes, A.A. (1982). The rainbow experiment. *Journal of the American Society for Psychical Research,* **76,** 197–215.
Morris, R.L., Nanko, M.J., & Phillips, D. (1982). A comparison of two popularly advocated visual imagery strategies in a psychokinesis task. *Journal of Parapsychology,* **46,** 1–16.
Morris, R.L., & Reilly, V. (1980). A failure to obtain results with goal-oriented imagery PK and a random event generator with varying hit probability. In W.G. Roll (Ed.). *Research in parapsychology 1979.* Metuchen, N.J.: Scarecrow Press, 166–167.

Moss, T. (1969). ESP effects in "artists" contrasted with "non-artists." *Journal of Parapsychology,* **33,** 57–69.

Munn, N.L. (1956). *Psychology: The fundamentals of human adjustment.* Boston: Houghton Mifflin.

Murphy, G. (1962). A qualitative study of telepathic phenomena. *Journal of the American Society for Psychical Research,* **56,** 63–79.

Murphy, G. (1963). Creativity and its relation to extrasensory perception. *Journal of the American Society for Psychical Research,* **57,** 203–214.

Murphy, G. (1966). Research in creativeness: What can it tell us about extrasensory perception? *Journal of the American Society for Psychical Research,* **60,** 8–22.

Murphy, G. (1970). Are there any solid facts in psychical research? *Journal of the American Society for Psychical Research,* **64,** 3–17.

Murray, D.M. (1983). The effect of schooling on the manifestation of clairvoyant abilities among Isnag children of the Northern Philippines. In W.G. Roll, J. Beloff, & R.A. White (Eds.). *Research in parapsychology 1982.* Metuchen, N.J.: Scarecrow Press, 245–248.

Mussig, G.F., & Dean, E.D. (1967). Mood as a factor in precognition. *Journal of Parapsychology,* **31,** 319–320.

Musso, J.R., & Granero, M. (1973). An ESP drawing experiment with a high-scoring subject. *Journal of Parapsychology,* **37,** 13–36.

Myers, F.W.H. (1903). *Human personality and its survival of bodily death.* London: Longmans, Green.

Mythili, S.P., & Rao, P.V.K. (1980). Rigidity and ESP. In W.G. Roll (Ed.). *Research in parapsychology 1979.* Metuchen, N.J.: Scarecrow Press, 167–169.

Nanko, M.J. (1981). Use of goal-oriented imagery strategy on a psychokinetic task with "selected" subjects. *Journal of the Southern California Society for Psychical Research,* **2,** 1–5.

Nash, C.B. (1958). Correlation between ESP and religious value. *Journal of Parapsychology,* **22,** 204–209.

Nash, C.B. (1978). Effect of response bias on psi mediation. *Journal of the American Society for Psychical Research,* **72,** 333–338.

Nash, C.B. (1985). A forced-choice ESP test with structural and semantic targets. In R.A. White & J. Solfvin (Eds.). *Research in parapsychology 1984.* Metuchen, N.J.: Scarecrow Press, 88–90.

Nash, C.B., & Nash, C.S. (1981). Psi-influenced movement of chicks and mice onto a visual cliff. In W.G. Roll & J. Beloff (Eds.). *Research in parapsychology 1980.* Metuchen, N.J.: Scarecrow Press, 109–110.

Nash, C.S., & Nash, C.B. (1968). Effect of target selection, field dependence, and body concept on ESP performance. *Journal of Parapsychology,* **32,** 248–257.

Nelson, R.D., Jahn, R.G., & Dunne, B.J. (1986). Operator-related anomalies in physical systems and information processes. *Journal of the Society for Psychical Research,* **53,** 261–285.

Nielsen, W. (1956). Mental states associated with success in precognition. *Journal of Parapsychology,* **20,** 96–109.

Nielsen, W. (1972). Mood, introversion, and precognition scores on individual and group targets. In W.G. Roll, R.L. Morris, & J.D. Morris (Eds.). *Proceedings of the Parapsychological Association, No. 8, 1971.* Durham, N.C.: Parapsychological Association, 88–90.

Orne, M.T. (1962). On the social psychology of the psychological experiment: With particular reference to demand characteristics and their implications. *American Psychologist,* **17,** 776–783.

Osis, K., & Carlson, M.L. (1972). The ESP channel—open or closed? *Journal of the American Society for Psychical Research,* **66,** 310–320.

Osis, K., & Haraldsson, E. (1977). *At the hour of death.* New York: Avon Books.

Osis, K., & McCormick, D. (1980). Kinetic effects at the ostensible location of an out-of-body projection during perceptual testing. *Journal of the American Society for Psychical Research,* **74,** 319–329.

Palmer, J. (1971). Scoring in ESP tests as a function of belief in ESP: Part I. The sheep-goat effect. *Journal of the American Society for Psychical Research,* **65**, 373–408.

Palmer, J. (1978). Extrasensory perception: Research findings. In S. Krippner (Ed.). *Advances in parapsychological research, 2: Extrasensory perception.* New York: Plenum Press, 59–243.

Palmer, J. (1982). ESP research findings: 1976–1978. In S. Krippner (Ed.). *Advances in parapsychological research, 3.* New York: Plenum Press, 41–82.

Palmer, J., Ader, C., & Mikova, M. (1981). Anxiety and ESP: Anatomy of a reversal. In W.G. Roll & J. Beloff (Eds.). *Research in parapsychology 1980.* Metuchen, N.J.: Scarecrow Press, 77–81.

Palmer, J., Khamashta, K., & Israelson, K. (1979). A Ganzfeld experiment with Transcendental Meditators. In W.G. Roll (Ed.). *Research in parapsychology 1978.* Metuchen, N.J.: Scarecrow Press, 65–67.

Palmer, J., & Kramer, W. (1984). Internal state and temporal factors in psychokinesis. *Journal of Parapsychology,* **48**, 1–25.

Parker, A. (1974). ESP in gerbils using positive reinforcement. *Journal of Parapsychology,* **38**, 301–311.

Parker, A. (1975). A pilot study of the influence of experimenter expectancy on ESP scores. In J.D. Morris, W.G. Roll, & R.L. Morris (Eds.). *Research in parapsychology 1974.* Metuchen, N.J.: Scarecrow Press 42–44.

Parker, A. (1977). Parapsychologists' personality and psi in relation to the experimenter effect. In J.D. Morris, W.G. Roll, & R.L. Morris (Eds.). *Research in parapsychology 1976.* Metuchen, N.J.: Scarecrow Press, 107–109.

Parker, A. (1981). In defense of introverts: A critical note on supposed personality differences between ganzfeld experimenters. *European Journal of Parapsychology,* **3**, 373–379.

Parker, A., Millar, B., & Beloff, J. (1977). A three-experimenter ganzfeld: An attempt to use the ganzfeld technique to study the experimenter effect. In J.D. Morris, W.G. Roll, & R.L. Morris (Eds.). *Research in parapsychology 1976.* Metuchen, N.J.: Scarecrow Press, 52–54.

Persinger, M.A. (1985). Geophysical variables and human behavior: Intense paranormal experiences occur during days of quiet global geomagnetic activity. *Perceptual and Motor Skills,* **61**, 320–322.

Pratt, J.G. (1973). A decade of research with a selected subject: An overview and reappraisal of the work with Pavel Stepanek. *Proceedings of the American Society for Psychical Research,* **30**, 1–78.

Pratt, J.G., & Price, M.M. (1938). The experimenter-subject relationship in tests for ESP. *Journal of Parapsychology,* **2**, 84–94.

Pratt, J.G., & Woodruff, J.L. (1939). Size of stimulus symbols in extra-sensory perception. *Journal of Parapsychology,* **3**, 121–158.

Price, A.D. (1973). Subject's control of imagery, "agent's" mood, and position effects in a dual-target ESP experiment. *Journal of Parapsychology,* **37**, 298–322.

Prince, W.F. (1915). The Doris case of multiple personality, Part I. *Proceedings of the American Society for Psychical Research,* **9**, 23–697.

Radin, D.I. (1982). Experimental attempts to influence pseudorandom number sequences. *Journal of the American Society for Psychical Research,* **76**, 359–374.

Radin, D.I., & Bosworth, J.L. (1985). Response distributions in a computer-based perceptual task: Test of four models. *Journal of the American Society for Psychical Research,* **79**, 453–483.

Radin, D.I., May, E.C., & Thomson, M.J. (1986). Psi experiments with random number generators: Meta-analysis, Part I. In D.H. Weiner & D.I. Radin (Eds.). *Research in parapsychology 1985.* Metuchen, N.J.: Scarecrow Press, 14–17.

Randall, J.L. (1971). Experiments to detect a psi effect with small animals. *Journal of the Society for Psychical Research,* **46**, 31–39.

Rao, K.R. (1979). Language ESP tests under normal and relaxed conditions. *Journal of Parapsychology,* **43,** 1-16.

Rauscher, E.A., & Rubik, B.A. (1980). Effects on motility behavior and growth rate of Salmonella Typhimurium in the presence of a psychic subject. In W.G. Roll (Ed.). *Research in parapsychology 1979.* Metuchen, N.J.: Scarecrow Press, 140-142.

Rhine, J.B. (1934). *Extra-sensory perception.* Boston: Boston Society for Psychic Research.

Rhine, J.B. (1941). Terminal salience in ESP performance. *Journal of Parapsychology,* **5,** 183-244.

Rhine, J.B. (1964). Special motivation in some exceptional ESP performances. *Journal of Parapsychology,* **28,** 42-50.

Rhine, L.E. (1981). *The invisible picture: A study of psychic experiences.* Jefferson, N.C.: McFarland.

Rogers, D.P. (1966). Negative and positive affect and ESP run-score variance. *Journal of Parapsychology,* **30,** 151-159.

Rogers, D.P. (1967a). An analysis for internal cancellation effects on some low-variance ESP runs. *Journal of Parapsychology,* **31,** 192-197.

Rogers, D.P. (1967b). Negative and positive affect and ESP run-score variance: Study II. *Journal of Parapsychology,* **31,** 290-296.

Roll, W.G. (1982). Mediums and RSPK agents as fantasy-prone individuals. In W.G. Roll, R.L. Morris, & R.A. White (Eds.). *Research in parapsychology 1981.* Metuchen, N.J.: Scarecrow Press, 42-44.

Roll, W.G., & Montagno, E. de A. (1983). Similarities between RSPK and psychomotor epilepsy. In W.G. Roll, J. Beloff, & R.A. White (Eds.). *Research in parapsychology 1982.* Metuchen, N.J.: Scarecrow Press, 270-273.

Rosenthal, R. (1966). *Experimenter effects in behavioral research.* New York: Appleton-Century-Crofts.

Ross, A.O., Murphy, G., & Schmeidler, G.R. (1952). The spontaneity factor in extrasensory perception. *Journal of the American Society for Psychical Research,* **46,** 14-16.

Ryzl, M. (1962). Training the psi faculty by hypnosis. *Journal of the Society for Psychical Research,* **41,** 234-252.

Ryzl, M. (1966). A model of parapsychological communication. *Journal of Parapsychology,* **30,** 18-30.

Sannwald, G. (1963). On the psychology of spontaneous paranormal phenomena. *International Journal of Parapsychology,* **5,** 274-292.

Sargent, C.L. (1980). A note on personality differences between psi-conducive and psi-inhibitory Ganzfeld experimenters. In W.G. Roll (Ed.) *Research in parapsychology 1979,* Metuchen, N.J.: Scarecrow Press, 114-115.

Sargent, C.L. (1981). Extraversion and performance in "extrasensory perception" tasks. *Personality and Individual Differences,* **2,** 137-143.

Schechter, E.I. (1977). Nonintentional ESP: A review and replication. *Journal of the American Society for Psychical Research,* **71,** 337-374.

Schechter, E.I. (1984). Hypnotic induction vs. control conditions: Illustrating an approach to the evaluation of replicability in parapsychological data. *Journal of the American Society for Psychical Research,* **78,** 1-27.

Scherer, W.B. (1948). Spontaneity as a factor in ESP. *Journal of Parapsychology,* **12,** 126-147.

Schlitz, M.J., & Haight, J. (1984). Remote viewing revisited: An intrasubject replication. *Journal of Parapsychology,* **48,** 39-49.

Schmeidler, G.R. (1943). Predicting good and bad scores in a clairvoyance experiment: A preliminary report. *Journal of the American Society for Psychical Research,* **37,** 103-110.

Schmeidler, G.R. (1952a). Rorschachs and ESP scores of patients suffering from cerebral concussion. *Journal of Parapsychology,* **16,** 80-89.

Schmeidler, G.R. (1952b). Personal values and ESP scores. *Journal of Abnormal and Social Psychology,* **47,** 757-761.

Schmeidler, G.R. (1960). ESP in relation to Rorschach Test evaluation. *Parapsychology Monographs,* **2,** 1-89.

Schmeidler, G.R. (1961). Evidence for two kinds of telepathy. *International Journal of Parapsychology,* **3,** 5-48.

Schmeidler, G.R. (1963). Tests of creative thinking and ESP scores. *Indian Journal of Parapsychology,* **4,** 51-57.

Schmeidler, G.R. (1964a). An experiment on precognitive clairvoyance, Part I: The main results. *Journal of Parapsychology,* **28,** 1-14.

Schmeidler, G.R. (1964b). An experiment on precognitive clairvoyance, Part IV: Precognition scores related to creativity. *Journal of Parapsychology,* **28,** 102-108.

Schmeidler, G.R. (1970). High ESP scores after a swami's brief instruction in meditation and breathing. *Journal of the American Society for Psychical Research,* **64,** 100-103.

Schmeidler, G.R. (1971). Mood and attitude on a pretest as predictors of retest ESP performance. *Journal of the American Society for Psychical Research,* **65,** 324-335.

Schmeidler, G.R. (1972). Respice, adspice, prospice. In W.G. Roll, R.L. Morris, & J.D. Morris (Eds.). *Proceedings of the Parapsychological Association No. 8, 1971.* Durham, N.C.: Parapsychological Association, 117-145.

Schmeidler, G.R. (1973). PK effects upon continuously recorded temperature. *Journal of the American Society for Psychical Research,* **67,** 325-340.

Schmeidler, G.R. (1978). Research findings in psychokinesis. In S. Krippner (Ed.). *Advances in parapsychological research, I: Psychokinesis.* New York: Plenum Press, 79-132.

Schmeidler, G.R. (1980). Does ESP influence the recall of partially learned words? In W.G. Roll (Ed.). *Research in parapsychology 1979.* Metuchen, N.J.: Scarecrow Press, 54-57.

Schmeidler, G.R. (1983a). ESP and memory: Some limiting conditions. *Parapsychological Journal of South Africa,* **4,** 51-69.

Schmeidler, G.R. (1983b). Interpreting reports of out-of-body experiences. *Journal of the Society for Psychical Research,* **52,** 102-104.

Schmeidler, G.R. (1983c). Psi scores and personality: Basic questions and a theory to encompass the answers. *Parapsychology Review,* **14(5),** 1-4.

Schmeidler, G.R. (1985). Field and stream: Background stimuli and the flow of ESP responses. *Journal of the American Society for Psychical Research,* **79,** 13-26.

Schmeidler, G.R. (1986). Subliminal perception and ESP: Order in diversity? *Journal of the American Society for Psychical Research,* **80,** 241-264.

Schmeidler, G.R. (1987). Psychokinesis: Recent findings and a possible paradigm shift. In S. Krippner (Ed.). *Advances in parapsychological research, 5.* Jefferson, N.C.: McFarland, 9-38.

Schmeidler, G.R., & Craig, J.G. (1972). Moods and ESP scores in group testing. *Journal of the American Society for Psychical Research,* **66,** 280-287.

Schmeidler, G.R., Friedenberg, W., & Males, P. (1966). Impatience and ESP scores. *Journal of Parapsychology,* **30,** 275.

Schmeidler, G.R., Gambale, J., & Mitchell, J. (1976). PK effects on temperature recordings: An attempted replication and extension. In J.D. Morris, W.G. Roll, & R.L. Morris (Eds.). *Research in parapsychology 1975.* Metuchen, N.J.: Scarecrow Press, 67-69.

Schmeidler, G.R., & Goldberg, J. (1974). Evidence for selective telepathy in group psychometry. In W.G. Roll, R.L. Morris, & J.D. Morris (Eds.). *Research in parapsychology 1973.* Metuchen, N.J.: Scarecrow Press, 103-106.

Schmeidler, G.R. & LeShan, L. (1970). An aspect of body image related to ESP scores. *Journal of the American Society for Psychical Research,* **64,** 211-218.

Schmeidler, G.R., & McConnell, R.A. (1958). *ESP and personality patterns.* New Haven, Conn.: Yale University Press.

Schmeidler, G.R., & Maher, M. (1981). Judges' responses to the nonverbal behavior of psi-conducive and psi-inhibitory experimenters. *Journal of the American Society for Psychical Research,* **75,** 241-257.

Schmidt, H. (1969). Precognition of a quantum process. *Journal of Parapsychology,* **33,** 99–108.

Schmidt, H. (1974). Comparison of PK action on two different random number generators. *Journal of Parapsychology,* **38,** 47–55.

Schmidt, H. (1975). A logically consistent model of a world with psi interaction. In L. Oteri (Ed.). *Quantum physics and parapsychology.* New York: Parapsychology Foundation, 205–228.

Schmidt, H. (1976). PK effect upon pre-recorded targets. *Journal of the American Society for Psychical Research,* **70,** 267–291.

Schmidt, H. (1984). Comparison of a teleological model with a quantum collapse model of psi. *Journal of Parapsychology,* **48,** 261–276.

Schmidt, H. (1986). Human PK effort on prerecorded random events previously observed by goldfish. In D.H. Weiner & D.I. Radin (Eds.). *Research in parapsychoogy 1985.* Metuchen, N.J.: Scarecrow Press, 18–21.

Schmidt, H., & Pantas, L. (1972). PK tests with internally different machines. *Journal of Parapsychology,* **36,** 222–232.

Schmitt, M., & Stanford, R.G. (1978). Free-response ESP during ganzfeld stimulation: The possible influence of menstrual cycle phase. *Journal of the American Society for Psychical Research,* **72,** 177–182.

Schouten, S.A. (1972). Psi in mice: Positive reinforcement. *Journal of Parapsychology,* **36,** 261–282.

Schouten, S.A. (1975). Effect of reducing response preferences on ESP scores. *European Journal of Parapsychology,* **1(1),** 60–66.

Schouten, S.A. (1976). Autonomic psychophysiological reactions to sensory and emotive stimuli in a psi experiment. *European Journal of Parapsychology,* **1(2),** 57–71.

Sheargold, R.K. (1972). Experiment in precognition. *Journal of the Society for Psychical Research,* **46,** 201–208.

Sherrington, C.S. (1906). *The integrative action of the nervous system.* New Haven, Conn: Yale University Press, 1947 (reprint).

Shields, E. (1962). Comparison of children's guessing ability (ESP) with personality characteristics. *Journal of Parapsychology,* **26,** 200–210.

Shields, E., & Mulders, C. (1975). Pleasant versus unpleasant targets on children's ESP tests and their relationship to personality tests. *Journal of Parapsychology,* **39,** 165–166.

Sidgwick, E.M. (1921). An examination of book-tests obtained in sittings with Mrs. Leonard. *Proceedings of the Society for Psychical Research,* **31,** 253–260.

Sidgwick, E.M. (1922). Phantasms of the living. *Proceedings of the Society for Psychical Research, 33,* 22–429.

Sinclair, U. (1930). *Mental Radio.* New York: Albert and Charles Boni.

Smith, M.J. (1972). Paranormal effects on enzyme activity. *Human Dimensions,* **1(2),** 15–19.

Smythies, J., & Beloff, J. (1965). The influence of stereotactic surgery on ESP. *Journal of the Society for Psychical Research,* **43,** 20–24.

Solfvin, G.F. (1982). Studies of the effects of mental healing and expectations on the growth of corn seedlings. *European Journal of Parapsychology,* **4,** 287–324.

Sondow, N. (1979). Effects of associations and feedback on psi in the ganzfeld: Is there more than meets the judge's eye? *Journal of the American Society for Psychical Research,* **73,** 123–150.

Sondow, N. (1984). Spontaneous precognitive dreams: A decline with temporal distance. In R.A. White & R.S. Broughton (Eds.). *Research in parapsychology 1983.* Metuchen, N.J.: Scarecrow Press, 75–77.

Sondow, N., Braud, L.W., & Barker, P. (1982). Target qualities and affect measures in an exploratory psi Ganzfeld. In W.G. Roll, R.L. Morris, & R.A. White (Eds.). *Research in parapsychology 1981.* Metuchen, N.J. Scarecrow Press, 82–85.

Stanford, R.G. (1964). Attitude and personality variables in ESP scoring. *Journal of Parapsychology,* **28,** 166–175.

Stanford, R.G. (1965). A further study of high- *versus* low-scoring sheep. *Journal of Parapsychology,* **29,** 141–158.

Stanford, R.G. (1966a). The effect of restriction of calling upon run-score variance. *Journal of Parapsychology,* **30,** 160–171.

Stanford, R.G. (1966b). A study of the cause of low run-score variance. *Journal of Parapsychology,* **30,** 236–242.

Stanford, R.G. (1970). Extrasensory effects upon "memory." *Journal of the American Society for Psychical Research,* **64,** 161–186.

Stanford, R.G. (1972). Suggestibility and success at augury-divination from "chance" outcomes. *Journal of the American Society for Psychical Research,* **66,** 42–62.

Stanford, R.G. (1973). Extrasensory effects upon associative processes in a directed free-response task. *Journal of the American Society for Psychical Research,* **67,** 147–190.

Stanford, R.G. (1974). Dr. Stanford's reply to Dr. Schmeidler's letter. *Journal of the American Society for Psychical Research,* **68,** 444–446.

Stanford, R.G. (1983). Possible psi-mediated perceptual effects of similarity of REG alternatives to the PK target: A double-blind study. In W.G. Roll, J. Beloff, & R.A. White (Eds.). *Research in parapsychology 1982.* Metuchen, N.J.: Scarecrow Press, 178–181.

Stanford, R.G., & Angelini, R.F. (1984). The role of noise and the trait of absorption in Ganzfeld ESP performance: The application of methods based upon signal detection theory. In R.A. White & R.S. Broughton (Eds.). *Research in parapsychology 1983.* Metuchen, N.J.: Scarecrow Press, 35–38.

Stanford, R.G., & Mayer, B. (1974). Relaxation as a psi-conducive state: A replication and exploration of parameters. *Journal of the American Society for Psychical Research,* **68,** 182–191.

Stanford, R.G., & Palmer, J. (1975). Free-response ESP performance and occipital alpha rhythms. *Journal of the American Society for Psychical Research,* **69,** 235–243.

Stanford, R.G., & Schroeter, W. (1978). Extrasensory effects upon associative processes in a directed free-response task: an attempted replication and extension. In W.G. Roll (Ed.). *Research in parapsychology 1977.* Metuchen, N.J.: Scarecrow Press, 52–64.

Stanford, R.G., & Stevenson, I. (1972). EEG correlates of free-response GESP in an individual subject. *Journal of the American Society for Psychical Research,* **66,** 357–368.

Stevenson, I. (1970). Telepathic impressions: A review and report of thirty-five new cases. *Proceedings of the American Society for Psychical Research,* **29,** 1–198.

Stevenson, I. (1987). *Children who remember previous lives.* Charlottesville: University Press of Virginia.

Szczygielski, D., & Schmeidler, G.R. (1975). ESP and two measures of introversion. In J.D. Morris, W.G. Roll, & R.L. Morris (Eds.). *Research in parapsychology 1974.* Metuchen, N.J.: Scarecrow Press, 15–17.

Taddonio, J.L. (1975). Attitudes and expectancies in ESP scoring. *Journal of Parapsychology,* **39,** 289–296.

Taddonio, J.L. (1976). The relationship of experimenter expectancy to performance on ESP tasks. *Journal of Parapsychology,* **40,** 107–114.

Targ, R., & Puthoff, H.E. (1977). *Mind-reach.* New York: Delacorte.

Tart, C.T. (1963). Physiological correlates of psi cognition. *International Journal of Parapsychology,* **5,** 375–386.

Tart, C.T. (1964). Experimenter bias in hypnotist performance. *Science,* **145,** 1330–1331.

Tart, C.T. (Ed.). (1969). *Altered states of consciousness.* New York: Wiley.

Tart, C.T. (1976). *Learning to use extrasensory perception.* Chicago: University of Chicago Press.

Tart, C.T. (1978). Space, time and mind. In W.G. Roll (Ed.). *Research in parapsychology 1977.* Metuchen, N.J.: Scarecrow Press, 197–249.

Tart, C.T. (1983). Information acquisition rates in forced-choice ESP experiments: Precognition does not work as well as present time ESP. *Journal of the American Society for Psychical Research,* **77,** 293–310.

Tart, C.T., Palmer, J., & Redington, D.J. (1979). Effects of immediate feedback on ESP performance: A second study. *Journal of the American Society for Psychical Research,* **73,** 151-165.

Tart, C.T., Puthoff, H.E., & Targ, R. (1981). Remote viewing: Examination of the Marks and Kammann cueing artifact hypothesis. In W.G. Roll & J. Beloff (Eds.). *Research in parapsychology 1980.* Metuchen, N.J.: Scarecrow Press, 24-25.

Tedder, W. (1977). Further investigation of nonintentional clairvoyance: Failure to replicate. *Journal of Parapsychology,* **41,** 379-380.

Tenhaeff, W.H.C. (1962). Summary of the results of a psychodiagnostic investigation of forty paragnosts. *Proceedings of the Parapsychological Institute of the University of Utrecht,* **2,** 53-79.

Terry, J.C., & Harris, S.A. (1975). Precognition in water-deprived rats. In J.D. Morris, W.G. Roll, & R.L. Morris (Eds.). *Research in parapsychology 1974.* Metuchen, N.J.: Scarecrow Press, 81.

Thalbourne, M.A., & Jungkuntz, J.H. (1983). Extraverted sheep versus introverted goats: Experiments VII and VIII. *Journal of Parapsychology,* **47,** 49-51.

Thomas, C.D. (1935). A proxy case extending over eleven sittings with Mrs. Osborne Leonard. *Proceedings of the Society for Psychical Research,* **43,** 439-519.

Thomson, A. (1973). The time factor in experimental ESP. In W.G. Roll, R.L. Morris, & J.D. Morris (Eds.). *Research in Parapsychology 1972.* Metuchen, N.J.: Scarecrow Press, 166-168.

Thouless, R.H. (1976). The effect of the experimenter's attitude on experimental results in parapsychology. *Journal of the Society for Psychical Research,* **48,** 261-266.

Tiller, W.A. (1977). A lattice model of space and its relationship to multidimensional physics. *Proceedings of the Association for Research and Enlightenment Medical Symposium.* Phoenix, Arizona.

Ullman, M., Krippner, S., & Vaughan, A. (1973). *Dream telepathy: Scientific experiments in the supernatural.* New York: Macmillan.

van Busschbach, J.G. (1961). An investigation of ESP in first and second grades in American schools. *Journal of Parapsychology,* **25,** 161-174.

Vassy, Z. (1985). Theoretical and methodological considerations on experiments with pseudorandom number sequences. *Journal of Parapsychology,* **49,** 127-153.

Waldron, S. (1959). Clairvoyance scores of sheep versus goats when subject's attitude toward the experimenter and the purpose of the experiment are manipulated. *Journal of Parapsychology,* **23,** 289.

Walker, E.H. (1975). Foundations of paraphysical and parapsychological phenomena. In L. Oteri (Ed.). *Quantum physics and parapsychology.* New York: Parapsychology Foundation, 1-53.

Walker, E.H. (1984). A review of criticisms of the quantum mechanical theory of psi phenomena. *Journal of Parapsychology,* **48,** 277-332.

Warcollier, R. (1948). *Mind to mind.* New York: Creative Age Press.

Warren, H.C. (1934). *Dictionary of psychology.* New York: Houghton Mifflin.

Watkins, G.K. (1972). Possible PK in the lizard *Anolis sagrei.* In W.G. Roll, R.L. Morris, & J.D. Morris (Eds.). *Proceedings of the Parapsychological Association No. 8, 1971.* Durham, N.C.: Parapsychological Association, 23-25.

Watkins, G.K., & Watkins, A.M. (1971). Possible PK influence on the resuscitation of anesthetized mice. *Journal of Parapsychology,* **35,** 257-272.

Watkins, G.K., Watkins, A.M., & Wells, R.A. (1973). Further studies on the resuscitation of anesthetized mice. In W.G. Roll, R.L. Morris, & J.D. Morris (Eds.). *Research in parapsychology 1972.* Metuchen, N.J.: Scarecrow Press, 157-159.

Watson, D., & Tellegen, A. (1985). Toward a consensual structure of mood. *Psychological Bulletin,* **98,** 219-235.

Weiner, D.H., & Haight, J. (1980). Psi within a test of memory: A partial replication. In W.G. Roll (Ed.). *Research in parapsychology 1979.* Metuchen, N.J.: Scarecrow Press, 52-53.

Weiner, D.H., & Zingrone, N.L. (1986). The checker effect revisited. *Journal of Parapsychology,* **50,** 85–121.

Wells, R.A., & Watkins, G.K. (1975). Linger effects in several PK experiments. In J.D. Morris, W.G. Roll, & R.L. Morris (Eds.). *Research in parapsychology 1974.* Metuchen, N.J.: Scarecrow Press, 143–147.

West, D.J. (1948). The investigation of spontaneous cases. *Proceedings of the Society for Psychical Research,* **48,** 264–300.

West, D.J., & Fisk, G.W. (1953). A dual ESP experiment with clock cards. *Journal of the Society for Psychical Research,* **37,** 185–197.

Wheeler, J.A. (1981). Not consciousness but the distinction between the probe and the probed as central to the elemental quantum act of observation. In R.G. Jahn (Ed.). *The role of consciousness in the physical world.* Boulder, Colo.: Westview Press, 87–111.

White, R.A. (1976a). The influence of persons other than the experimenter on the subject's scores in psi experiments. *Journal of the American Society for Psychical Research,* **70,** 133–166.

White, R.A. (1976b). The limits of experimenter influence on psi test results: Can any be set? *Journal of the American Society for Psychical Research,* **70,** 333–369.

White, R.A. (1977). The influence of experimenter motivation, attitudes, and methods of handling subjects on psi test results. In B.B. Wolman (Ed.). *Handbook of parapsychology.* New York: Van Nostrand Reinhold, 273–301.

White, R.A., & Angstadt, J. (1965). A review of results and new experiments bearing on teacher-selection methods in the Anderson-White high school experiments. *Journal of the American Society for Psychical Research,* **59,** 56–84.

Wiesinger, C. (1973). Two ESP experiments in the classroom. *Journal of Parapsychology,* **37,** 76–77.

Wigener, E.P. (1981). The extension of the area of science. In R.G. Jahn (Ed.). *The role of consciousness in the physical world.* Boulder, Colo.: Westview Press, 7–17.

Williams, L.B., & Duke, D.M. (1980). Openness versus closedness and their relationship to psi. In W.G. Roll (Ed.). *Research in parapsychology 1979,* Metuchen, N.J.: Scarecrow Press, 96–98.

Willis, J., Duncan, J., & Udolfia, J. (1974). ESP in the classroom: Failure to replicate. *Psychological Reports,* **35,** 582.

Winkelman, M. (1981). The effect of formal education on extrasensory abilities: The Ozolco study. *Journal of Parapsychology,* **45,** 321–336.

Wollman, N. (1982). Personality traits correlated with particular psi tasks. In W.G. Roll, R.L. Morris, & R.A. White (Eds.). *Research in parapsychology 1981.* Metuchen, N.J.: Scarecrow Press, 199–201.

Woodruff, J.L. (1960). The effect on ESP scoring of an unexpected qualitative change in ESP material. In J.G. Peatman & E.L. Hartley (Eds.). *Festschrift for Gardner Murphy.* New York: Harper, 106–116.

Index

C

D

E

F

G

H

I

J

K

L

P

Q

R